The History of British Society
Britain in the Nineteen Twenties

The History of British Society

Edited by E.J.Hobsbawm, Professor of History,
Birkbeck College, University of London

Britain in the Nineteen Twenties

Noreen Branson

University of Minnesota Press, Minneapolis

Published in the United Kingdom by
Weidenfeld and Nicolson
11 St John's Hill London SW11

Library of Congress Catalog Card Number: 75-27162
ISBN 0-8166-0770-2

Printed in Great Britain

Contents

Acknowledgements

The author and publisher would like to thank the following for
supplying photographs for use in this book:
The National Coal Board for plate 1; the Radio Times Hulton
Picture Library for plates 2, 4, 9, 10, 11, 12, 13, 14 and 15; the
Transport and General Workers Union for plate 3; Dr S.D.
Chapman (*The History of Working Class Housing*, published by David
and Charles) for plate 5; the Greater London Council for plates
6 and 7; Warrington County Library for plate 8.

General Editor's Preface

Social history is a comparatively new *genre*, though the name itself has long been familiar. It has been widely used as part of the combination 'social and economic history', as a label for the history of labour and popular movements and other topics of interest to scholars of the left, for miscellaneous studies of customs, social behaviour and everyday life, or even, as with the late G. M. Trevelyan, as a residual category of traditional history; 'history with the politics left out'. Its aim today is the ambitious one of writing the history of society. Ideally, it ought therefore to embrace and coordinate the numerous historical specialisms, since all are relevant to its task. In practice, social historians are, at least for the present, likely to concentrate on a number of topics which have tended to be neglected, or to be treated only peripherally, by the general and specialist historians, with some honourable exceptions.

Class and social structure is the most obvious of these, but the historical demographers have also opened up the study of the pattern of birth, marriage, death, household and kinship; 'urban studies' has explored the cities, while the pattern of culture (in the anthropologists' sense of the word) and ideas has attracted what the French call the historians of 'mentalities'. More generally, all aspects of the life and activities of the common people, that is to say those who have left little documentation behind as individuals, have been studied with increasing intensity. A great deal of work in social history has concentrated in these areas since 1950, when the subject began to be systematically developed. However, these studies have been unsystematic, both because the topics themselves have been treated patchily, and because other and equally relevant ones have been neglected. Though of course a good deal of important material has been accumulated by historians of one kind or another in other contexts.

The present series attempts to bring together, for the period from the industrial revolution on, what we know (and don't yet know) about the structure and changes in British society. Since social history is itself in the process of development, the individual authors have been left free to define their field, though they have all agreed to treat certain common questions and subjects. Though they are all experts, they have not written for a specialist public, but for students of history, sociology, or indeed of any subject which requires some understanding of British society since 1780 and for the general reader, who, contrary to a widespread opinion, is not a myth. Not everyone who wants to know about the past and the present also wants to pass an examination. However, it may be hoped that the attempt to draw together the threads of our present knowledge, and at least some of those of historical discussion, may help to advance the work of the numerous and active force of social historians, if only by stimulating them to do better than the authors of this series.

E.J. HOBSBAWM

Preface

I am very grateful to all those who have given me expert advice and help in the writing of this book. Robin Page Arnot threw light on many aspects of the General Strike in the course of discussion. Yvonne Kapp read some early drafts of the book, and her suggestions were of much value to me. Both Betty England and Peter Kerrigan read and commented on the trade union chapters. Margot Heinemann whom I consulted on many questions gave most generously of her time; so did Margaret Morris. John Mahon gave me valuable information and advice on the Hands Off Russia episode, Max Morris on education, Roger Simon on the economic background and Harry Watson on dockers. To all these friends I record my warmest thanks.

I would like to express my appreciation of the great kindness shown me by Dr Brenda Swann at the Public Record Office and Mr E. Brown of the TUC Library.

Finally I owe a very special debt to the Labour Research Department and its staff.

Neither the LRD nor the friends I have mentioned are responsible for anything in the book, and any views expressed in it are my own.

NOREEN BRANSON

I

The Political Setting

The Armistice was signed on Monday, 11 November 1918. The news
was given out at 11 o'clock in the morning. In the industrial areas of
the Midlands and the North, the factory hooters and sirens sounded and
munition workers stopped work and ran out in their overalls cheering.
In Manchester girls with shawls over their heads flocked out from their
factories and mills into the wintry sunlight, and formed a procession
which gathered numbers as it rolled along. They shouted and sang and
danced the foxtrot as they went. Soon all the trams had gone home, all
traffic had stopped, and the streets were entirely given over to joyful
celebration.

In London, the crowds round Buckingham Palace sang Tipperary,
and Land of Hope and Glory, and shouted rhythmically, 'We-want-
King-George.' King George V came out on the balcony and spoke.
'Few could hear him,' recorded *The Times*. 'But his message was well
chosen. "With you," he said, "I rejoice and thank God for the victories
which the Allied Armies have won bringing hostilities to an end and
peace within sight." '

In the City, office girls tore up paper and threw it out of the windows
– it floated down like giant white confetti on to the noisy crowds
below. The open tops of the London buses were crammed with
people, swaying and shouting; every lorry and van was commandeered
by soldiers and sailors and girls blowing horns and beating tin trays. 'I
got a taxi,' complained one man, 'but when fourteen other people got
into it, I left it and walked.' Innumerable little flags appeared – the
Union Jack, the Stars and Stripes, the Belgian flag, the French flag.
People bought them and stuck them in their hats. The rain came down,
and all the colours ran, and nobody cared.

As dusk fell, the fountains in Trafalgar Square began to play for the
first time in four years, and Big Ben, silent for so long, began to chime

the hours. On the packed pavements little rings of laughing, clapping, dancing people formed and reformed. Some of the street lamps, masked for so many months, shone out, and people said: 'Isn't it beautiful to see the lights again.'

In the beginning nobody had realized how long the war would last and how terrible it was going to be. Now Britain had lost 800,000 men, an incomparably greater number than had ever been killed in any other war. Another 2 million had been wounded and nearly half of these were badly enough disabled to be entitled to a pension. The worst among them were crippled or blinded. Others were shell-shocked and seemed turned to stone. Gas casualties numbered over 180,000 and although the majority of gas cases were officially classified as 'slight' the after-effects would cling to them as a minor handicap until they died. Everywhere were families who had lost their breadwinner. As many as 2 million relatives of the dead or disabled – parents, widows, wives, children – were on war pensions or allowances.

The war casualties had accentuated the disparity in the numbers of men and women. There had always been more women than men in the population (which by now numbered 43 million), but the inequality as between the sexes had not been quite so marked before. Now, between the ages of 20 and 40 there were 7 million women to only 6 million men. Soon people were going to begin talking about the problem of 'surplus women'.*

The war had unleashed revolution in Tsarist Russia and toppled thrones in other parts of Europe. But in Britain the basic structure of society had survived the great upheaval intact. The major sources of wealth were still concentrated in the hands of very few. 90 per cent of the wealth had been owned by 10 per cent of the population before the war and it still was so.† Included in this 10 per cent were the big industrialists, the big landowners, the big financiers. There were also the comfortably-off rentiers, all those who, as the Webbs disapprovingly put it at the time, 'live by owning instead of by working'.[1] Collectively they and their relatives and associates formed the upper class. Beneath them came the middle strata: small working employers, shopkeepers and farmers; professional people ranging from the affluent to the underpaid; clerical and administrative workers. There

* See Table 1 end chapter.
† See Table 2.

had been some considerable increase in the numbers in white-collar occupations; even so about three quarters of the population were manual workers or belonged to manual workers' families.

When the war ended some people, particularly among the top 10 per cent, hoped for a return to the comforts and certainties of the pre-war world. Many working-class people, on the other hand, were hoping for a new and better world. Indeed they had been promised it by the politicians. The Prime Minister, Lloyd George, was aware that if there were an early general election the tide of joy and relief at the ending of the war could sweep him back to office, whereas if he delayed the mood might change. So a few days after the Armistice, before the soldiers had come back from the front, before people's ideas had crystallized, an immediate general election was announced.

The voters had no radio or television to bring the election into their homes. True, the political speeches could be read in the closely-printed columns of the newspapers. But people who wanted to see the party leaders in the flesh, to get a whiff of their personality, had to go to a meeting to do so. The politicians of the day had no microphones. Like actors they had to know how to throw their voices to the topmost row of the gallery, how to make themselves heard by an audience even of Albert Hall proportions. The most talented among them gave great theatrical performances, rousing their audiences to excitement, reducing them to laughter, carrying all before them on the wave of a peroration.

In these respects the election campaign of 1918 was little different from those of earlier years. But in other ways it revealed how greatly the war had changed things. Thus, before the war about one fifth of all working men had been unable to qualify for inclusion on the electoral register. Now, in recognition of the great service performed by the millions who had gone out to the front, universal suffrage for all men over 21 had been established by Act of Parliament. Even more striking, about half the adult female population were given the vote for the first time. The long struggle for women's suffrage had ended in 1917 in a compromise measure which permitted women over 30 to vote provided they were householders or the wives of householders. They could also stand as candidates, and some were actually doing so.

Just as significant as the extension of electoral rights were the shifts in political allegiance. For many decades people had been accustomed to think in terms of the two main rival political parties, Conservative and Liberal. Labour had seemed little more than a wing of a Liberal alliance. The 1918 election saw the beginning of the Liberal disintegration and the emergence of the Labour Party as a serious independent political force.

It also saw a change in the composition of the Conservative Party, which after 1918 became increasingly identified with industrialists and businessmen. In the 1906 Parliament, over half the Conservative MPs had been either 'gentlemen' (i.e. men of independent means) or members of the armed forces.[2] There were powerful landowning interests among them but not more than a quarter of them had been businessmen. Among Liberal MPs, on the other hand, 41 per cent had been businessmen, about half of whom had started in well-to-do circumstances, while the other half were of humble origin. The Liberals also had more barristers, solicitors and writers among them than the Conservatives. 27 per cent of Conservatives had been at Eton; only 8 per cent of Liberals. The Conservatives were thus clearly identified with the upper class, the Liberals much less so.

To its supporters the Liberal Party had appeared to champion the rights of the small man against the privileged few, in particular against the landed aristocracy. It was the Liberal leader Lloyd George who before the war had posed the famous rhetorical question: 'Who made 10,000 people owners of the soil and the rest of us trespassers in the land of our birth?' Combining as it did a deep-rooted faith in the progressive role of capitalist free enterprise with a belief in the importance of individual liberty and the need for social reform, the Party had commanded the allegiance not only of nonconformists but of many trade union leaders.

The Liberals had dominated Parliament ever since 1906, though after 1910 they had held office only with the help of Irish Nationalists and a group of about forty Labour MPs who had supported them against their more numerous Conservative opponents. But since 1916 Lloyd George had been Prime Minister in a wartime coalition government comprising Conservatives, Liberals and one or two Labour men, but excluding the previous Liberal leader, Asquith, and his close supporters. And during this time Lloyd George had increasingly shown more confidence in his Conservative than in his own Liberal colleagues.

Now, as the 'man who won the war', he asked the electorate for a mandate to continue with a coalition government in time of peace, and shortly afterwards 541 candidates were endorsed by his headquarters as coalition candidates. However, the breach between Lloyd George and Asquith had not been healed, and it soon transpired that far more Conservatives than Liberals were being endorsed as coalition candidates. Though 159 Liberal candidates received Lloyd George's blessing, this was withheld from another 253 Liberals and given instead to their Conservative opponents. The habitual Liberal voter was thus faced with a curious situation. He might have a coalition Liberal candidate who had received Lloyd George's blessing or a non-coalition Liberal candidate who had been repudiated.

Angry and confused, many within the Liberal Party believed they had been betrayed, and in later years attributed their party's decline to the splits and rivalries between their leaders which persisted from that time onwards. But the truth was that once working people had begun to identify themselves with the Labour Party, there was going to be little room for a Liberal Party.

The Labour Party in 1918 was making clear that it was an independent party with an independent policy. During the war most of the 42 Labour MPs had supported the coalition, though there had been a minority group opposed to the war and refusing support for the government. Now, in the week following the Armistice, a Special Emergency Conference voted to leave the coalition and fight the election free from ties with any other parties.

Up to 1918 the Labour Party had been a purely federal body, having by that time 131 affiliated trade unions with a membership of nearly 3 million and a group of affiliated socialist societies, the most important of which was the Independent Labour Party with a membership of over 30,000. Formed in 1893, the ILP had been one of the founder bodies of the Labour Representation Committee in 1900. It had played a significant part in the spread of socialist ideas within the Labour Party and among trade unionists. The other socialist societies affiliated to the Labour Party were the Fabian Society with about 2000 members and the British Socialist Party with about 10,000. The BSP was avowedly Marxist and was shortly to play a leading part in founding the Communist Party of Great Britain.

Despite this organizational link with the socialist societies many trade union leaders had before the war looked on themselves as Liberals, and the group of Labour MPs as part of a Liberal alliance with a special mission to press for working-class demands. But under a constitution adopted at the beginning of 1918 the Labour Party had made two momentous changes. Firstly, arrangements for individual membership of the Party had been introduced. Secondly, the Party's socialist aim had been made clear. For though the word 'socialism' was not used in the new constitution, one of the objects embodied in it was 'to secure for the producers by hand and by brain the full fruits of their industry . . . the basis of the common ownership of the means of production.'

Of course this formulation meant very different things to different people. Some in the Party thought it must involve workers' control of industry. Others looked upon this as syndicalist folly. Others again, like Ernest Bevin, the dockers' leader, were in the habit of talking about giving 'Labour' responsibility without making clear whether by 'Labour' was meant the working class, a group of trade unionists, or a political party. In this respect Bevin and others who talked like him were reflecting the instincts of a new generation of working people who just thought of 'Labour' as 'us', without any very clear distinction between the political party and the class it was supposed to represent.

Most of the Party leaders saw the transition to socialism as an evolutionary process of social reform within the framework of capitalism. Gradually one enterprise after another would be taken over and run by publicly appointed bodies which would be far more efficient than those they were superseding. A minority in the Party, including all in the BSP and also many in the ILP, disagreed with this approach. To them the first step in the transition to socialism was the revolutionary seizure of power by the working class. They had been filled with hope by the revolution in Russia and the subsequent revolts in other parts of Europe. 'Every morning has brought a new victory for the Revolution. The old order is cracking about our ears,' the *Herald* told its readers a week after the war ended. 'The essential thing is that these are no bourgeois revolutions but Social Revolution; that the Imperial standards have gone down, not before the national tricolours, but before the Red Flag itself.'[3] The *Herald* was a weekly paper with a fighting socialist line, and was edited by George Lansbury, himself a pacifist. With the help of 'Herald Leagues' in the localities it was busy raising money to launch itself as a daily newspaper. This it succeeded in doing a few months later and quickly became the acknowledged

Labour newspaper. However the views of its left-wing contributors were often at variance with those of the Labour leaders, many of whom in particular looked on the Russian revolution with the deepest misgivings.

This did not prevent Lloyd George from asserting during the 1918 election that the men running the Labour Party had pulled it out of the coalition because 'what they really believed in was Bolshevism'.[4] Such accusations rose to a crescendo towards the end of the election campaign. Moreover coalition candidates were earning wild applause for their promises to 'make Britain a fit country for heroes to live in' and for demands to hang the Kaiser and make Germany pay. All candidates outside the coalition were made to appear unpatriotic, and this did not only apply to Labour candidates, but to non-coalition Liberals as well. They were equated by Lloyd George with an enemy who had poured poison gas on British soldiers and then cried 'Kamerad'.[5]

When the results of the election were declared it was found that the coalition candidates had won an overwhelming victory: 478 seats out of 707. Of the 478 coalition MPs, 335 were Conservatives and 133 were Liberals. The non-coalition Liberals were reduced to a handful of 28 seats. And Labour got only 63 seats which, although a considerable advance on the previous 42, was nevertheless a severe disappointment, since the Party's hopes had been high.

There was one part of the British Isles in which all the issues concerning the coalition were irrelevant. 101 out of the 707 seats in the Commons were Irish, and in Ireland, dominating all else, was the question of Irish independence. In this election no less than 73 seats were captured by the uncompromisingly republican Sinn Fein candidates, 36 of whom were in jail when elected. All 73 refused to take their seats at Westminster.

This meant that the coalition government had an even bigger majority in the House than would otherwise have been the case. Yet the voting pattern in Britain had shown a result which was much less decisive: coalition candidates had received barely half the votes cast. On the other hand, 22 per cent had voted Labour as compared with 7 per cent in pre-war elections. Only 58 per cent of the electorate had actually voted, the lowest poll for any general election this century, partly because the soldiers were yet to be demobilized, and only one soldier in four managed to vote. Many never got their voting papers.

The coalition government was to last for four years, during which time the similarities in the outlook of Liberals and Conservatives were much more apparent than the differences, and the Labour Party established itself as the chief opposition party. When the coalition at last came to an end in 1922, Labour won 142 seats, and in 1923, 191 seats, as a result of which the first minority Labour government was established. Though a Conservative government was reelected only nine months later, Labour's share of the poll continued to rise, and by 1929 it commanded 37 per cent of the total poll and became the largest party in the House. (For figures of various elections see Tables 3 and 4, pp. 11-12.)

Labour's growing strength came primarily from former Liberal strongholds: the industrial areas in the north of England, in Wales and in Scotland, the working-class constituencies in the East End of London. Most of its support came from areas where the workers were relatively highly organized and the trade unions strong. At the same time a significant number of radical intellectuals came over to the Labour Party as they saw the Liberal Party losing its zest for reform.

After the coalition ended the Liberals maintained their support intact in certain non-industrial areas of Scotland and Wales, and in a dozen or so provincial towns where the Liberal tradition was deep-rooted. And many salaried and professional people continued to identify themselves with the Liberals. But all the time those who feared and distrusted Labour, including not only lower middle-class people but many unorganized working people, were turning more and more to the Conservatives as the stronger alternative. At the same time employers who had formerly been Liberal supporters became increasingly identified with the Conservative Party. This shift was encouraged by the fact that an increasing number of industrialists were looking to 'protection' as a way out of their difficulties. One of the few issues which still divided Liberals from Conservatives was that of 'free trade' versus 'safeguarding'.

All these tendencies became apparent gradually over the ensuing decade. But immediately after the 1918 election it was already clear that the Conservative Party's links with finance, industry and commerce were more marked than hitherto, while those of the Liberals were not quite so strong.* Taking both together there was a more

* Of 374 Conservatives in the House (coalition and non-coalition), 163 or 43 per cent were listed in the Directory of Directors in 1921. Of 164 Liberals (coalition and non-coalition), 58, or 35 per cent were so listed.

formidable concentration of businessmen and industrialists in the House than had been seen there for many years.

There were directors of colliery companies, iron and steel men, textile men. At least thirty MPs were directors of railway companies. Coal and railways had been under government control during the war and over their future hung a question mark. Now the owners could be certain that they would have the ear of the Cabinet when controls were removed. The same was true of shipping. The big steamship lines were represented in the Commons in force: P & O, Cunard, Union Castle and others.

Vickers, the largest engineering combine in the country, was represented by its chairman, Douglas Vickers. Many other famous engineering firms had directors in the House. The new rising industries were represented as well, including the thrusting electric power companies and the rapidly expanding chemical firms. Thus Brunner Mond was represented by Sir Alfred Mond, later to become the first chairman of Imperial Chemical Industries. There were directors from Shell and from Dunlop rubber. Familiar names from well-known products were scattered around the benches: Austin, head of the Austin Motor Company, a Bird from the firm that made Bird's Custard, a Lyle from Lyle's Golden Syrup, one or two Guinnesses, a Wills from Imperial Tobacco. And this list did not include those holding government office who were obliged to resign their directorships but who retained their family connections and their big shareholdings, like Stanley Baldwin of Baldwin's steel firm.

The concentration of big business in the House of Commons was reinforced by that in the House of Lords. Here, where the representatives of the old noble families still greatly outnumbered the rest, were to be found the biggest coalowners and, in addition, shipowners, railway directors, bankers and financiers.* In spite of a tendency over the previous half-century to sell land and invest the money in industry, the landowning interest in the House of Lords was still formidable. 305 peers owned between them 10 million acres, more than one eighth of the territory of the British Isles.† 1·7 million out of the 10 million

* For an analysis of business interests in the House of Lords, see *Labour and Capital in Parliament* (Labour Research Department, 1923). This showed that 227 peers were directors of 425 companies.

† 31 of these peers had no seat in the Lords, either because they were Scottish or Irish

were in Ireland. Apart from their great possessions at home, the hereditary peers had close connections with the British Empire. Their younger sons were commonly to be found serving as officers in the regular army in India or other colonial territories, or launched on careers as colonial administrators.

Though the formal political power of the Lords had been weakened by the Parliament Act of 1911 its actual power was still very great and its social influence immense. Politically, 70 per cent of the peers were Conservatives,* and to them at least the general election had proved reassuring. But their world had changed out of all recognition. Sons, brothers, nephews, cousins, heirs, had been killed in the war. The Empire which covered a quarter of the earth's surface was seething. There was unrest in India, rebellion in Ireland. Early in 1919 a general strike for a forty-hour week was proclaimed on the Clyde, and troops were sent to occupy Glasgow. Other strikes were in progress or threatened in nearly every industry. Soldiers were mutinying and demanding to be demobilized.

Such was the turbulent foreground. Few people recognized the underlying truth, that Britain's economic position in relation to the rest of the world had been permanently undermined.

---

* In *British Political Facts* (1963) by David Butler and Jennie Freeman the political composition of the House of Lords in 1919 is given as 481 Conservatives, 130 Liberals, 66 politics not stated, 21 minors: total 698. The authors state that the figures should be treated with caution.

---

peers without an additional English title or because they were peerages temporarily held by peeresses. The figures of landownership are derived from *Who's Who*, 1918, where it was still the custom to set out the number of acres owned. However the custom was beginning to be abandoned, partly because various new forms of landownership, such as transfer to a private company, were becoming popular after the introduction of death duties. The totals given above of the numbers of landowners among the peers are therefore likely to be understated. For the great wave of land sales which took place soon afterwards in 1919 and 1920, see F. M. L. Thompson, *English Landed Society in the Nineteenth Century* (1963).

Table 1   Composition of the population in 1921

Total population of Great Britain: 42·7 million. Composed as follows:

	Males	Females	Surplus or deficit of females over males
	000	000	000
Age 0–20	7,977	7,944	−33
Age 20–40	6,023	7,102	1,079
Age 40–60	4,641	5,054	413
Age over 60	1,780	2,246	466
Total	20,421	22,346	1,925

(Source: *Statistical Abstract for the United Kingdom*, No. 78, Table 16)

Table 2   Pattern of Ownership of Wealth

Proportion of population %	Proportion of total wealth % 1911–13	1924–30
1	69	62
5	87	84
10	92	91

(Source: A. B. Atkinson, *Unequal Shares* (1972))

Table 3 Percentage Share of Total Vote in General Elections

	Labour	Liberal	Conservative	Other
1910 (Dec)	7·2	43·8	46·3	2·7
1918	23·7a	25·6b	38·7c	12·0
1922	29·5	29·1d	38·2	3·2
1923	30·5	29·6	38·1	1·8
1924	33·0	17·6	48·3	1·1
1929	37·1	23·4	38·2	1·3
1931	32·3e	10·7f	55·3	1·7

(a) Including 1·5% Coalition Labour.
(b) 13·5% Coalition Liberal and 12·1% Non-Coalition Liberal.
(c) Including 3·4% Non-Coalition Conservatives and 2·7% Irish Unionists.
(d) 11·6% National Liberals and 17·5% Liberals.
(e) Including 1·6% National Labour.
(f) Including 3·7% National Liberal.

(Source: D. Butler and J. Freeman, *British Political Facts 1900–1960* (1963))

Table 4 Political Parties in the House of Commons

	Labour	Liberal	Conservative	Other
December 1910	42	272	272	84
December 1918	73a	161b	383c	90d
November 1922	142	116e	345	12
December 1923	191	159	258	7
October 1924	151	40	419	5
May 1929	288	59	260	8

(a) Including 10 Coalition Labour.
(b) 133 Coalition Liberals, 28 Liberals.
(c) 335 Coalition Unionists, 25 Irish Unionists, 23 Conservatives.
(d) Including 73 Sinn Fein, 7 Irish Nationalists.
(e) 62 National Liberal, 54 Liberal.

(Source: D. Butler and J. Freeman, *British Political Facts 1900–1960* (1963))

2

The Post-War Industrial Confrontation

The economic pattern of the years 1918 to 1931 shows four distinct phases. From the Armistice until the middle of 1920 there was an uncontrolled inflationary boom during which output never reached pre-war standards but prices soared and fortunes were made overnight. The second phase saw the collapse of the boom, a slump in 1921-2 of a severity previously unknown and unemployment at a level not seen for a hundred years.

In the third phase, beginning in 1923, came partial recovery with new industries forging ahead, and some major technological advances. Standards of living improved for many and some social legislation of great consequence was introduced. But side by side with seeming prosperity, unemployment never fell below a million, largely because the old staple export industries - coal, cotton, shipbuilding, iron and steel - failed to shake off the depression into which they had been plunged. Anxious to restore Britain's position as the centre of the world money market, the government pursued a relentlessly deflationary policy which, if anything, accentuated the difficulties of these older industries. Meanwhile the employers saw wage reductions as their only hope. It was these pressures which led to the major crisis over the coal industry in 1926.

The fourth phase came after 1929 when, following the Wall Street crash, Britain was engulfed in a world economic crisis which made even 1921 look, in retrospect, like a comparatively mild recession.

During the first of these four phases, the post-war inflation, expectations of a better life were high among manual workers. From the turn of the century up to the outbreak of war in 1914 real wages had failed to rise and for some workers had actually declined. Discontent had erupted in a series of extensive and even violent industrial disputes. The war had intervened and industrial conflict was to a great extent postponed. Now it was clear that large sections of workers were not prepared to go on being treated in the old way and were getting ready for a trial of strength with their employers. For some, the contest would not be confined to wages and conditions but would go further, involving a challenge to the system of ownership in industry. This was an urgent issue, since the government had taken charge of some industries during the war. Whether the industries would be handed back to their owners and in what form was thus a crucial question.

Over three quarters of the occupied population were manual workers, numbering nearly 15 million. Of these some 5·6 million were skilled workers; 6·5 million could be classed as semi-skilled, and about 2·8 million as unskilled. These broad categories could be found in every industry but in very varying proportions. During the war, while prices had doubled, wage increases had tended to give proportionately more to the unskilled than to the skilled, so that the gap between their pay had narrowed. The lowest-paid generally had been raised onto a new plateau, acquiring as a result a new confidence and self-respect. The wages of the higher-paid, on the other hand, had often failed to keep pace with the rise in prices.

When the war ended the skilled workers ceased to be restrained by feelings of solidarity with those at the front. Both government and employers knew that the demand for the eight-hour day could no longer be withstood. It had been central to the programme of the trade unions for many decades, had indeed inspired the first May Day demonstration in 1890. Now it was granted to large numbers of workers. Then, as prices rose between 1918 and 1920 by a further 30 per cent, wages were pushed up even faster, while weekly earnings increased by about 50 per cent. Many workers in 1920 had a glimpse of a prosperity they had not known before.

The trade unions had grown in strength. Total membership rose from 4 million in 1913 to 6·5 million in 1918 and 8·3 million in 1920. The numbers affiliated to the Trades Union Congress rose in the same period from 2·2 million to 6·5 million. The most powerful organization in the trade union movement was the Miners Federation of Great Britain, which early on had taken the initiative in trying to form closer links with other unions. An agreement for a Triple Industrial Alliance

had been concluded between the MFGB, the National Union of Railwaymen and the Transport Workers Federation, which organized the
dockers, among others. This alliance was the result of pre-war experience when a strike of miners had thrown railwaymen and dockers
out of work and vice versa. All three groups had a key place in the
economy. The kind of work they did, their relationship with their
employers and the attitudes of these employers had a close bearing on
the industrial conflicts which culminated in the General Strike of 1926.

Miners and Coalowners

The coalmining industry occupied a unique place in the British
economy. In the nineteenth century Britain's economic supremacy in
the world had been based on coal, and in the early part of the twentieth
century almost all industries still depended on it. The railways ran on
steam engines which were fuelled with coal, and the railways were still
the main method of transporting goods and passengers, since the petrol-
driven road vehicle was relatively new. Ships ran on coal, for con-
version to oil had only just begun. Coal was a major export and coal
carrying contributed to the prosperity of the shipping lines. It was the
basis of power for nearly all industrial processes. Every ton of steel
made required four tons of coal. Domestic heating in Britain's nine
million homes came almost entirely from open coal fires and much of
the cooking was done on coal ranges.

   The mineworkers, who numbered over a million, represented
together with their families one tenth of the population of Great
Britain. They were organized in district associations which functioned
as separate trade unions with separate wage agreements. These associations were joined together in the Miners Federation (MFGB), one of
whose aims was nationally negotiated wages. During the war this had
been achieved to a limited extent under government control. Uniform
wage awards had been made throughout the coalfields and a system of
pooling part of the profits of the colliery companies meant that the
highly profitable coalfields had been used to support the less profitable,
high-cost mines.

The colliery companies varied greatly in size. The majority were linked through district associations of colliery owners with a national body, the Mining Association of Great Britain.

It was in 1919, while the industry was still under government control, that the whole issue of its future ownership came to a head. Early that year the Miners Federation put forward a claim for a 30 per cent increase in earnings (which would have meant an extra 3s a day on average throughout the coalfields) and a six-hour day in place of the existing nominal eight-hour day. At the same time the union raised once more a demand for the nationalization of the mines. The government in reply offered 1s a day and a Committee of Inquiry. This offer was rejected outright by the miners' leaders, who took a ballot throughout the coalfields for or against a national strike. The result of the ballot was a six to one majority for a stoppage.

When it became clear that the miners meant business, Lloyd George took action, and after much negotiation and recall conferences the miners agreed to postpone their strike in return for the setting up of a Royal Commission to inquire into all aspects of the industry. They were able to make it a condition, however, that not less than six members of the Commission should be either nominated or endorsed by the miners. The six were three MFGB leaders, Robert Smillie, Herbert Smith and Frank Hodges, and three eminent intellectuals, Sir Leo Chiozza Money, R. H. Tawney and Sidney Webb. On the employers' side were three from colliery companies and three appointed by the government from other industries: a shipowner, the head of a steel firm and the chairman of a group of engineering companies. The Commission was chaired by Mr Justice Sankey.

It soon transpired that the employers' side was far from united. This was underlined when on 20 March the Commission produced its first interim report divided into three parts. One was from the six miners' representatives, sticking to the miners' demands. One was from the three colliery owners offering 1/6d a day and a reduction in hours to seven and a half. But the three independent employers deserted their coalowning colleagues and joined Mr Justice Sankey in the main report advocating an advance of 2s a day, an immediate seven-hour day, and a further reduction of hours in 1920. And this report included the following momentous passage:

Even upon the evidence already given, the present system of ownership and working in the coal industry stands condemned and some other system must be substituted for it, either nationalization or a measure of unification by national purchase and/or by joint control . . . It is in the interests of the country that the colliery worker shall in the future have an effective voice in the direction of the mines.[1]

The government then announced that it accepted the award of 2s a day and the reduction in hours to seven, with a further reduction in 1920. The Commission was to continue its work and produce a final report on the proposed nationalization or reorganization of the industry. On this understanding the miners called off the national stoppage altogether and the Commission continued sitting throughout May and part of June.

The colliery owners were aghast. They had gone into the Commission intending to secure a favourable financial position in preparation for the time when government control would be lifted and the industry fully handed back to them. Now it began to look as though this might never happen. They were furious with the independent employers on the Commission, with Sankey and, above all, with the government. They set about trying to redress the situation, rallying all forces in their defence.

But meanwhile, as the Commission continued its sittings, it began to look as though the colliery companies were on trial. Indeed, as witness followed witness with evidence of technical backwardness, mismanagement and waste, and above all as the bitter antagonism between employer and employee was revealed, it was said in Labour circles that capitalism itself was on trial.

Miners were by no means among the worst paid at that time – indeed the earnings of a skilled collier averaged nearly £4 a week – but as Vernon Hartshorn, a miners' MP, told the Commission: 'If the miners get all they asked for as to wages and hours they will still have an existence which very few outside mining circles would exchange with them'.[2] 'It is a very arduous occupation and very laborious,' he said, recalling how, as a growing lad, he used to get home from the mine and 'lie down on the hearthstone in front of the fire feeling too tired and stiff and lifeless to get a bath and rest.'[3]

Hours worked underground were limited by law to eight, but this did not include one 'winding time' – the time taken to get the whole shift into the cage and down the shaft – so that in practice the actual hours underground were nearer nine than eight. And the miners said that if their six-hour day was granted, it would still be nearer seven than six.

Only a minority of mines had mechanical coalcutters. Most coalgetting was done manually with a pick. The hewer undercut the coal, often lying on his side in a cramped position. Supports were then withdrawn to let the overhang fall, or it was brought down by blasting. The roof of each excavated section had to be supported by packing in stones and putting in props as the coal was removed. Conveyors for carrying away the coal were only just beginning to come into use. The hewer and his helper – often a son or a nephew – would shovel the coal into tubs or 'trams', which were then hauled to the shaft by rope and pulley or by pit ponies.

Since most of the work was carried on in half-darkness, many men went sick with an eye disease known as miners' nystagmus. Much work was done in great heat. One medical witness told the Commission he had visited a seam where the temperature was over 90 degrees. He took the temperature of the men during the meal break. 'I found in each case the temperature was over 100 degrees and the pulse rate was over 100. I thought it was a very bad thing for the workmen to be working at such a high temperature with such a high pulse rate when the whole of the conditions could be improved by ventilation,' he said.[4]

One miner in six met with an accident every year. In 1918 there were 1300 killed and 160,000 injured, 12,000 in such a way as to be incapacitated for more than a year. Sir Malcolm Delevigne, an official Home Office witness, told the Commission:

> The industry is carried on in face of an enemy against whom a ceaseless watch has to be maintained, and the operations are not carried on in the light, as in a factory; the men are scattered singly or in twos and threes through the workings often a long distance from the shaft and with no illumination except that of a miner's lamp or candle . . . A careless or reckless act of any single individual working by himself in some distant part of a mine, the negligence of an official in carrying out some statutory examination or the like, may bring disaster . . . The need of a highly trained and highly disciplined force – at any rate in the more dangerous mines – is hardly less than it is in actual warfare.[5]

The main causes of death and injury were not the dramatic explosions which, when they happened, killed men by the score, but the continual roof falls, which crushed and maimed, and the innumerable haulage accidents.

Many of the miners lived in houses put up by the colliery companies which, they alleged, had not been built to last, since the companies had an eye to the length of time it would take before a pit should be worked out. 'If you pay a visit to the Rhondda you will see what kind of a place it is,' said Mrs Elizabeth Andrews, a miner's wife from South Wales. 'All these industries have ruined all its beauties and stripped the trees and made it a drab and sordid place . . . The houses are built practically within a few yards of the pit tops. The result is that the women who live in those houses before they can think of washing clothes have to go out to find which way the wind is blowing.'[6]

Mrs Agnes Brown, a Scottish miner's wife, said that the miners' rows had no sanitation. 'The ashbin is at the back. They have a square brick thing to which they carry out the ashes, and put them in . . . the children just run about there.'[7] She said that many mining families lived in one room. Mrs Mary Hart, a miner's wife from Wigan, said the miners lived in 'back-to-back' houses with no water supply. 'The conveniences are totally inadequate to the number of houses; in many instances two or three families use the same convenience, and as this is usually a pail it is both unhealthy and disagreeable.'[8]

The colliery owners were indignant at these criticisms; they claimed that they had done more about housing their workmen than other industrialists. Joseph Shaw, chairman of the Powell Duffryn Steam Coal Company (which employed 18,000 in South Wales and had an output of 4 million tons a year), blamed the miners themselves. 'A great many of these difficulties about the houses is that the bad tenant makes a bad house,' he observed. 'We built houses that were too roomy and the people did not want them.' He added: 'All it did was to encourage two families living in a house.' He agreed that his newly-built houses for miners had no bathrooms. 'You often find the cocks and hens in the bathroom . . . We would provide baths tomorrow if the people would use them.'[9]

Sir Thomas Watson, another colliery owner, expressed similar views. 'When we have built a good house for a collier the condition inside is deplorable,' he said. 'Of course they are not all alike; there are good men and bad men.' He contrasted the Welsh collier's wife unfavourably with French and German miners' wives. 'If the Welsh collier's wife was as good a manager as the French collier's wife, the Welsh collier would be a great deal happier and healthier man.' The miners' representatives, Hodges and Smillie, hit back. 'You must know,' said Hodges, 'that the houses that your company own . . . have their back doors abutting on your own coke ovens.' 'They were built before the coke ovens,' answered Sir Thomas. 'Then you built the coke ovens on top of them,' said Smillie.[10]

The union wanted pithead baths, where the miner could wash and change and leave his pit clothes to be dried. At present he came home in filthy, wet clothes; he would strip and wash in a tub filled from a pan of water heated on the fire. The pit clothes might be all night drying. A woman with husband and sons on different shifts would be lifting and filling tubs and drying clothes for a large part of the day and night. In Scotland, where the family often had only one room, they would sleep in the room with the drying clothes. 'I have known of a case where there were children, and a baby lying in the cot at the fire, and three men's clothes being dried round the fire, and that baby lying ill with pneumonia,' said Mrs Brown.[11]

The mining community had the highest infant mortality of any section. In 1911 it had been 160 per 1000 births, as compared with 96·8 for agricultural labourers, who were less well paid than miners and certainly as badly housed. Sidney Webb suggested that the main cause of the difference between mining and agricultural families was the exceptionally heavy work of the miner's wife as a result of the dirt brought into the house.

The employers alleged that the issue of infant mortality had been raised by the miners' representatives in order to create prejudice, and insisted that much of the high infant death-rate was due to ignorance. They also said that the miners did not want pithead baths. The miners' wives agreed that there was some prejudice against baths among the older men, but said if the baths were there the men would begin to like it. And Mrs Andrews told of a big conference which had been held by the women in South Wales to demand baths.

The miners put their hardships down to the system of mine ownership. By English law anyone owning the surface of the land owned the minerals under it. The coal seams therefore belonged to the landowners. There were nearly 4000 of these; very few of them worked the coal themselves; most of them leased the right to mine their coal to a colliery company which paid them a royalty on each ton extracted. Apart from royalties there were payments for wayleaves: i.e. charges made for hauling coal over an owner's property.

In certain areas the coal seams belonged to many small landowners. Sometimes they could not be traced, and this made difficulties for companies trying to mine the coal. The boundaries between one owner and another were haphazard; they inhibited the most economical arrangements for drainage and pumping and meant that a lot of coal between one property and another remained unworked.

The large royalty owners nevertheless argued that the system on the whole led to efficiency, since the owner had a strong financial incentive to make certain that the output of coal was as large as possible. The biggest royalty owners were the Ecclesiastical Commissioners, whose royalties and wayleave rents had amounted to £317,000 in 1917. Most of the other big royalty owners came from the old landed nobility. The Duke of Northumberland had 244,000 acres of proved mineral rights with an annual output of nearly 2 million tons of coal. His gross income from royalties and wayleaves in 1918 had been £82,450. His net income from this source, after deduction of a special wartime excess mineral rights duty and what was at that time an exceptionally high rate of income tax and super tax imposed temporarily during the war, had been just under £24,000. The Marquess of Bute owned 128,000 acres of land, including 48,000 acres of proved mineral rights, mostly in Glamorgan but partly in Dumfries, with an output of over 3 million tons per annum. His gross income from royalties and wayleaves was £115,000. The Duke of Hamilton owned 56,000 acres in Lanarkshire, Stirlingshire and Linlithgow, from which the output of coal was 4 million tons a year and his 'lordships' totalled £113,000 a year. The Earl of Dunraven, a big Irish landowner, also owned 17,000 acres of coal in Glamorgan with an output of over 2 million tons a year; his royalties and wayleaves averaged £64,370. The Earl of Durham owned 12,411 acres of land in County Durham with an output of coal in 1918 of 1½ million tons; his gross income from royalties, wayleaves and rent from a surface railway used for hauling coal was £40,000; his net income from this source was £20,000. Lord Tredegar owned 82,000 acres in Monmouthshire, Breconshire and Glamorganshire, including 18,000 which contained minerals and produced 3½ million

B

tons of coal a year. His royalties and wayleaves came to £83,000 gross. He also owned the Tredegar Park Railway (popularly known as the 'golden mile') which carried the coal across his property. The railway had cost £40,000 to build, and it brought in £19,000 a year. The Marquess of Londonderry, who owned coal royalties in Durham, was unusual in that he was also the proprietor of a colliery company.

The big royalty owners were informed that the Royal Commission was considering the principle of nationalization of minerals, and were invited to attend and give evidence. As they appeared, one by one, the public benches became packed.

The miners contended that many of the royalty owners were not legally entitled to the lands they held. Their ancestors had been granted the land by the Crown in return for services which were obsolete, such as the provision of soldiers for the monarch when required. In some cases, it was said, the land had actually been stolen. Thus Smillie and Hodges alleged that the Marquess of Bute's forerunners had obtained the estates by a fraud practised on a 10-year-old Tudor king. They demanded that the title deeds of the leading owners should be brought before the Commission for examination. The landowners objected that it would take many months to sort out the deeds and that they would need to be delivered in van-loads. Lord Tredegar observed that his land had been owned by his family 'from time immemorial, prob- ably long before the Norman Conquest'[12] and that many of the deeds were in dog Latin.

However the main argument of the miners' representatives was one of principle: that since no man created the land no individual was entitled to own it; it should be held by the whole community. In this stand the miners were not only voicing the opinion of all socialists, but also of many Liberals who had long believed that the private owner- ship of land inhibited the development of free enterprise. When Lord Tredegar commented: 'If you are entitled to confiscate the land, you are entitled to confiscate anything, so far as I can see,' Smillie's answer was: 'Is there not a wonderful difference between what can be created by human effort and confiscating something which the Creator made for the use of all people and which no one can reproduce?'[13]

The royalty owners defended their position with spirit. 'There is a very old book, and there is a statement in it that "the earth is the Lord's

and the fullness thereof",' said Smillie to the elderly Earl of Durham.
'It appears in the Bible . . . Would you deny that authority?' 'I prefer
another authority which says "Render unto Caesar the things that are
Caesar's, and unto God the things that are God's",' replied the Earl
amid loud laughter.[14]

The Duke of Northumberland declared that he intended to do his
utmost to oppose nationalization both in the House of Lords and in the
country. He alleged that the Miners Federation were 'only going in for
this scheme of nationalization as a step to something far more drastic
and for measures more revolutionary.' 'It seems to me,' he said, 'that
the Miners Federation are trying to get a monopoly of the coal for
themselves.' 'You think it is a bad thing for the miners to have such a
monopoly? . . . Then do you not think it is a bad thing for a man to
own as much as you do?' he was asked. 'No, I think it is an excellent
thing in every way,' he replied.

Asked by Herbert Smith, the representative of the Yorkshire miners
on the Commission, whether he knew about the infant death-rates in
Northumberland and Durham, the Duke said: 'You think landowners
have nothing to do but examine statistics. I am a hard-worked man. I
am not a privileged man like you. I cannot afford to waste time sitting
on a Commission like this.'[15]

The Marquess of Londonderry did not believe that his collieries
would be run more efficiently or the conditions of the workmen better
under state ownership. 'I believe in the ownership of private property,'
he said. 'I believe in holding my own property like the coat on my
back . . . I am an individualist, and I think that as soon as we get back
to individuality the better for the country.'[16]

The employers who represented the colliery companies on the Commission were meanwhile in a certain dilemma. That there was a conflict
between themselves and the landowners could not be doubted. Yet the
attack now being made upon the royalty owners was not of a kind that
they could support. So while the Commission was sitting, the colliery
representatives tried to smooth the path for them, putting questions
to them which would show the advantages of keeping the coal seams
in private hands. But though they made common cause with the
royalty owners in the open sittings, at the last they deserted them. In
the final minority report, signed by five employers, they recommended nationalization of all mineral rights, differing from the miners,

of course, in that they urged that the royalty owners should be paid compensation.

The colliery companies were themselves in a vulnerable position. It was alleged that as compared with their foreign rivals they were technically backward. Many of the small units lacked capital, so that they could not afford to modernize but went for the coal that could be got easily, sometimes in such a way as to ruin unworked seams. Sir Richard Redmayne, the government's Inspector of Mines, thought that the system was 'extravagant and wasteful'.[17]

The colliery companies' chief witness, Lord Gainford, endeavoured to refute these criticisms, arguing that the industry was run on highly efficient and progressive lines, that it had always produced as much coal as the nation wanted, and that mechanization had been retarded by the attitude of the miners. The industry did not earn excessive profits, he said, and the friction alleged between employers and their workpeople had been grossly exaggerated. Above all, coalmining was unsuitable for public ownership, since it was a highly speculative industry that could only be run successfully on the basis of private enterprise, prepared to take risks. This latter argument was stressed by Joseph Shaw, the Chairman of Powell Duffryn. 'People like myself and Boards of Directors go into a speculative concern, and we ask people to subscribe,' he said, 'If they are satisfied with me and that I am a fairly sound man to back up they will come in . . . Nationalization means this . . . that you are going to let people whose name would not get a brass farthing in the City gamble with the taxpayers' money.'[18]

The Royal Commission produced its Final Reports on 23 June 1919. The chairman, Mr Justice Sankey, in his report came down on the side of the miners in proposing nationalization of both coal royalties and collieries. The six miners' representatives endorsed the chairman's report but wanted greater provision for workers' representation in the administration of the industry than Sankey had allowed. A third report, signed by five of the employers, proposed nationalization of coal royalties but rejected colliery nationalization or any form of compulsory reorganization. The fourth report, that of Sir Arthur Duckham (one of the independent employers nominated by the government, and a professional engineer), proposed reorganization and unification of the industry on a privately-owned basis.

The coalowners had for months past been mounting a vigorous anti-nationalization campaign, issuing circulars, lobbying MPs, enlisting newspaper support. With the publication of the Sankey Reports which showed a majority recommendation for nationalization, these efforts were redoubled. Dislike and distrust of the Prime Minister boiled up. 'Concessions made as a result of fear do not tend to remove the danger of Bolshevism,' protested Earl Brassey, initiating a debate on the Sankey Report in the House of Lords on 16 July 1919. 'The people of this country voted overwhelmingly against Bolshevism at the last election . . . They certainly did not put the present Government into power to "bolshevize" British industry . . . Unless the people come to their senses it is my belief that we are in for a disaster similar to that which befell the Roman Empire in its last days.'

Finally on 18 August the government announced its decision. It could not accept the policy of nationalization of the mines. State purchase of mineral rights was agreed to but, for the rest, almost everything proposed by the Final Report of the Commission was rejected.

The miners' leaders now believed that they had been deceived. The government had accepted the first Sankey Report which had said that there must be a new system of ownership; on this understanding they had called off their national stoppage, persuading their membership to do so with some difficulty. True, they had won higher pay and shorter hours. But they remained convinced that there could be no permanent change for the better until private ownership of the mines was ended. In the bitter years that followed this belief was to be fortified rather than dispelled. Meanwhile even the proposal for state purchase of mineral rights was quietly dropped in the ensuing months. Sankey and all the hopes and beliefs that it represented became a dead letter.

Railwaymen and the Government

The directors of the railway companies had been as apprehensive about the future as the coalowners. During the general election, Winston Churchill, a leading member of the coalition Cabinet, had twice stated that it was government policy to nationalize the railways.

There were thirty or forty main railway companies, as well as numerous local ones. During the war the government had controlled the industry through a Railway Executive Committee composed of railway managers. It had guaranteed to the railway companies a revenue equal to that of 1913, which had been a good year, and had been obliged to subsidize them as a result, partly to permit increases in wages to offset the rise in prices. Now that the war was over the question was when, and on what terms, the government intended to relinquish control.

Churchill's statement that the railways were to be nationalized caused an immediate advance of a point or two in the leading railway stocks.[19] A few days later he elaborated his statement, suggesting that in the hands of the state it might be expedient to run the railways at a loss if this helped private industry and trade to develop. He envisaged honest and fair treatment for the stockholders should the state take over.[20] Austen Chamberlain, soon to be leader of the Conservative Party, observed it was 'unthinkable that we should ever allow the railways to go back to the old disorganized system where each was in unlimited competition with the other'.[21] He added that with the abolition of the old pre-war hours and wages the financial position of the railway companies was so much changed that he should not be surprised if they were the first to ask that the state should take them over.

The election was no sooner held, however, than the railway directors made clear that, far from wishing to be taken over, they were determined to prevent it. The Federation of British Industries declared against it; the Railway Companies Association began to exert pressure; railway director MPs joined forces with their coalowning colleagues to block any form of state ownership. And railway nationalization, which had initially received the sober endorsement of *The Times* city columns, began to be spoken of as a concession to bolshevism and an attack on freedom. In the debate on the Sankey Report in the House of Lords, the railways received almost as much attention as the coal mines. Lord Inchcape, shipowner, chairman of P & O and also a director of the Great Western Railway, spoke of the insidious attempts to attack the liberty of the British people. 'The first of these attempts was aimed at shipping. That has gone by the board. The second is aimed at the coal mines. The third . . . is aimed at the railways. The public are now getting thoroughly alarmed. They realize that if the two great industries, coal and railways, built up by private enterprise, are taken over by the Government, all other industries in the country will be endangered.'[22] By this time a clause in a Ways and Communications Bill, which had conferred on the state powers of compulsory purchase of the railways, had been dropped by the government itself.

Part of the anxiety of the coalowners, shipowners and railway owners arose from the changed attitude of the workers they employed. Trade union organization had become much stronger in recent years. By a series of amalgamations before the war the National Union of Railwaymen had been established, and now accounted for a membership of over 480,000 out of the 640,000 workers employed. True, its aim of establishing one union for the industry had not been achieved. 58,000 of the footplate men (drivers, firemen and engine cleaners) were in the Associated Society of Locomotive Engineers and Firemen, and 86,000 railway clerks and supervisory grades were in the Railway Clerks Association. Relations between these unions were not always happy. However, the centralized direction of the railways under the wartime control had for the first time led to national negotiations on wages and conditions, in place of the old method by which the unions had dealt with each company separately.

Before the war railway workers had included some of the most poorly paid. 100,000 of them had earned less than £1 a week, a sum well below what was then held to be subsistence level for a family. Hours were long: most railwaymen entered the war with a minimum working week of sixty hours, or a ten-hour day, and some were working a twelve-hour day. During the war many had joined the forces and, in spite of the recruitment of women as porters, cleaners and ticket collectors, a much increased volume of goods and passenger traffic was handled by fewer staff. Inevitably hours became still longer. Wages were also a cause of discontent. Increases had taken the form of flat-rate war bonuses which, by the end of the war, amounted to 33s added on to the pre-war wage, whatever that had been. Thus the permanentwayman who was paid 20s a week before the war was, by 1919, receiving 53s, an increase of 165 per cent. At the other end of the scale an express train driver who before the war got 48s would now be receiving 81s, an increase of only 69 per cent over his pre-war earnings. Since the cost of living had risen by at least 120 per cent the skilled grades had suffered a severe cut in their standards of living. The wages situation on the railways thus illustrated the trend in much of industry, where the gap between skilled and unskilled had narrowed.

However, the wages of the lower grades on the railways were still very poor, and during the war the trade union leaders had had great difficulty in restraining members from strike action. Now that the war had ended, the railwaymen, like the miners, were not prepared to go on in the old way.

The first step forward was important. Together with a large number of other workers, the railwaymen were granted an eight-hour day in February 1919. But the main negotiations on wages still lay ahead. The union leaders met the Railway Executive and the Board of Trade and found them in no mood to concede more than marginal improvements.

On 20 March 1919 a Special General Meeting of the NUR resolved to ask their partners in the Triple Alliance to support them in calling a national strike. The leaders of the Triple Alliance then met Bonar Law, the Conservative leader, and other members of the government who, already preoccupied with the mining crisis, appeared conciliatory. At the time, men doing exactly the same work for different railway companies were paid at different rates; indeed it was estimated that there were over 500 grades with separate rates of pay. The unions wanted to reduce the number of grades and make wages and conditions for each grade uniform throughout the country on the basis of a rate equal to that of the best-paid man in that grade, whichever company he worked for. It was around this issue of 'standardization upwards' that Bonar Law offered hope. As a result the strike threat was withdrawn.

By August it began to look as though the decision to call off the strike had been justified. The claim of the drivers and firemen, the highest-paid, was settled on extremely favourable terms. The principle of 'standardization upwards' was fully implemented; to the war bonus of 33s was added the highest rate of pay prevailing in each category in June 1914. For drivers of eight years' standing it meant a weekly wage of £4 10s compared with a previous average of £3 18s.

But it soon became apparent that the kind of settlement reached for the minority of skilled footplate men was not envisaged for the vast mass of railwaymen in the lower grades. The union leaders pursued their goal of 'standardization upwards' for the guards, porters, shunters platelayers, ticket collectors and all the other grades, but appeared to be making little progress. At last, on 19 September 1919, they received the government's offer. It came as a shock. Far from conceding advances, the new rates proposed involved serious reductions in many existing wage-rates, even though these reductions were hedged about with provisos on the cost of living. It was proposed that ultimately a porter earning between 51s and 53s would receive 40s; passenger guards would have their wages reduced by 4s to 7s 'a week; ticket collectors by 5s to 10s a week. In an accompanying letter, Sir Auckland Geddes, the President of the Board of Trade, stated that the proposals were not put forward for negotiation but as the government's 'definitive' offer. To the NUR executive, 'definitive' meant 'final' with no room left for argument. At a meeting on Wednesday, 24 September, they drew up a message to be sent to all branch secretaries, telling them that unless they heard to the contrary, all union members were to strike at midnight on Friday.

No one was less anxious to have a strike than J. H. Thomas, the general secretary of the NUR. In previous crises he had always managed somehow to get a compromise settlement and for the next two days he worked hard to get an offer which would justify calling off the strike. But he came up against men who were determined on a confrontation. Foremost among them were the Geddes brothers: Sir Eric, who was Minister of Transport, and Sir Auckland, President of the Board of Trade. Eric had formerly been general manager of the North Eastern Railway, Auckland a Professor of Anatomy. Both had been given a succession of key posts in the Lloyd George wartime administration. The sons of a Scottish civil engineer, they reflected the attitudes of a new managerial class. But they shared with the old-established industrialists the opinion that if Britain's competitive position in the world was to be restored, wages must be got back to pre-war levels – not, perhaps in money terms, while prices remained so high, but in real terms. Only so did they believe the railways could be put on a sound basis for the time when government control should be relinquished. They also believed that what was decided for the railways would create a precedent for all industry.

At the eleventh-hour talks, the NUR leaders got the impression that the Geddes brothers really wanted a strike. No doubt the rest of the Cabinet thought that Sir Eric, with his experience as a railway manager, knew what he was doing. In fact he was making one of the major miscalculations of his career. The strike which began on 26 September 1919 lasted for nine days. It ended with a settlement which the railwaymen as a whole greeted as a victory. And though in fact its terms were a compromise, they represented, beyond all doubt, a major defeat both for the government and the railway employers.

From the first the plan to buy off the skilled men and divide the railwaymen failed. The drivers and firemen belonging to the rival ASLEF decided to support their lower-paid fellows. Rivalry and jealousy between ASLEF and the NUR had been bitter at times, and now the ASLEF men had no economic interest in the outcome of the strike. But a few days before the strike began the Executive of ASLEF sent a message to the NUR: 'If you want help we are standing by.' When it became clear that the strike was on, a telegram was sent to all ASLEF branches: 'Executive decided to support NUR. Our members must strike at midnight tonight.'

At headquarters the NUR was quite unprepared for action and had hardly any ready cash available for strike pay. However, the Co-operative movement came to the rescue. The CWS Bank advanced the money and made it payable through local Co-operative societies all over the country.

The strike was due to begin at midnight on Friday 26 September but large numbers of railwaymen left work at 10 o'clock that evening. The majority of them, indeed, entered the strike with unprecedented enthusiasm, almost as though a longed-for day had come at last. 'All out to a man'; 'One hundred per cent solid'; 'Stoppage complete'; the telegrams poured into the NUR headquarters. It was clear that this was quite a different kind of railway strike from the last one which had taken place eight years previously. The 1911 strike, though unprecedented at the time for size and militancy, had started spontaneously in a series of unofficial waves. A large proportion of the strikers had been non-unionists and the number taking part had not exceeded 200,000. This strike was a united disciplined affair, involving half a million trade unionists.

All over the country local strike committees went into action. They had received strict instructions from union headquarters that they were not to break the law and that pickets must rely on peaceful persuasion only. In fact their main activities were concentrated on publicity for their cause, social functions to keep up morale and the collection of funds, particularly for the relief of strikers with children. Strike pay was only 12s a week, with 1s for each child. A day-to-day account from Watford[23] showed that during the week of the strike, three football matches were arranged (locomen versus permanentway men), there were several marches with bands and banners, teas were laid on by the strikers' wives in the local Co-op Hall where marchers from neighbouring depots were welcomed, in the evenings there were singsongs and concerts, with music and turns laid on by other sections of the Labour movement. When strike pay day came on Saturday, local print workers distributed 500 loaves of bread and 165 pots of jam.

The actions of the government, however, suggested that it was preparing for insurrection. It was reported that three warships had anchored off Southend and a cruiser had been sent to the Mersey. Troops occupied all railway stations and were ordered to protect bridges and signal boxes. In some stations, as at Woking, guns were mounted, though a proposal from Winston Churchill to place machine-guns at the entrances to railway tunnels was turned down by the Cabinet.

Simultaneously an emergency transport plan was put into operation, for the railways were Britain's lifeline. Though motor-buses were common for passenger transport, there were estimated to be not more than 65,000 commercial motor-vans in the whole country. Now Hyde Park was turned into a transport centre from which thousands of army lorries were directed. They were used to bring milk to London daily and to take food out to the rest of the country. This was divided into sixteen regions in each of which food controllers, still in existence as part of the wartime Ministry of Food, were given power to requisition vehicles. The existing sugar and butter rations were reduced and rationing of meat reimposed.

A determined effort was made to mobilize the general public against the strikers and involve them in strike-breaking activities. This was not a strike for wages or better conditions, declared the Prime Minister in a widely publicized telegram cancelling a speaking engagement in Caernarvon on 27 September. The strike, he said, had been engineered by a small but active body of men who 'wrought tirelessly and insidiously to exploit the labour organizations of this country for subversive ends'. He characterized the strike as an 'anarchist conspiracy'.

In a leader on 29 September *The Times* appeared anxious that everyone should be clear:

> Mr Lloyd George is not quite correct in calling it an 'anarchist conspiracy' though it is directed against the Government. It is really something new – neither Socialism, nor Syndicalism, nor Sovietism nor Anarchism. It comes nearest to Syndicalism because what the men behind the movement aim at is the control of industry. But they go beyond Syndicalism ... They aim at controlling the Government ... If successful it would mean the end of representative Government and the power of Parliament. For the Government therefore the conflict is one of life and death ... Like the war with Germany, it must be a fight to a finish.

Appeals made for volunteers to man the railways and for men to enrol as special constables had a big response. Volunteers offered their services on the railways in large numbers so that towards the end of the strike the government was able to maintain a skeleton service for passengers on some lines. A *Times* reporter described the activities of these volunteers on the London underground:

> They seemed chiefly to be of what is classed roughly as the public school type of man. Many were ex-officers, and nobody could have wished for a more cheerful, courteous and considerate body of public servants. Here and there one of the new race of porters instinctively raised his hat after telling a lady that the next train did not stop at Goodge Street.[24]

In such a mood of mutual congratulation strike-breaking was developed. The government propaganda was unremitting. But here again it was revealed how greatly the world had changed, for it transpired that in this field also the lumbering forces of labour were able to compete. The unions authorized the Labour Research Department to take charge of counter-propaganda, and that body enlisted the help of various leading intellectuals, including Bernard Shaw. Posters and handbills were printed and a series of full-page paid advertisements began to appear in the newspapers putting the railwaymen's case. 'Don't blame the Railwaymen for the strike, blame the Government that forced the strike upon them,' ran one in bold letters covering a full page of *The Times*. 'The Prime Minister said there must be "A land fit for heroes to live in." Does he make "the land fit for heroes" by forcing down Railwaymen's wages? If the Government set the example every private employer will follow suit . . . Browbeating the poorest workers is worse than a scandal. It is a crime.'[25]

The reiteration day after day that the government was trying to cut railwaymen's wages had a certain effect. Gradually there began to be mutterings about government mishandling and blunders, even in those newspapers formerly most hostile to the railwaymen. Ernest Bevin, one of the leaders of the Transport Workers Federation, was confronted by demands from busmen, tramwaymen and dockers that they should be called out on strike in support of the railwaymen. A conference of leading unions and the Labour Party sent a statement to the Prime Minister warning him that unless a more reasonable attitude was adopted it would be impossible to avert a widespread extension of the strike.

On this the Cabinet capitulated and agreed to negotiate with the railwaymen, as a result of which a compromise settlement was arrived at. The government's original proposals were dropped. Wages were to be stabilized at their existing level for a year; negotiations on standardization were to proceed; no adult railwayman was to receive less than 51s a week so long as the cost of living stood at a certain level above 1914.

After the strike there was some criticism of the NUR from members of other unions – particularly from the left-wing secretary of the Transport Workers Federation, Robert Williams – because the railwaymen had not asked for the support of the Triple Alliance from the beginning. The truth was that J.H. Thomas was much afraid that if the railwaymen called for the help of other unions, the dispute might end by having political and constitutional implications. The railwaymen were attacked by the government throughout for striking for political ends; the leaders were appalled at the idea that this untruthful allegation might in time become true. Whatever the criticisms from the other unions, the mass of the railwaymen were convinced that their settlement represented a historic victory.

Meanwhile, nationalization was no longer a live issue. Instead the Railway Companies were forced by Act of Parliament two years later to follow the trend and reorganize themselves into the four main-line companies.

Dockers and Shipowners

In October 1919 the National Transport Workers Federation made a claim on behalf of 125,000 dockers for a minimum wage of 16s a day.* The figure of 125,000 men was an estimate; no one really knew how many dock labourers there were. The claim for 16s a day (or 8s a half day) compared with existing minimum rates varying from 11/8d a day in London and Liverpool to 14s a day on the Clyde.

The employers began by resisting the claim, and then offered to submit it to a public Court of Inquiry to be appointed by the Minister of Labour. After some hesitation – for the dockers themselves wanted action, particularly those who had just come back from the war – the Executive of the Transport Workers Federation agreed to the Court of Inquiry and appointed one of its members, 39-year-old Ernest Bevin, to present the dockers' case.

The port employers had no national machinery for collective bargaining, being accustomed to individual negotiations, port by port, in which they saw much advantage. But they hurriedly formed an ad hoc organization called the National Council of Port Employers and briefed an eminent K C, Sir Lynden Macassey, to act on their behalf.

The Court of Inquiry, which was chaired by Lord Shaw of Dunfermline, opened its proceedings on 3 February 1920 and held sittings in public for five weeks. It attracted almost as much publicity as the Sankey Commission had done the year before, and Ernest Bevin became known as the Dockers' K C.

The dockers' employers were a heterogeneous group. Most important among them were the shipowners. The big lines which had ships sailing regularly to and from certain ports would hire their own labour to load and unload. In addition there were firms who acted as contractors for dock labour – in particular, master stevedores who undertook contracts to load vessels, and master porters who contracted to unload vessels and to clear goods from the quay. Among other dock employers were wharfingers who owned warehouses at the docks;

---

* The NTWF was a Federation of over 30 unions including a number of dockers', stevedores', and other port workers' unions. Also in the Federation were seamen's unions, several unions catering for carters and lorry-drivers, and others catering for tramway men and busmen.

waterside manufacturers whose raw materials came in by water; innumerable merchants who employed men to handle certain types of goods; master lightermen, responsible for goods discharged 'overside' into barges – and in ports like Hull nearly everything was discharged 'overside' to be taken to destinations along canals and inland waterways. In some ports, where everything was removed by rail, the railway companies employed dock labour. At Liverpool, where almost everything was removed by road, the employers of the carters (or, to a growing extent, the lorry drivers) tended to overlap with the employers of dock labour.

Superimposed on all this were the harbour authorities, who managed the ports in return for fees paid by the port users but were themselves, to some extent employers of dock labour. Most of these harbour authorities were ostensibly public, non–profit-making bodies, but they tended to consist primarily of the dock employers. This was so in Liverpool and in London. Bristol on the other hand was entirely municipally owned, while the docks at Southampton were owned by the railway companies.

The shipowners were enjoying a boom based partly on the shortage of shipping space and correspondingly high freight-rates. In the middle of the war there had been public outcry about war profiteering in shipping, and towards the end of 1916 the government had been forced to take control. Despite the atmosphere of public disapproval, the shipowners had fought off proposals for the government to retain control when the war ended and, indeed, to nationalize the industry. Bit by bit they had gained release from government interference. Big capital gains were now being made by selling off old ships at very high prices. Some of the companies formed to buy such ships later went bankrupt, but at the beginning of 1920 it was not yet clear that the boom would come to an end.

It was against this background that Bevin argued to the Court that the whole of the dockers' pay claim could be paid for by the shipowners.

The dock labourers' work was among the hardest known, much of it involving continuous lifting and carrying of very heavy loads. There were cranes, of course, but mechanical aids were still rudimentary. In the grain ports men carried loads of up to 280 lbs – 2½ cwt – on their backs; during the course of a single day a man could hump 70 tons over his shoulders. 'They pick out the strongest men and discourage the old ones and the cripples and as long as these men can work hard they will keep them on, but they ruin them very quickly,' Bevin told the Court. And he described how grain porters had been 'ruptured and ruined, and laid out with asthma and things of that kind';[26] how the warehouses which held the grain were ill designed, so that the loads had to be lifted from awkward levels;[27] and how wheat cargoes coming from the East were 'filled with dust and sand and asphyxiating gases' which led to tuberculosis and asthma.[28]

Some cargoes were highly dangerous. An official of the Liverpool Dockers Union, called as a witness, described what it was like to handle $2\frac{1}{2}$ cwt bags of soda-ash. 'Now that is burning hot on the man's back. He has to stand that; he has to work through it. I have known many a man working alongside of me, happening to work, perhaps, a little longer than me and they went to their graves with a hole as big as the palm of your hand on the back of their neck. It burns right through. It will go through clothes, or anything.'[29]

The employers continually suggested that though a docker's work might be heavy it was unskilled. 'There is nothing in a dock labourer's profession that he cannot learn in a week,' observed the dock superintendent for the Ellerman-Wilson line at Hull,[30] and added that shovelling iron ore and things of that sort didn't require much skill. But included in the many categories involved in the claim for the 16s minimum were some who were highly skilled, particularly the stevedores who had to stow all classes of cargo into the hold of a ship in such a way that it would not endanger the ship and would arrive undamaged. Bevin called as witness a working stevedore from Birkenhead who, as a skilled man, got preference for any work going. He was pressed by the employers' counsel to agree that piecework would lead to greater output and higher earnings. He disagreed on the grounds that rush methods did not lead to safe stowage, and that different cargoes had to be stowed in different ways. 'If you are stowing cases of glass, if they were being paid piecework, and there was no one to watch them, they would tumble that glass in any way,' he said. 'Now there is only one recognized method, so far as Liverpool is concerned, of stowing glass; it must be stowed on its edge athwart the ship, not fore and aft. It is very difficult to stow glass; a narrow case of glass will be put athwart the ship, and someone may have to stand by that case of glass after you have stowed it for fear it might tilt; it is only narrow, and it might possibly stand four or five feet high.'[31] He said that over six months or so his average wage had been £3 10s – this included overtime. His earnings had been reduced by a dock accident in which his shoulder had been broken.

The main characteristic which distinguished the docker's life from others was neither its danger nor its back-breaking toil, but the fact that the work was casual, intermittent and insecure. Very few men were employed on a regular basis. From the employers' point of view there were good reasons for this. Much of the trade was seasonal, with cargoes which came in or went out at certain times of the year only. There were the hazards of the weather; ships due in or out could be delayed. One week there would be dozens of ships coming in, and work for hundreds, including a demand for work at night so that a ship could sail; the next week there would be no ships at all, and work for nobody.

To meet these circumstances the employers were in the habit of hiring men for a day or even for half a day to deal with the loading or unloading of one particular consignment of goods only or one particular ship's cargo. The older members of the Court could remember, indeed, how not much more than 30 years previously starving men had fought one another at the dock gates for what might turn out to be a single hour's work. But then in 1889 the impossible had happened; in the Port of London these men, looked on by those in more settled callings as shiftless, declassed and impossible to organize, had come out on strike, and in the battle for the 'dockers' tanner' had shown an unexpected solidarity with one another. Moreover the stevedores, already organized in craft unions, had come out in support of what they called their 'poorer brothers'. As a result of that strike the minimum pay had been fixed at sixpence an hour and, even more important, the minimum spell of work at four hours. So that men could no longer be hired for a single hour, but if taken on at all had to be paid for at least four hours.

The docker of 1920 was very different from his father. He was better educated and had the habit of trade union organization. But the employers' behaviour towards the men had changed little. They took men on and laid them off as seemed convenient, and no man knew at the beginning of a week whether he would get a full week's work, or three days' work, or half a day's work or nothing. The men would assemble at the dock gates, or the call-on stands, and from among those who turned up the foreman would take his pick, deliberately leaving out any who might be 'awkward'.

'Take the case of a man who takes a prominent part in looking after the men's welfare,' said Patrick McKibbin of the Liverpool Dockers Union: 'directly that man shows himself prominent in that way in Liverpool he does not immediately get the sack, but they have a habit of leaving him standing on the stand the next morning, and he is not employed.' Having chosen his men, McKibbin said, the foreman would try to force the pace. He told the Court about the type of foreman 'who tries to get as much as he can possibly get with the least number of men working in the gang. That man becomes a very prominent official in the firm; they pay him on results.'[32]

Meanwhile those not called to a job at 8 in the morning would have to wait until 1 o'clock for their next chance, and might fail again. Those who lived close might go home in the interval; for the others there was nowhere to go. The Court observed in its final report: 'there does not appear even yet to exist on any appreciable scale within the docks, ports and harbours of our Kingdom any refuge, place of rest, or even proper or sufficient canteen accommodation, although in the case of thousands of men their homes may be miles from their place of labour.'[33]

Though some dockers got work on only two or three days a week, jobs often involved working beyond normal hours. Part of the union's claim was for increased overtime pay, not so much, they said, to get more money, but to make it more expensive for the employer and so give him an incentive to better organization that could bring more regular hours for the men. Bevin told the Court:

In dock life there has been very little regard at all paid to any convenience of the men. A broker rings up a dock authority or a stevedore, and says, 'I want that ship tonight' or 'I want it tomorrow. I want it to sail; I have another freight.' He could have given that order at 11 o'clock in the morning, possibly, because he knew, but perhaps he went to his own lunch and did not bother. Then he came back and let it go on into the afternoon. If the workman says 'I have arranged to go somewhere this afternoon, I have a wife and children and I do not feel like working,' he outrages the sense of that broker. Fancy a docker declining![34]

There was also competition from unemployed men in other trades, who would try to pick up casual work at the docks to tide them over a bad patch. To protect their members the dockers' union had been fighting for a system of registration. This was seen as a first step towards decasualization. Under such a scheme the employers would be able only to take on dockers who were registered with the trade union.

But in practice, when the union leaders tried to get registration schemes adopted, they found themselves up against not only the employers but, to a large extent, their own members. One reason for this was that in return for such a scheme the employers insisted on an agreement obliging those registered to accept any job offered them. A man who could make a tolerable livelihood for himself under a foreman he knew and with a gang he knew, working on a type of cargo that he understood, might find himself put on unfamiliar work with strangers. There was also a deep-rooted belief among the dockers that when anything new was introduced by the employers the object must be to apply the screw in some way. And finally there were, of course, some who had got used to the system, who had managed to some extent to get it to work their way. It was such a mixture of motives that had recently caused the membership to torpedo a registration scheme agreed between the employers and the union on the Clyde. And though there was in existence a registration scheme at Liverpool, it had provoked strikes at Birkenhead. In London a scheme had just been inaugurated.*

In resisting the dockers' claim for 16s a day the employers had enlisted the help of A. L. Bowley, Professor of Statistics at London University and a former member of a government committee on the cost of living, to compile a minimum weekly budget for a man, wife and three children. The budget prepared by Bowley totalled £3 13s 6d. The striking thing about this budget, since it was the employers them-

---

* The Port of London Registration Scheme had been drawn up in 1919 by the Port of London (Casual Labour) Committee, on which both sides of the industry were represented; its object was to reduce the number of casual labourers in the Port and to prevent workers from other trades from resorting to the docks and wharves when unemployed and so making conditions of employment more irregular than before. The Scheme was inaugurated in January 1920; regular dockworkers were registered and issued with a numbered brass tally as a means of identification. Initially 62,000 workers were registered: by 1924 they had been reduced to 34,000. Other ports adopted similar schemes on a national basis. In 1930 the Minister of Labour instituted a Port Labour inquiry; the outcome was unanimous approval of registration schemes.

selves who put it forward, was that it was admitted to cost more than the earnings of the average docker. Evidence given to the Court by Sir Alfred Booth, Chairman of Cunard, suggested that in Liverpool weekly earnings of dock labourers, including overtime and the rather higher earnings of 'preference' men, were under £3 6s a week.

To construct his minimum budget, Bowley had taken Rowntree's pre-war estimates made in his book *The Human Needs of Labour* for all the non-food items and had repriced them. For food, however, Bowley had taken the actual diet in 1914 of a railway goods porter, with a wife and three children and had not only repriced it but considerably modified it. The budget looked like this:

	£	s	d
Food	2	0	0
Rent		6	6
Clothing		12	6
Fuel		4	8
Sundries:			
Household		3	4
Personal		6	6
Total	£3	13	6

The allocation of £2 for food assumed that the breadwinner, being a very heavy worker, required 3700 calories a day. The original diet on which it had been based had, however, been considerably altered by Bowley in order to cut out the more expensive items and replace them with cheaper substitutes. Part of the argument for doing this was that some of the items had been rationed during the war and were still in short supply. Thus butter, which had been in the original diet, was removed and margarine put in its place; the original 11 pints of milk were reduced to 8; 6 eggs had been cut out altogether; the allowance of vegetables and fruit had been much reduced. In compensation Professor Bowley had increased the allowances of potatoes, flour, rice and, to a small extent, cheese.*

At the time vitamins and other nutrients later recognized as essential

---

* The actual diet of 1914 and Bowley's proposed diet are compared in Table 5, p. 46. Beside them is set out the actual average diet of a family of this size in 1967.

to a healthy diet had hardly been heard of; discussion of an adequate diet among experts normally centred around protein and calories. But Bevin's reply to this diet did not concern itself with calories; instead he concentrated on some visual demonstrations. He bought the exact amount of potatoes and cabbage allowed in the diet and cooked them, bought the requisite allowance of cheese, divided the whole into seven portions to represent the seven days of the week, redivided them into five portions for the five members of the family and brought the resultant scraps of food into Court on five plates. This demonstration not only delighted the dockers in the public gallery, it was seized on by the press.

Professor Bowley appeared as a witness in defence of the diet he had devised, and for a day and a half was subjected by Bevin to the kind of heavy-handed sarcasm which his own colleagues in the Labour movement tended to resent when directed against themselves. The visual demonstrations were continued; the entire portion of bacon allowed in the diet was brought to the court and dividing it into seven, Bevin asked if it was sufficient breakfast for a man who was to go and discharge ships and carry grain. 'I am willing to cook it,' he said, 'and when that is cooked I want to ask any employer, or you, or the Court whether a Cambridge professor is a competent judge of a docker's breakfast. (Laughter.) Do not laugh, please; I am quite serious on this, because the point is this, that we have to examine it in the light of a man, and not of a gentleman who sits down to see how little we can live on.'[35] In defence of the bacon allowance, Bowley suggested that the fish in the diet might help for breakfast on one morning in the week. Bevin's response was to buy sixpennyworth of fish at a stall in Canning Town which was selling off cheap to prevent waste, cook it and bring it to Court divided as a breakfast between five. 'Do you think that is sufficient for a docker to go to work upon, handling heavy cargo?' he asked.[36]

Every item in the diet was challenged. 'We will be quite prepared to cook the whole daily budget in proportionate ingredients by the most scientific method of cooking and submit it to your Lordships' Court,' said Bevin. 'And I challenge Professor Bowley to live on it.'[37] Bowley answered that he and his wife and three children *had* lived on it for three weeks – except that they had 22 pints of milk in place of the 8 pints in his diet. After which he was asked how much manual work he had done in that three weeks and replied that he had been digging in his garden, in 'stiff clay, I may tell you'. 'But you have not done eight hours' digging right off, have you?' 'No.' 'And you have not had somebody come and say to you at the end of eight hours "Now work on for another four hours"?' 'No, not on the gardening work.' 'Dockers do!'[38]

Bowley held his ground and argued his case, as the Court subsequently suggested, 'with great ability'. But Bevin throughout the proceedings continued to object to the very concept of a minimum budget which 'is just like calculating the cost of keeping an animal.'[39]

Apart from the lengthy arguments about minimum budgets, the employers' case fell into three parts. The first argument was that increased handling charges would have to be passed on in higher prices to the consumer. The London Chamber of Commerce, claiming to represent 9000 firms, many with a vital interest in import, export or entrepot trade, expressed anxiety that transport charges should not be increased. Lord Devonport, chairman of the Port of London Authority and a businessman with interests mainly in food firms, observed that London, as the great entrepot port of the world, was in sharp competition with the continental ports of Antwerp and Rotterdam.

The employers also argued that if the dockers were granted 16s a day, which meant 2s an hour, there would be immediate demands for wage increases from other workers. 'It is bound to affect the analogous trades of labour – particularly such trades as the carters and other men working alongside the docks,' said Sir Alfred Booth, chairman of the Cunard Steamship Company. 'I understand there has been an application put in for the carters already to bring them up to the same level as the dockers would be brought to if this application were granted. It gets, of course, beyond the docks because the engineers and ship repairers are working on the ships in the docks alongside the dock labourers, and from them it spreads to the whole engineering and shipbuilding trades of the country.'[40]

This was not just an argument to impress the Court; it signified genuine apprehension, There was considerable interlocking between the railway companies and the shipping companies; some of the shipowners were also large employers in shipbuilding, ship repairs, marine engineering, coal and oil. For example the chairman of Ellerman Lines, Sir John Ellerman, had a big holding in John Brown & Co, who were coalowners in South Yorkshire, shipbuilders on the Clyde, marine engineers in various parts of the country, and also owned iron mines.

The main argument of the employers, however, concerned the alleged fall in output by the dockers. Like the railwaymen and other sections, the dockers had gained a reduction in hours from nine to eight for a normal day when the war ended. But the employers said that the fall in output was out of all proportion to the reduction in hours. The union argued that the fall was partly the result of the acute congestion in the docks, valuable warehouse space being still occupied by government-controlled stocks. Secondly the union stressed that the fittest dockers had gone to fight in the war, leaving the less fit to man the docks. Hull, for example, had lost half its labour force during the war. 'The good type of man, the healthy and strong type of man were all called up to go to the war,' McKibbin of Liverpool told the Court. 'It left the docks with old men and, I might say respectfully, cripples.' He added that the majority of those who had come back again had been impaired in health.[41]

The employers denied the statements about the men's health and were full of the difficulties they were having as a result of the behaviour of the men. Sir Alfred Booth complained that the Liverpool employers had signed a new agreement on overtime with the National Union of Dock Labourers, but that then the Liverpool men had turned the agreement down by ballot vote; subsequently the Annual Congress of the Union had turned down the agreement also and had elected a new executive committee which refused to consider itself party to the agreement.

The director of a Liverpool firm of master stevedores complained that the men were constantly accepting jobs and then going off, so that half an hour later the foreman would find the gang short; at other times they found a whole gang would be taking an hour off in turns continuously throughout the day. He said that the firm had had to take on machines because the men would not now attempt to lift anything approaching the weights that had been lifted ten years before; in practice they would not lift more than 2 cwt by hand.[42]

A representative of the Liverpool Coastwise Association complained of constant stoppages and demands for extra money for certain cargoes. For example, men were paid an extra shilling a day for handling Pernambuco sugar which was 'very dirty and sloppy stuff to handle', but now they had refused to handle drier West Indies sugar because they wanted a shilling extra for this too.[43]

A Glasgow employer told of an electrically-driven grain-weighing machine which did the work of weighing and bagging. It was meant to replace the hand weighing machine which involved humping 2 cwt bags; with the new machine the bag was never lifted over the shoulder at all. Though the employers offered the men a much higher rate of pay to work the machine, the men had refused and the machine had remained idle. The reason was that whereas the old system employed fifteen men the new machine needed only six, and the workers wanted more men employed on the new machine.[44]

A Humber shipowner said that though there might be a full week's work for a man, 'a lot of the men are quite satisfied with two, three or four days' wages and will not work any more.' Like the Bristol employers he spoke about the bad time-keeping. 'If we were to get an honest day's work for an honest day's pay, we think we could give them a little bit more money,' he said.[45] A warehouse manager at the Port of London spoke of a dispute with deal porters who were breaking off for 15 minutes in each working hour and were declining to unload timber from barges unless cranes were provided. He complained that grain porters at Surrey Commercial Dock were taking 10- to 15-minute breaks morning and afternoon.

'We have not got the 8-hour working day; in some parts it is down to 6, in others $6\frac{1}{2}$, in others 7,' said Sir Lynden Macassey on behalf of the employers.[46] And he urged that the unions should fine those of their members who failed to carry out agreements made by their own unions.

Bevin took up this point in his closing remarks:

That is not the way, my Lord, to accomplish the result that we require. If you want Labour to accept responsibility it must carry with it corresponding power . . . I would never be a party and I am quite sure my colleagues of the Federation never will be a party to converting the Trade Union movement into merely an instrument of punishment for its members, because it declines to carry out the orders of somebody else. But give us the power to have the making of the orders, and we will not shirk the responsibility of carrying them out.[47]

On 31 March 1920 the Court of Inquiry issued its findings. The majority report signed by seven out of the nine members recommended that the demand for a minimum wage of 16s a day should be granted in full. The Report made an all-out condemnation of the casual system and recommended that a system of registration coupled with maintenance by the industry of its unemployed casuals should be introduced.

Two employers dissented from the recommendation in a minority report. But after some hesitation the employers as a whole finally agreed to the Court's recommendation and conceded the 16s minimum.

At the tenth Annual Meeting of the National Transport Workers Federation on 3 June 1920 the result was hailed as a great victory. In a special report the executive of the Federation described it as:

the greatest triumph which the Federation has gained during the past year. The Report of the Court of Inquiry is the most sweeping vindication of the claims of the workers that has ever been elicited from any tribunal. It must destroy for all time the notion that the casual worker is merely the spare part of the industrial machine. It established the right of the docker to decent human conditions, both as regards his work and his home. It gave him status – and status, as was said at one of the demonstrations held during the negotiations, is the greatest thing in life.[48]

The new minimum came into operation on 10 May 1920. It was on that same day that some London dockers refused to load a ship with arms intended for the war against Russia.

Table 5   Diets 1914–67

	Actual diet of railwayman, wife and three children, 1914		Bowley's proposed diet for a docker family, 1920	Average diet of man, wife and three children, 1967	
	lbs	oz	lbs oz	lbs	oz
Butcher's meat	7	8	6 0	4	1
Sausages	—	—	} 2 0*	2	14
Fish		(8)‡		1	3
Bacon	1	0	1 0	1	4
Total meat, fish, bacon	9	0	9 0	9	6
Cheese		7	11½		11½
Eggs (number)		6	—		21
Milk (pints)		11	8		26
Butter	1	3	—	1	6
Margarine		—	2 0		11½
Lard, suet etc	1	0	1 0		11½
Potatoes	12	0	14 0	16	14
§Peas		8 }			
§Carrots	1	10	(1s) }	8	3
§Cabbage		(6d)			
§Fruit		(1s 2d)	(10d)	6	15
Bread	22	0	21 0	10	1
Flour	2	0	7 0	1	6½
†Oatmeal	1	0	1 0	2	7
†Rice		8	2 0		
Cake		5		1	6½
Biscuits		—	12	1	11
Sugar	4	5	2 8	4	4
Jam	1	0	2 8		12
Tea		10	10		6
Cocoa		—	4		1
Coffee		—	—		1

* Actually 3/–. According to Reid of the Liverpool Dockers' Union (See Appendix 39 Transport Workers Court of Inquiry Cmd 937) sausages cost in 1920 1/4d to 1/10d a lb. Cod cost 1/4d, hake 1/10d, 'Finnie Haddie' 1/4d. Bowley's allowance of 3/– might therefore have procured 2 lb of fish or sausages.

† Breakfast cereals, rice, etc.

‡ Actually 6d. This would have procured at least 8 oz of fish in 1914 – possibly more.

§ Since fresh fruit and vegetables are given in money terms for 1914 and 1920 it is not possible to compare them except to say that Bowley's recommended diet clearly provided much less than the 1914 diet, and the 1967 diet (for which the quantities are known) far more than either.

(Sources: The 1914 diet of a railwayman's family is an actual one shown in Appendix No 58 to the Transport Workers Court of Inquiry. The diet proposed by the employers and compiled by Bowley for a dockers family in 1920 is in Appendix 55 ibid. The 1967 diet is the average for a family of that size shown in *Household Food Consumption and Expenditure*, 1967 published by the National Food Survey Committee.)

3
The Attitude to the Outside World

Germany and the Peace Treaty

In the summer of 1919 the Versailles Peace Treaty was signed. All through the spring, while the heads of state were negotiating in Paris, British newspapers expressed fears that the promise to 'make Germany pay' might be broken. In April 1919 370 coalition MPs sent a telegram to the Prime Minister, Lloyd George, reminding him of his election pledges, and saying that their constituents expected that Britain's bill for reparations would be presented in full.

However when the terms of the treaty were published in May 1919 it appeared that these fears were groundless. Germany was not only to be disarmed and her fleet scuttled, she was to lose all her colonies, to suffer drastic revision of her frontiers, to submit to the occupation of the Rhine for fifteen years, and to hand over the Saar coalfields. She was to pay massive reparations, and yet was to be largely deprived of the means of payment. 'She is first stripped naked and then told to turn out her pockets,' was how the *Daily News* put it.[1] But despite the doubts expressed in one or two Liberal newspapers about the economic terms of the treaty, the independent Liberals made no stand against them. The view that the peace terms were too harsh was not a popular one. Germany would have been harder on us had she won the war, it was said.

All-out opposition came only from the left. A peace of reconciliation was the Labour Party's stated aim, and the Party's National Executive now issued a statement condemning the treaty, while the Union of Democratic Control* pointed out that Britain's quarrel had been with

* The UDC had been formed by a group of Liberals and Socialists during the war and worked for a democratically-controlled foreign policy.

the rulers of Germany who had now been overthrown, and that the apparent purpose of the Allied governments was to reduce the new democratic Germany to the position of a vassal state.[2] Labour's newspaper, the *Daily Herald*, declared that the treaty was the revenge of the imperialist powers; it would mean economic disaster and would sow the seeds of a future war. Its cartoonist, Will Dyson, portrayed a child crying outside the peace conference chamber. The child was '1940 Class'.[3]

Towards the end of 1919 appeared J.M.Keynes's book *The Economic Consequences of the Peace*. It argued that the treaty would not only ruin Germany but would destroy the prosperity of Europe, including Britain. Later events appeared to justify such forecasts. Germany defaulted on her reparations payments and by 1923 she was suffering from a runaway inflation. The French moved in and occupied the Ruhr and the name of Adolf Hitler was mentioned in British newspapers as leader of a fascist movement which had tried unsuccessfully to overthrow the German government.

The decision to form a League of Nations was also embodied in the Peace Treaty. The League came into existence in January 1920 'in order to promote international cooperation and to achieve international peace and security by the acceptance of obligations not to resort to war.'[4] Its members bound themselves not to use force for settling disputes but to submit them first to the League for decision. Articles in the League Covenant were aimed at the control of the private manufacture of arms and the abolition of secret treaties. Gradual progress towards international disarmament was envisaged.

In Britain the acceptance of such ideas showed how profoundly the climate had changed. Before the war an unquestioning nationalism had been normal, jingoism common. Only minority groups – socialists, pacifists and some Liberals – had urged the need for international cooperation and disarmament. Now most statesmen were talking in these terms. Scepticism about the League's peace-keeping role was widespread, and here and there was open hostility. But a belief in the League's aims was at least respectable.

A League of Nations Union was formed consisting of people from various political parties, and, though it had more Liberal and Labour supporters than Conservatives, its chairman was Lord Robert Cecil, a Conservative MP and son of the Marquess of Salisbury. The aim of the

Union was to build up a body of opinion in support of the League's purposes and the ideals embodied in its Covenant.

Russia

To the Labour movement in the year 1919 the continued war of intervention in Russia was a matter of more urgency than the German peace treaties. Russia had been an ally of Britain and France for the first years of the war. But in 1917 had come the March and October revolutions; and a Soviet government was established which after unsuccessful efforts to secure a general peace, signed a separate peace with Germany. Since the spring of 1918 British troops, along with those from other countries, had invaded Russian territory and were cooperating with the anti-Bolshevik forces which were trying to topple the Soviet regime. Originally the stated object of these operations had been to protect allied military stores in Russia and to prevent her resources falling into German hands. But when the war against Germany came to an end in November 1918, intervention in Russia still went on.

'Impossible and contrary to human nature, and cannot last,' were the words used by Bonar Law about the Soviet government.[5] They summed up the shocked incredulity which still prevailed two and a half years after the 1917 revolution. For generations society had been plagued by revolutionary theories which envisaged the destruction of the existing social order. Now a great country was actually engaged in implementing a revolutionary theory. If the new system could survive it would be a challenge to the old system in every country in the world.

There were, nevertheless, sharp divisions as to the wisdom of continuing military intervention in Russia. Some, including certain members of the Cabinet such as Winston Churchill, wanted greatly intensified military operations. Others, including Lloyd George, had the deepest misgivings about continued British involvement. The result was that throughout 1919 the words spoken by Lloyd George and some of his colleagues seemed to be out of step with the events taking place. Repeatedly it was said that British troops were to be withdrawn, while simultaneously they were reported as going into action.

At the opposite pole from those who wanted to crush the Soviet system was a handful of people who, in November 1917, heard the news of the Bolshevik revolution with excitement and hope. Some of these were members of the Independent Labour Party, others of much smaller left-wing socialist groupings such as the British Socialist Party, the Socialist Labour Party and the Workers' Socialist Federation. Some were socialist war resisters, spending the war years in prison.

The news of the revolution caused excitement too in the Shop Stewards and Workers Committee movement which had grown rapidly during the war, particularly in the big munition and engineering centres. It appeared to some active shop stewards that it was workers like themselves who had seized power in Russia. They were gripped by a confused idea of transforming their own workers' committees into organs of revolution. This enthusiasm for Russia felt by individual shop stewards was not shared by the workers as a whole. And the enthusiasm was certainly not shared by the majority of the trade union and Labour leaders who believed in the gradual transformation of society by means of the ballot box, and regarded the Bolshevik revolution with abhorrence and fear.

However in the twelve months that followed the Armistice in 1918, the enthusiasts for the Soviet Republic who had been obstinately swimming against the current suddenly found themselves swimming with it – indeed pushed along by it. To some extent this was the reflection of a growing sympathy with what the Soviets were said to be doing: throwing out the landlords, giving land to the peasants, putting industry under workers' control. To a much larger extent it was a sign that people were sick of war and angry that the British government were proposing a new Bill to continue conscription. Moreover many were moved by horror at the reports of famine and devastation which the allied blockade and intervention were creating in the Soviet Union. In such a situation even those who disliked the Soviet regime began to say that Russia's form of government was her own affair. So that when in April 1919 the *Daily Herald* issued a call to workers to unite against 'militaristic maniacs' who wanted to 'plunge us into a new Armageddon in Eastern Europe' it evoked a wide response in the trade union movement.

A national 'Hands Off Russia' Committee was formed, which assiduously circularized organizations, in particular trade union branches, urging action to stop the war against Russia. Enthusiastic 'Hands Off Russia' meetings were held in the Albert Hall in London and in the largest halls in Manchester, Glasgow, Edinburgh, Sheffield.

By the spring of 1919 it was hardly necessary to argue the case against the war of intervention at trade union conferences. The most urgent debates were concerned with what action, if any, could be taken to stop it. Resolutions and deputations are not enough, it was said. The trade unions must force the issue by 'direct action'.

The phrase 'direct action' had come into use before the war and signified a certain change in the attitude to strikes. Formerly these had been viewed as symptoms of a breakdown in collective bargaining. Now it began to be suggested that they could be used for a wider purpose altogether. To some extent the phrase 'direct action' had been associated with the spread of syndicalist ideas. These included the concept of industrial action for a political purpose, and indeed the economic and political emancipation of the working class by means of a general strike. The whole issue of whether a strike for a political purpose was legitimate was to be debated time and again during the Twenties and, allied with this, the political implications of a general strike.

Thus in 1919 an argument developed between those who urged that the war against Russia be ended by 'direct action', which meant industrial action of a nature not very clearly defined, and those who thought that industrial action for a political purpose was unconstitutional. The leaders of the Triple Industrial Alliance (miners, railwaymen and transport workers) asked the Parliamentary Committee of the TUC to call a special conference to discuss what action could be taken to compel the government to abolish conscription, withdraw troops from Russia and raise the blockade. The Parliamentary Committee avoided calling such a conference and sent yet another deputation to the government instead. But at the Trades Union Congress in September 1919 the merits of 'direct action' versus 'constitutional action' were much discussed.

Among the supporters of 'direct action' were John Bromley, General Secretary of ASLEF, the railway drivers' union, and Robert Smillie, President of the Miners Federation. They argued that by continuing conscription and military involvement in Russia, the government was violating its election pledges. 'This government was elected upon certain definite promises, and I have the right to say that if those pledges are broken we should use our power to see that they honour them,' said Bromley.[6] Smillie made the same point and went so far as to say that if a Labour government were returned to power on certain pledges and then refused to redeem them 'it would be the duty of the nation to take any and every action to turn that government out.' He added that the Russians were 'fighting the fight of Socialism against the whole world.'[7]

It was J. R. Clynes, of the National Union of General Workers, who deployed the arguments against direct action most effectively. First, he said it would mean violence. 'You cannot bring millions of men out to begin a great struggle like this without anticipating a condition of civil war,' he argued, 'It would, I believe, immediately begin the breaking of workmen's heads and the breaking of women's hearts.' Secondly, it was undemocratic. It would give to every other section of the community the right to follow Labour's bad example in the case of a future Labour government, and to resist by unconstitutional action the measures of a Labour Parliament. He underlined the uncertainty of the response of the mass of the workers to a call for industrial action. 'Do not delude yourselves with the conviction that your class is united,' he said. 'If they are not united enough to go willingly and intelligently to the ballot box, you deceive yourselves by thinking that you can drag them out of the workshop against their will, or that, having succeeded in getting them out, they will fight intelligently and unitedly until victory is reached.'[8]

In the end Congress adopted, with only one dissentient vote, a resolution instructing the Parliamentary Committee to demand the repeal of conscription and the immediate withdrawal of British troops from Russia and, failing this, to call a Special Trades Union Congress immediately to decide what action should be taken.

A Special Congress was called, but before it met events had intervened. In November it was announced that all British troops had been withdrawn from Russia and sailed for home. So the Special Congress held on 10 December 1919, which was in any case preoccupied with the coal crisis, limited itself to urging an end to the blockade and preparing for a trade union delegation to visit Russia.

C

Direct action when it came was not in fact initiated from above but from below. And it came after the mass of British troops had been withdrawn from Russia and a new stage in the war of intervention had opened. At the beginning of 1920 it seemed clear that Allied intervention had failed; the anti-Bolshevik armies had collapsed. But in April 1920 Poland, whose armed forces had been organized and equipped by the Allied governments, mounted an offensive against the Soviet Union, drove deep into the Ukraine and on 7 May announced the capture of Kiev. The British 'Hands Off Russia' Committee sent out one more circular to every local trade union branch and local Labour Party: 'Fellow Trade Unionists, don't allow this fearful crime to go on.'

In Poplar there was a small 'Hands Off Russia' group led by Harry Pollitt, a 29-year-old boilermaker, and Sylvia Pankhurst, a former leader of the left-wing women's suffrage movement, and leader of the Workers' Socialist Federation. Pollitt was well-known in the Boilermakers' Union in which he had earlier held office as London District Secretary. Now he and his group were distributing Lenin's *Appeal to the Toiling Masses* amongst dockers and shipyard workers. On Sunday nights they conducted meetings at the East India Dock gates. The meetings grew in size. Then the firm which employed Pollitt ordered him to work on two Belgian barges to be adapted for carrying war material to Poland. He refused and was dismissed. He was deeply disappointed when in spite of his influence in the shipyards, he failed to get strike action on the job from men who would willingly have followed him on a purely trade union issue. The predictions of Clynes – 'you deceive yourselves by thinking that you can drag them out of the workshop against their will' – were, it appeared, being fulfilled.

But during the first week in May occurred an event which signified that Clynes had misjudged the mood. The *Jolly George*, a Walford Line vessel, was being loaded with a cargo of munitions destined for Poland, including aeroplanes and forty 18-pounder guns with their limbers and carriages. The dockers working on the cargo sent a deputation to Fred Thompson, London secretary of the dockers union, and then to Ernest Bevin, the General Secretary. Both gave assurances that if the men declined to load the boat the union would stand by them. And at noon on 10 May 1920, they decided to stop loading it. Moreover the coal heavers refused to coal it, so that the ship could not leave. The owners capitulated and a few days later those munitions already on board were unloaded and the ship left port carrying only a general cargo.

This *Jolly George* episode caused a great stir. The export branch of the Dock, Wharf and Riverside and General Workers Union, which had a membership of over 4000, pledged itself on 11 May 'not to handle any form of munitions consigned to Poland or any other country at war with Soviet Russia'. At the National Conference of the dockers union held at Plymouth on 18 May, the London members were congratulated on their refusal to load the guns and the whole movement was called upon to follow their example, Ernest Bevin saying amid cheers: 'I am not going to ask the dockers to put a gun in the ship to carry on this wicked venture. The workers have a right to say how their labour shall be used'.[9]

In June however the Red Army threw the Poles out of the Ukraine and by the end of July had swept forward into Polish territory. The British government demanded that the Russians halt their advance, failing which military aid would be given to Poland. And on 5 August Lloyd George told a tense House of Commons that in view of the Soviet offensive, military action might be necessary to preserve Polish independence.

In this new crisis the Labour and trade union leaders took unprecedented action. On Sunday 9 August a joint meeting of the Parliamentary Committee of the Trades Union Congress, the Labour Party and the Parliamentary Labour Party declared itself for 'direct action' to stop the war, and set up a National Council of Action. The *Daily Herald* issued a special Sunday edition with a banner headline 'Not a man, not a gun, not a sou'. And by this time there was no doubt whatever about the response of the mass of the workers to such a call. A national Labour Conference met on 13 August and decided unanimously to empower the Council of Action to call a general strike to stop the war on Russia. The most unexpected speeches were those by J. R. Clynes, who said that if the League of Nations could not avoid war they must have 'an effective League of Labour action', and J. H. Thomas of the NUR who said:

> I have always opposed direct action because I believed that the same results could be achieved through the ballot-box. But I ask those who share my views ... whether we are not justified today in saying that no vote at the ballot-box

could prevent war today. We believe that the disease is so dangerous and the situation so desperate that only desperate and dangerous methods can provide a remedy . . . I believe that giving effect to this resolution does not mean a mere strike. Do not be under any misapprehension that you are merely voting for a simple down-tools policy . . . If this resolution is to be given effect to it means a challenge to the whole constitution of the country.[10]

This declaration was greeted with prolonged cheers from the thousand delegates. Following the conference 350 local Councils of Action were formed.

However it was soon clear that the danger of Britain's direct military involvement was over. Indeed, no government could have gone to war in such a situation, and Lloyd George hastily told a Labour deputation that they were 'pushing at an open door'. The French gave some assistance to the Poles, but in the meantime Russia's peace terms had been published, and by October an armistice had been signed. The Labour movement was convinced that it was their stand that had prevented the war, and it generated a confidence hitherto unknown.

In that same month of August 1920 the main existing Marxist groups – the British Socialist Party, the Socialist Labour Party, the Workers Socialist Federation, and others from among the Shop Stewards and Workers Committee Movement – came together and formed the Communist Party of Great Britain. Until 1917 their ideas about socialism and the way to achieve it had been purely theoretical. Now they saw their theories in process of being tested by reality.

Ireland

Throughout 1920 the Irish crisis was running parallel with that over the Soviet Union. After the 1918 general election, the Sinn Fein candidates, who had won 73 out of 105 Irish seats, refused to participate in the Westminster Parliament. Instead they met in Dublin and instituted the first Dáil Éireann, or Irish Assembly, and adopted a declaration of independence, establishing an Irish Republic. An independent republic which would involve total separation from Britain was very different from 'Home Rule', which had been seen as a small measure of Irish self-government under the main authority of Westminster. A republic was even more extreme than 'Dominion status', which the government were not prepared to grant but which would at least have kept Ireland within the Empire.

Early in 1919 the Dáil set up ministries, raised a public loan, and called on the people to boycott the Royal Irish Constabulary as 'agents of a foreign power'. The RIC was a semi-military police force of 10,000. In addition there were still 43,000 regular British troops occupying Ireland. Before long a guerrilla force was operating against both the RIC and the British army. Volunteers were joining an illegal Irish Republican Army, which came to be known as the IRA. Men of the RIC and of the British army were ambushed and shot, barracks were raided, arms stolen. Irish juries refused to convict IRA men caught and charged. Irish witnesses refused to give evidence against them.

The British government, after some months of indecision, declared Sinn Fein illegal, arrested several hundred leading Sinn Feiners, and early in 1920 set up recruiting depots in England for men prepared to 'face a rough and dangerous task'. The recruits, who ultimately numbered 7000, became known in Ireland as the Black and Tans.* Up against a war of sudden ambushes, shots in the dark, hole-and-corner murders, they soon answered their attackers with reprisals on the civilian population.

At home, a Bill for the Better Government of Ireland (commonly called the Partition Bill) was started on its slow legislative journey. It divided Ireland into two parts, one to consist of six of the nine counties of Ulster (those that had a majority of Protestants), the other of the remaining 26 counties of Ireland which were predominantly Roman Catholic. Each part was to have a separate Parliament with powers not much wider than those of a county council. Members of both Parliaments would be required to take the oath of allegiance to the King: foreign affairs, taxation and the armed forces would all be outside their jurisdiction. The Bill also allowed for the eventual fusion of these two Parliaments.

---

* They were English recruits to the Royal Irish Constabulary, but since there were not enough green RIC uniforms to go round they were equipped with a mixture of khaki, dark green and black belts. When they appeared in Limerick they were promptly nick-named the 'Black and Tans' after a once-famous pack of hounds. See Richard Bennett, *The Black and Tans.*

Before the war the opposition to Home Rule by the Ulster Protestant Unionists, under the leadership of Edward Carson, had reached
the point of open rebellion. Carson had been supported by key officers
in the British army and by Conservative political leaders in London.
As a result a former Home Rule Bill had been made inoperable. Now,
in the eyes of Sinn Fein, the partitioning off of part of Ulster was
simply an English device to avoid admitting the right of the Irish to
govern themselves.

For Lloyd George and his colleagues the strategic question had
always been in the forefront. Ireland as a possible base for enemy
operations seemed to them a potential threat, as it had to Britain's
rulers for hundreds of years before. The Admiralty stressed the need
for Irish ports in time of war to deal with enemy submarines.

At the same time the statesmen were convinced that to give in to
Sinn Fein would lower British prestige the world over, and would
have incalculable effects on other restless elements within the Empire.
They looked on the Empire as Britain's birthright. It was unthinkable
that any part of it should be given up voluntarily. If challenged on the
ethics of this attitude they suggested that the Irish were not capable of
governing themselves. This comfortable assumption was widespread.
The Irish, it was said, had a wonderful gift for talking and were undoubtedly charming people, but they were like children, and could not
be trusted with adult matters.*

When the news first came of IRA shootings and ambushes, the initial
reaction was anger. There were calls to the government to stop shilly-
shallying and put the Irish down with a firm hand. But as time went
on and more and more reports told of reprisals by the Black and Tans,
opinion in Britain became divided. Many were critical of the violence
used by the British and claimed that it solved nothing. The Liberal
press suggested that the Partition Bill was a disaster, since it satisfied no
one. Some trade unions demanded withdrawal of British troops from
Ireland.

There was, however, a minority of people in Britain who were more

---

* Sir Alfred Cope, Assistant Under Secretary for Ireland, 1920–2, wrote privately from
Dublin Castle to Thomas Jones during the 1921 negotiations, saying: 'Many of us have
said time and again that the people this side are children in politics and statesmanship, and
having said so we can't very well turn round now when we come to deal with them and
expect them to act as big men' (Thomas Jones, *Whitehall Diary*, vol III, p. 99).

than onlookers; they had direct ties with Ireland, and felt themselves passionately involved in the outcome of the struggle. Most of them were grouped at opposite poles of society. At one end were the land-owners with a stake in Irish soil and, to a less extent, businessmen with a stake in Irish industry. At the other end was a much larger group: the Irish immigrants, most of whom had come from poor homes. Of the 43 million inhabitants of Great Britain, some half a million had been born in Ireland. They were only the latest wave of Irish immi-grants; there had been one wave after another ever since the Irish famine of the 1840s.

The Irish clustered in Liverpool, in Glasgow, in certain parts of London, and in some other towns. Many of the young men found work in the docks or went on to building jobs. Many of the young girls went into domestic service. First-generation immigrants could be recognized by their speech, but their children usually grew up talking like their English or Scottish neighbours, and in time there were only two things left to show their origin: their names and, often, their Roman Catholic religion. There were some Protestant Irish groupings – particularly in Liverpool – but the majority of Irish were Catholics. Those who could manage it went back to Ireland to visit relatives. Those who could not afford it still thought of Ireland as the old country.

During the spring of 1920, after Sinn Fein had been declared illegal, the government began to transfer interned Sinn Fein prisoners to English jails. On 26 April the Home Secretary told the Commons that there were 179 Irish prisoners in Wormwood Scrubs, all of whom had gone on hunger strike. They had not been brought to trial, he said, because in Ireland fear of being murdered prevented people from giving truthful evidence.

On the night before this statement was made there occurred the first of a series of disturbances outside Wormwood Scrubs. The Irish Self Determination League had called on its members to march to the prison on the evening of 25 April. Between 7000 and 8000 went and marched in procession behind the building, accompanied by three bands of Irish pipers, and carrying the green, white and orange flag of the Irish Republic. They formed up 100 yards from the prison wall while a priest recited prayers in Irish. It was then seen that handker-chiefs were being waved through the barred windows, a cheer from outside was answered by a cheer from inside, and excited messages were shouted back and forth. 'We will stick it to the death,' cried one prisoner.

On the following night there were what the newspapers described as 'riotous scenes'. A much bigger crowd assembled, singing Irish songs; some prisoners smashed the upper portion of a large window as well as its iron bars, and through the gaps thrust heads and shoulders, cheering and waving flags. They then asked for silence and from inside the prison could be heard the chorus of the Sinn Fein song: 'Wrap the green flag round me, boys.' The emotion outside was very great; some women were in tears. The prisoners then set fire to sheets of newspaper and tried to throw them over the prison walls and, as darkness fell, the crowd, now 20,000 strong, joined in the singing of 'The Wearing of the Green'. As if stunned by these unusual proceedings, the police, who were lined up in front of the prison wall, made no attempt to interfere.

On subsequent evenings, however, there was a changed atmosphere. While thousands of people turned up nightly, partly to see the fun, they were increasingly set upon by hostile groups who pelted them with mud and bricks and endeavoured to drown their singing with 'Rule Britannia' and 'Three Cheers for the Red, White and Blue'. By the end of the week broken bottles were being thrown, the mounted police had been brought in, batons were being freely used and the injured taken to hospital.

In Liverpool a deputation representing Irish societies met the Lord Mayor on 27 April and told him that unless the hunger strikers were released within 48 hours, the labour of all Irish workers would be withdrawn and the Port of Liverpool brought to a standstill. This angered the officials of the Dock Riverside and General Workers Union, to which most of the Liverpool dockers belonged. The General Secretary was James Sexton, a Labour MP, and he expressed his indignation in the Commons: 'The action will be entirely unofficial and irresponsible. I am vigorously opposed to the policy which is known as direct action. I will protest and continue to protest as long as I live against the industrial weapon being used for political purposes.'[11]

To an angry May Day meeting in St Helens a few days later he said that his union was composed of Irishmen and Orangemen, and to call them out on strike would mean 'the breaking up of my union. Already religious strife and hatred have been engendered in Liverpool.'[12]

Several thousand Liverpool dockers disobeyed their leaders' call and came out on strike on 29 April. They succeeded in closing one dock only, which enabled the newspapers to claim that the strike was a failure. But the government were by this time concerned lest prisoners who had never been brought to trial should die on their hands. They began to release the hunger strikers in groups and by the second week of May all had been set at liberty.

In that same month Dublin dockers refused to unload war materials for the Black and Tans, and when soldiers were brought in to do the work 400 members of the National Union of Railwaymen in Dublin went on strike.* The executive of the NUR in England told the Dublin members to go back to work, an instruction which they disobeyed, continuing on strike until the following Christmas. But the NUR referred the matter to the Triple Alliance, which in turn decided that the handling of munitions of war for Ireland ought to be considered by a special TUC.

In June 1920 two officials from the Irish Trades Union Congress came to the annual meeting of the National Transport Workers Federation and asked for help to stop the flow of munitions: to 'do for Ireland what you did by the Jolly George,' as one of them put it.[13] On 13 July, when the special TUC met under the chairmanship of J. H. Thomas, a resolution tabled by the miners was indeed carried by 2,760,000 votes to 1,636,000, demanding withdrawal of British troops and the cessation of production of munitions of war for use against Ireland and Russia – 'and in case the Government refuses these demands, we recommend a general down-tools policy and call on all the trade unions here represented to carry out this policy, each according to its own constitution, by taking a ballot of its members or otherwise.' But so far as Ireland was concerned this resolution was never implemented. The trade unionists were much divided on the question; before the resolution was passed, they had spent half a day arguing about the relationship between Great Britain and Ireland and moving and rejecting amendments to a resolution asking for dominion status for Ireland. Some were fortified in their desire for compromise by the

* Churchill's comment at a Cabinet meeting on 31 May 1920 was: 'The transport workers won't allow arms to go to the Poles to smash the Bolshevists nor to save the police from the Irish Bolshevists. We ought to take the transport workers by the throat' (Thomas Jones, *Whitehall Diary*, vol III, p. 22).

attitude of their Belfast members. And just after the TUC met, Protestant dockworkers in Belfast turned on their Catholic workmates, beat them up and threw them into the water. Groups of Catholics retaliated, after which there were several days of rioting. From then on the trade unions in Britain were more and more preoccupied with the problems arising from the dismissal and persecution of their Catholic members in Ulster, problems which largely defeated them owing to the attitude of the Protestant members. In such circumstances the call to the British trade unions to 'do for Ireland what they did by the Jolly George' ceased to be a realistic one.

The government had meanwhile hastily rushed through Parliament a new law which enabled it to try political prisoners by court martial, and on 12 August 1920 Terence MacSwiney, the Lord Mayor of Cork, was arrested and sentenced to two years for the possession of documents 'likely to cause disaffection to His Majesty'. MacSwiney said when sentenced: 'I have decided I shall be free alive or dead within a month,' and immediately went on hunger strike. But the month dragged into two months and longer. He lingered on for 75 days while his sufferings were reported daily in newspapers all over the world.

MacSwiney died in Brixton prison on 25 October 1920. His body was released and taken to St George's Roman Catholic cathedral in Southwark. The lying-in-state lasted for twelve hours, while 20,000 people reverently filed past. Irish people came from all parts of Britain to attend the requiem mass held on the morning of 28 October, and some failed to get in after waiting for hours. Many of the mourners were boys and girls hardly out of their teens. In the afternoon the coffin, wrapped in green, white and orange, was taken in procession to Euston Station. The procession was a long one, watched in silence from the pavements by large crowds. 'Are we to take it that all these people are Sinn Feiners?' said one man to his neighbour as he stood on the pavement. 'It's rather a serious thing for London, isn't it? I never guessed we had so many of them and right in our midst.'[14]

Apart from the hard-pressed Irish immigrants there was another group acutely concerned with the outcome of the Irish struggle. They included at least 69 peers who between them owned 1¾ million acres of Irish land.* Most of their ancestors had been associated with the

---

* This figure is compiled from *Who's Who*, 1918, and is therefore by no means complete. In 1873 a survey showed that 197 peers had between them owned 5 million acres

waves of English 'planters' who had settled in Ireland over the previous 200 years and helped to bring her under British rule. The majority of them were Protestants in a country which was overwhelmingly Catholic.

They tended to have connections on both sides of the Irish Sea. The Marquess of Londonderry was a landowner in Ulster, but also a colliery owner in Yorkshire. The Earl of Dunraven owned property in Limerick and was Lord Lieutenant of that county, but he was also a coalowner in Wales. The Irish peers customarily sent their sons to English public schools, they mixed and intermarried with the old titled families in England and Scotland, talked with the same accent, thought in the same way. Many of them had London addresses; some of them left the management of their Irish estates entirely to agents, only travelling to Ireland for the fishing season. Like other governing-class families they put their sons into politics, the diplomatic service or (increasingly) into business. They provided recruits for the Irish administration which, with its headquarters at Dublin Castle, was alleged to be out of proportion to the size of the population. The most common profession for the younger sons of peers, whether English or Irish, was the army.

It was 'their' Ireland just as it was 'their' Empire, and to most of them the separation of the two was unthinkable. Since the 1890s every Bill for Irish Home Rule had been overturned in the House of Lords. Moreover the issue of Home Rule had caused profound splits and realignments in the existing political parties. The opponents of Home Rule in the Liberal Party had fused with Conservatives in what had been called for some years the 'Unionist' Party.

By November 1920, against a background of raids, shootings, burnings, reprisals and hunger strikes, the Partition Bill had wound its tedious way through the Commons and had reached the House of

---

of Irish soil, one quarter of Ireland's total territory. Since that time there had been land reform laws, under which the state purchased the land from the landowner and sold it on an annuity basis to the Irish peasants and small farmers. Since rents were uncomfortably dependent on the vicissitudes of the potato crop, many of the large landowners had taken advantage of this scheme to sell off part of their land. Some had got rid of thousands of acres of bogland, but had retained their big house and grounds and, perhaps, the ground rents from a neighbouring town, some fishing rights, an odd bit of valuable farm land. In the years just before the war this process had been going on rapidly, but the possessions of the big landowners were still formidable in 1920.

Lords. All along the peers had been the chief barrier to Home Rule in Ireland; now they were paying for their intransigence. Having been determined to relinquish nothing, they faced losing everything. But a catastrophe is not more acceptable to people because they have brought it on themselves. Commonly they look round for a scapegoat. In this case it was the Lloyd George government and its blunders.

In some despair the peers assembled to discuss their future. Some had hardly ever been seen before at a House of Lords session and would hardly be seen again. In the debates that followed, the lists of speakers sounded like a roll-call of Irish place-names: the Earl of Wicklow, Lord Donoughmore, the Marquess of Sligo, the Earl of Mayo, the Marquess of Londonderry, Lord Oranmore and Browne. When an Englishman, Lord Harris, wanted to speak – 'is it not time that England had a word in the matter?' – he was hastily silenced. The Irish peers must have their say; they were the victims of a terrible misfortune and must be treated with the courtesy befitting the occasion. But nothing that they found to say could prevent what was about to happen.

Ireland was to be divided into two parts, each with a separate Parliament. One part was to cover six of the nine counties of Ulster; the other the 26 counties in the rest of Ireland. Very reluctantly the Ulster Unionists had been persuaded to support the Bill; if they could not maintain the status quo, they could at least safeguard their own position. Most of the peers who had links with the six counties had been mobilized to lend the Bill their support.* But the peers from the 26. counties were in despair. For one thing they were certain that the Bill was not one over which the Sinn Fein would be prepared to negotiate, and they saw no end to their troubles this way. Secretly many of them now believed that Dominion status offered the only way out. But Dominion status for the whole of Ireland was one thing; cutting off the six counties quite another. It meant that, as loyalists and, for the most part, Protestants, they were being abandoned by those in the North who should be their allies. If the Bill ever came in to effect, they would be cut adrift in a sea of republican hostility. 'The men whom you are going to put in this position are the men who have built up the whole prosperity of the south of Ireland,' said the Earl of Midleton.

---

* Including the Duke of Abercorn, the Marquess of Dufferin & Ava, the Marquess of Londonderry, the Earl of Kilmorey, the Earl of Roden, Viscount Charlemont, Viscount Templeton, Viscount Massarene, Lord Deramore, Lord Ranfurly.

'The men who are behind us in the protest I am making are the men who hold all the greatest businesses in Dublin and throughout the South, all the largest owners of land, those to whom the country owes most.'[15]

The Marquess of Dufferin and Ava, a man with a long diplomatic career behind him, who was also Deputy Lieutenant of County Down, gave the answer on behalf of the Ulster Unionists:

We dislike most intensely having to abandon our fellow-Protestants in the South and West, but we cannot help it . . . We Protestants in Ireland are in the position of shipwrecked mariners. We in the North are those who have been lucky enough to get onto a raft in comparative safety. The Southern Unionists are like the remainder of the crew who have been unable to get into safety and wish to upset our frail bark simply with the idea that 'if we cannot be saved, blest if you should be.'[16]

40 peers from the 26 counties failed to mobilize enough support among the English and Scottish peers, and the Partition Bill was carried by 164 votes to 75.

In the six counties it was put into effect. Elections were held and the Parliament of Northern Ireland duly opened by the King in June 1921. But in the 26 counties Sinn Fein treated the election as a means of re-electing the Dáil, to which 124 Sinn Fein candidates were returned unopposed. Fighting still went on and there was total deadlock.

At last in July 1921 a truce was arranged, and by the end of the year a treaty had been negotiated which provided for an Irish Free State for the 26 counties on terms equivalent to Dominion status. Since this fell short of total independence, and did not provide for the ending of partition, the Dáil only endorsed the treaty by a very narrow majority and, as British troops began to withdraw, civil war between pro- and anti-treaty sections broke out and continued for many months.

In Britain the Ulster Unionists tried to get the treaty rejected; they had only acquiesced in partition because they believed it had been designed to keep the whole of Ireland in the British Empire. But in the Commons they only mustered 60 against 343 who supported the treaty.

In the House of Lords the protest against the treaty was led by the Duke of Northumberland, who said that Sinn Fein had been 'to a large extent a Bolshevik movement masquerading under the guise of a national revolt'.[17] Carson, who had just been elevated to the Lords, spoke bitterly of the 'splendid obsequies of the Unionist Party' which was 'dead and buried from today'.[18] And indeed the Unionist Party henceforth reverted to the name of Conservative Party except in the six counties of Ulster. The Earl of Wicklow voiced the feelings of most southern Unionists when he gave the treaty his blessing and hoped it would mean peace at last. 'It is no thanks to noble Lords opposite or to their colleagues in another place if there are any of us alive to come here and talk at all,' he said bleakly.[19] The anti-treaty motion was defeated by 168 votes to 49.

The Empire

The troubles in the more distant parts of the Empire had much less impact on the British working people than those in Ireland. In India a wave of revolt just after the war had been met with extraordinary measures of repression, but little of this was reported in the British press. In April 1919 General Dyer ordered troops to fire on an unarmed crowd in Amritsar. Most of the crowd were sitting on the ground listening to a speaker. 379 people were killed and 1200 wounded. But news of this event did not reach Britain for over seven months; when it finally broke into the newspapers it was received with incredulous shock and horror. General Dyer was ordered to resign. This decision, however was received with dissatisfaction in the House of Lords, where a motion was carried in July 1920 deploring the conduct of Dyer's case as 'unjust to that officer and establishing a precedent dangerous to the preservation of order in the face of rebellion'.[20]

The peers who supported General Dyer felt a personal involvement in Empire affairs. So did the families of colonial administrators or of those who had business or commercial interests in the overseas territories. Others had relatives in the regular army or navy whose turns of duty had taken them to the colonies or dominions. But for most working people the Empire was only at the edge of consciousness. They had been taught about it at school, of course. In geography lessons they had learnt that it covered one quarter of the earth's surface. Their history books dwelt upon Britain's great civilizing mission among backward peoples. Empire Day on 24 May, chosen because it had been Queen Victoria's birthday, was celebrated in most schools as a special occasion. Adventurous young men emigrated to the white Dominions: Canada, New Zealand and Australia. But with the peoples of India or Africa or the West Indies there was little contact. They were commonly referred to as 'natives', so that in many minds this word was exclusively associated with black or brown faces. In most parts of Britain such a face was an oddity. Most people took it for granted that non-whites were inferior to whites.

That the peoples of the Empire were heirs to a glorious heritage was stressed when the British Empire Exhibition was opened by the King at Wembley on St George's Day, 23 April 1924. In the newly built stadium, which held 110,000 people, massed choirs sang 'Land of Hope and Glory' conducted by its composer, Sir Edward Elgar. As the advertisers put it, the exhibition brought to visitors 'the wondrous reality of Britain's might and magnitude – her grandeur and her glory . . . The scene is without parallel in the history of mankind. Within the master gateway of Wembley are a hundred inner gates of Empire. They give access to the five continents and all the seas; to the mystic East, the stirring West, the sterner North, the romantic South.'[21]

The exhibition covered 219 acres and was, among other things, held to be 'the greatest demonstration there has yet been for the virtues of reinforced concrete'.[22] Huge palaces and pavilions housed the treasures of the Dominions, India, the Crown Colonies, the Protectorates, and the Mandated Territories.

Shining domes and minarets topped the Indian pavilion within which could be seen 'the splendour of the East', including silks, carpets, embroideries, marble and silverware. West Africa was represented by a red-walled township where Nigerian women could be seen pounding rice. The Hong Kong pavilion had a replica of a street with shops and a restaurant where you could sample shark's fins. Burma displayed ivory figures and lacquer bowls. There were diamonds and ostriches from South Africa; tea, rubber and coffee from Ceylon; sugar and bananas from Jamaica; petroleum products from Trinidad. Australia had merino sheep on show as well as a model of Jack Hobbs, the cricketer, in butter. Canada displayed her forest wealth and a statue of the Prince of Wales, also in butter. There was a 'never-stop' railway which ran round and through the exhibition, slowing up for passengers to get on and off. Part of the grounds were set aside for a huge amusement park. Catering was in the hands of Messrs J. Lyons and Co; apart from a small government grant the affair was financed by private enterprise.

The plan for the exhibition had taken shape two years earlier, but it was opened somewhat ironically at a time when the first Labour government had just taken office. The Labour Manifesto of 1918 had promised 'freedom for Ireland and India' and the right of self-determination to all subject peoples; the Labour Party Conference in 1920 had again passed a resolution demanding self-determination for India. The *Daily Herald*, conscious of its readers' susceptibilities, dwelt on the scientific wonders in the exhibition when describing the opening ceremony. It told of the 'amazing' loudspeaker equipment in the stadium, through which the voices of the Prince of Wales and of the King 'could be heard clearly and distinctly in every corner of the vast structure,'[23] and of how a telegram announcing the event had been flashed round the world in 80 seconds.

J. H. Thomas, Labour's Colonial Secretary, was free of such inhibitions. 'Nothing is more mistaken than the idea, prevalent in some circles, that Labour is hostile to the Empire and to the Imperial idea,' he wrote in a special article in *The Times* on Empire Day.[24] Admitting that the working classes of Great Britain had not always been alive to the scope and diversity, the resources and possibilities, of the Empire, he observed: 'That however is no fault of theirs. Very few of them have had any opportunity to acquire such knowledge of the Empire beyond what is conveyed by looking at the parts coloured red on a map of the world.' He hoped that the exhibition would correct that 'excusable ignorance'.

And so it may have done. On the other hand it may have been the delights of the giant switchback, the Queen's Doll's House, or the 'Wild West Rodeo' that made the more lasting impression on the thousands of children who were taken to the exhibition that summer. There were 17 million visitors. Financially it was not a success.

4
Slump: the Dole and the Poor Law

In 1921 came the slump. Already in the last few months of 1920 unemployment had been rising. By March 1921 it had reached 1,355,000, or 11·3 per cent of the insured workers. By December 1921 it was over 2 million, or nearly 18 per cent.

That Christmas was a bleak one. Unemployed ex-servicemen wearing medals were shaking collecting boxes in London's West End. Many workplaces closed down for an extended unpaid Christmas holiday. In shipbuilding the situation was catastrophic. There were 128,000 out of work: more than one man in three. The outlook in nearly all the engineering trades was gloomy; 310,000 engineering workers were unemployed – one in four of the total work force – and a great many others were on short time. In iron and steel the position seemed beyond belief: 107,000 had lost their jobs, representing 38 per cent of those employed. Over 45,000 dockers – one fifth of the work force – were wholly unemployed, and once more men struggled with one another on the dockside for jobs, as they had done before the war. The *Labour Gazette*, surveying the industrial scene in January 1922, reported that employment was 'bad' in trade after trade. In pig-iron it 'continued bad', the total number of furnaces in blast were 77 compared with 274 the previous year. In the cotton trade employment in December 'continued bad' and was 'even worse than in November'; in woollen and worsted, employment 'continued bad'; in hosiery it was 'fair'; in jute it was 'bad'. In the boot and shoe trade it was 'very depressed'; in paper, printing and bookbinding it 'continued bad'; in food preparation it was 'only moderate'. In woodworking and furnishing it 'remained bad'. The building trades were worse off than usual. One quarter of all seamen were out of work.

Before the war a trade cycle with alternating booms and slumps had been a familiar pattern, but nobody could remember a depression like this. Indeed, it was said that such unemployment had not been known for a hundred years.

Initially the exceptional severity of the slump was attributed to the abnormal post-war circumstances. Shortages in every country had led in 1919 and 1920 to feverish buying, and had driven up prices. In Britain an illusion of prosperity had prevailed, partly owing to the very high prices paid for British exports. But merchants in all parts of the world had overstocked and were now left with unsold goods on their hands. In a frantic attempt to find outlets British exporters reduced their prices, but without success. During 1921 British exports went down to less than half their pre-war volume.

The view in Labour circles was that the collapse of the export trade was directly linked with the elimination of Germany as the chief European trading centre, and that the 'make Germany pay' strategy combined with the wars of intervention in Russia had led to economic disaster. The employers on the contrary argued that the depression had been caused by the high wages and excessive demands of the trade unions during 1919 and 1920. The solution to the problem, they thought, was to bring down prices by cutting costs, which meant in their view lower wages and lower taxation. Already in 1920 the government had entered upon a deflationary policy which had as its ultimate aim the return of Britain to the gold standard at pre-war parity. And it concurred in the view that the weight of taxation was too great, initiating a policy of financial stringency. In August 1921, amid a chorus of warnings from industrialists and bankers about the precarious state of the national finances, it announced the formation of a Committee on National Expenditure under the chairmanship of Sir Eric Geddes to advise the Cabinet on economies. The Geddes Report which appeared early in 1922 became known as the 'Geddes Axe'. It proposed cutting government expenditure in many directions, particularly in education and armaments. About half the proposed cuts were implemented, and in the spring of 1922 a reduction in the standard rate of income tax from 6s to 5s in the £ was announced.

Among the first to be faced with demands for big wage reductions were the miners. This was at the beginning of 1921. The government simultaneously announced that the mines were to be decontrolled and handed back to their owners by 31 March. The owners were determined to go back to the pre-war system of fixing wages on a district basis, so that they depended on the financial circumstances of each district independently of the prosperity or otherwise of the others. So they gave notice to all miners and offered to re-engage them at new rates of wages, which meant a drop in pay of 40 per cent for a skilled collier in South Wales, and of 24 to 28 per cent in Scotland, Northumberland and Durham, but only of 10 per cent in Nottingham. In Yorkshire there was to be no drop. Prices had come down by about 12 per cent since the autumn of 1920, but the reductions in pay proposed for most districts could not be accepted without a severe cut in living standards.

The new terms were rejected by the miners' leaders, and a national stoppage began on 1 April 1921. The miners then appealed to their partners in the Triple Alliance, the railwaymen and the transport workers, to take strike action in their support. The National Union of Railwaymen and the Transport Workers Federation did indeed issue a strike call. But after a great show of military preparations by the government and some widely-publicized signs of splits and indecision on the miners' executive, those leaders, such as J. H. Thomas of the NUR, who had all along wanted to avoid a strike were able to prevail upon their colleagues to call it off. The strike was cancelled at the last moment on 15 April 1921, a day which became known in the trade union movement as 'Black Friday'. Innumerable trade unionists at local level who had been actively preparing for the great conflict were thrown into a state of confusion and bitterness, while the miners fought on alone until the end of June and were then forced to accept defeat. It was the end of the Triple Alliance and all the hopes centred on it, including the belief that it would be able to withstand successfully the attacks on standards which everyone had seen coming. The whole trade union movement suffered a loss of confidence. Trade union membership, which had been 8·3 million in 1920, fell to 6·6 million by the end of 1921.

As prices came tumbling down, wage reductions were enforced in every industry. In some cases, as with the miners, the reductions were more drastic than the fall in prices. Thus the engineering employers were able to impose substantial wage cuts in the second half of 1921, and to these the union leaders reluctantly acceded. However, when the Engineering Employers Federation tried to alter accepted workshop practice so that, among other things, the employer should be the sole judge of when and where overtime was to be worked, the new proposal was turned down by a ballot vote of the members of the Amalgamated Engineering Union. The employers' response was to lock out all AEU members in March 1922 and, ultimately, the members of 46 other unions who had stood by the AEU. The lock-out dragged on for 13 weeks, after which the AEU had to accept defeat. Shortly after, the employers insisted on still further wage reductions, with the result that by September 1922 the average weekly rate for fitters and turners had been pushed down to 57/6d as compared with 89/6d in December 1920, a cut of 35 per cent in money wages. And, though prices were falling, they had not fallen quite as much as this.

By the end of the year there were some sections of manual workers whose real wages (i.e. purchasing power) had fallen below 1914 levels. True, this was not the case for the majority, and in particular it was not so for the lowest-paid unskilled workers, whose position had improved greatly since 1914. However, the levels of 1914 did not seem relevant to the average worker, even if his employer looked back on those days with longing. Since that time there had been a considerable improvement in living standards and the workers in 1922 could compare their position with that in 1919 and 1920.

Meanwhile unemployment persisted. At the beginning of 1923 many industrialists thought that industry would soon have turned the corner. And some sections did. But many of the old-established industries remained in the doldrums. Unemployment as a whole fell to 1·3 million in the middle of 1923 and to 1 million in June 1924, but there it seemed to stick. Indeed, for the whole period between the wars it never fell below 1 million. It seemed that a sickness which had formerly plagued society only from time to time had now become chronic. How the unemployed should be dealt with, what to do with them, how they should be treated, became a major preoccupation for statesmen, political parties, trade unionists, administrators, councillors, charitable organizations. Above all for the unemployed themselves.

Unemployment Insurance

One thing which the employers believed was helping to prevent the wages of the lower-paid coming down far enough was the existence of new forms of insurance benefit and relief for the unemployed. Before the war only 2½ million workers had been covered by the state unemployment insurance scheme.* Now in 1920 unemployment insurance had been extended to 12 million wage-earners.† Moreover the 1920 Act was no sooner in force than the benefits it conferred had to be improved and then improved again, as the administration, faced with a situation it had not known before, lurched from one expedient to another. While this went on, some pre-war assumptions about the economy were destroyed, while pre-war attitudes to those out of work were challenged by a new working-class and socialist philosophy.

The pre-war Insurance Act had been based on the conviction that a man should stand on his own feet. If he was out of work for a short time only, it was assumed that he ought to have enough savings to tide him over, or some sort of private insurance, perhaps through a friendly society or a trade union. State unemployment insurance under the 1911 Act had been intended to add something to these resources, it was never intended to be sufficient to live on. 'It was,' as one government report put it, 'too small in amount to offer any inducement to idleness.'[1]

Further the 1911 scheme was based firmly on the 'insurance principle', which meant that it was financed by weekly contributions from employers, employees and the state, and was meant to be 'self-supporting' – meaning that payments out of the Insurance Fund by way of benefit were not to exceed the contributions paid into it. The result was that benefit was not merely small, but was paid for only a very limited number of weeks, the period of benefit being strictly conditional on the number of contributions previously paid. Underlying all this were other assumptions, such as that if a man was out of

---

* This scheme had been extended during the war, and after the war a temporary out-of-work donation had been introduced for ex-soldiers and those displaced from war industry.

† That is to say to nearly all manual workers except agricultural workers, domestic servants and most railwaymen. Non-manual workers were included if they earned less than £250 a year.

work for long it probably indicated some defect either physical or moral. And in any case continuous financial assistance which did not carry with it an obligation to render any service in return was demoralizing. So nobody ought to get benefit unless they had paid for it.

These assumptions underlying the 1911 Act were implicit in the 1920 Act. At 15s for an adult man, with nothing for his dependent wife or children, there was no pretence that unemployment benefit was more than a supplement to other resources to help a man over a bad time. And the number of weeks' benefit which could be drawn was strictly related to the number of contributions previously paid,* and in no case could exceed 15 weeks' benefit in any single year.

By the time the scheme came into operation in November 1920 the depression had already set in and hundreds of thousands of men and women were out of work, with no immediate possibility of accumulating the contributions needed to qualify them for benefit. So before Christmas an amending Act was rushed through Parliament to enable such people to draw benefit for the next 8 weeks. By March 1921 a further Act had been passed raising the amount; by June 1921 the Insurance Fund faced insolvency, so benefits were hastily reduced to their former level: 15s for a man, 12s for an insured woman. Meanwhile duration of benefit had been increased, and was now 22 weeks in a 35-week period.

Lest the insurance principle be lost, these extensions of the period for which benefit could be drawn were regarded as advances on future contributions and called 'uncovenanted benefit' which, in turn, was subject to a series of interruptions which came to be known as 'gaps': several weeks of entitlement would be followed by a few weeks without.

In the autumn of 1921 the government hastily brought in yet another Act, this time to give allowances of 5s for a dependent wife and 1s for each dependent child of an unemployed man. This decision to add allowances for dependants was the first admission that unemployment benefit ought to bear some relation to the cost of maintenance. It was described as 'a temporary expedient in a grave emergency'[2] and was introduced when it was clear that a second winter of unemployment lay ahead. But by April 1922 dependants' allowances

---

* The contributions were initially fixed at 4d each from a man and his employer and 2d from the state.

had been made a permanent feature of the insurance scheme. Further Acts in 1922 and 1923 continued to tinker with 'gaps' and with devices to overcome the Fund's constant tendency towards insolvency.

Even after the grant of dependants' allowances, unemployment benefit was still below what was currently regarded as subsistence level and was particularly inadequate where there were children.* How then did the unemployed manage? The normal expedients – turning to relatives, friends, or even the landlady – were less readily available than usual. Such relatives and friends were often themselves working short time. Many skilled workers had savings accumulated during the good years just after the war; in addition most of those who were in trade unions were entitled to trade union benefit: normally a few shillings a week added to the basic unemployment benefit. It was when unemployment began to run from weeks into months that the pinch was really felt. Savings were exhausted while trade union benefit ran out. Rent got into arrears, clothing deteriorated, there was no way of keeping the children in boots. Furniture had to be sold, blankets pawned. And then, just when you thought you had touched rock bottom, would come one of the incomprehensible 'gaps' in benefit; the Labour Exchange would tell you there was *nothing* for you this week – no money at all. Your only resort was to go to the Poor Law Guardians, and there was no guarantee either that they would give you anything.

During this period many previously-held assumptions were shattered. Skilled men who had worked for half a lifetime for a single firm, and expected to stay with it into old age, suddenly found their firm had shut down, and with it had gone all their sense of security. People who had prided themselves on their steadiness, who had privately looked on their more feckless neighbours with pitying contempt, found themselves living on the savings carefully hoarded for their old age. The savings went, and they were then as badly off as their neighbours after all. Their past endeavours, it seemed, had been futile. To go to the Guardians was the final blow to self-respect.

---

* Benefit was 15s for the man, 5s for his wife, 1s for each child, amounting to 23s for a family with three children. Bowley's minimum diet (set out in Table 5, p. 46) for the dockers, which in 1920 cost £2, would by January 1922 have cost roughly 23s. So that to reach even Bowley's standard would have meant spending the entire amount on food with nothing for fuel, rent or clothing.

The authorities were perturbed that many of the younger unemployed were forming committees under the auspices of what later became known as the National Unemployed Workers' Movement. The leader of this movement was 25-year-old Wal Hannington, a former engineering shop steward and a Communist. Under the slogan 'work or maintenance' the movement organized marches and deputations, invaded outraged Poor Law Guardians while in session, and by 1922 was organizing the first national Hunger March on London. The leaders of the movement and many of its followers were convinced that unemployment was a disease of capitalism, and wanted the overthrow of the system. For the individual the activities meant, among other things, the preservation of self-respect. Shabbiness was not looked on as a badge of inferiority in the NUMW; the activities meant a lot of excitement, some adventure and, indeed, some amusement. Getting together with others and truculently demanding your 'rights' was infinitely preferable to trying to hide your circumstances away in shame.

The Poor Law

The main job of the Poor Law Authorities was to look after the old, the sick, the disabled, the widows and the orphans. Poor relief could be 'indoor' – i.e. in workhouses or other institutions – or 'outdoor' – i.e. given in cash or in kind to people in their own homes. The rules made it very difficult for an able-bodied unemployed man to get outdoor relief (or 'out-relief' as it was commonly called).

Between the beginning of 1921 and July 1922 the numbers on poor relief rose alarmingly from 750,000 to over 2 million. Some of this was the indirect result of unemployment, which among other things prevented workers from supporting aged parents. But some of the increase arose because the unemployed themselves were getting relief in spite of the rules. By mid-1922 it is possible that one unemployed person in six was getting relief; in some industrial areas it was one in three or four.* This development seemed like a violation of

---

* It is not possible to do more than estimate the numbers of unemployed on poor relief, because the Ministry of Health returns did not distinguish between a man and his depend-

all the principles on which the Poor Law was supposed to operate.

Poor relief was administered by Boards of Guardians† which had been originally established to enforce the principles of 'deterrence' and 'less eligibility' laid down in 1834. On paper they were still expected to uphold these principles, in spite of the condemnation of the whole system by a Royal Commission in 1909. The Boards now numbered over 600 in England and Wales, and the relief they dispensed was largely financed from local rates. This fact was in itself an inducement to most Guardians to keep the cost as low as possible. But in addition they were obliged to obey the regulations issued by the Ministry of Health, and if they spent money in unauthorised ways they could be surcharged.

The Guardians were elected locally and, up to the end of the war, had been drawn primarily from the middle and lower middle class. But the extension of the Parliamentary franchise in 1918 had been matched by an expansion in the voters' lists for local councils and Boards of Guardians. And the disqualification from voting of people receiving out-relief was abolished, so that they could now help to choose their own Guardians. These developments had meant a change in the composition of many Boards; in particular there were many more Labour Guardians than before the war.

According to the rules an able-bodied man who applied for relief should be offered the workhouse. Alternatively, he could be given outdoor relief but only if he underwent a 'labour test', which usually meant an eight-hour day stone-breaking in a labour yard in return for less than half a day's wages or its equivalent in kind. Unconditional out-relief without a labour test could be given to an unemployed man only in cases of 'sudden or urgent necessity'. The Guardians however were allowed to depart from these regulations 'upon consideration of

† In Scotland, poor relief was in the hands of Parish Councils.

---

ants. In June 1922 the number of unemployed insured people and their dependants on relief was over a million in England and Wales. It was normally assumed that three quarters of these were dependants, which leads to the conclusion that 250,000 were unemployed themselves. The Scottish figures, however, classified the able-bodied unemployed separately from their dependants, and in September 1922 the number on relief was 50,000. Since there were 1·5 million registered unemployed in July 1922 it can be assumed that probably 300,000 of them, or about one in five, were on relief.

the special circumstances of any particular case', provided the case was individually reported to the Ministry of Health.

When the unprecedented wave of unemployment hit the country early in 1921, the Boards of Guardians were overwhelmed. Some of them, particularly in non-industrial areas where unemployment was not so severe, tried to adhere to the old rules. But over great areas of the country neither the workhouse test nor the labour test appeared applicable or indeed possible, and the Guardians took refuge in a new procedure: they granted unconditional out-relief, but automatically reported 'special circumstances' to the Minister in almost every case. Asked in June 1921 how many Boards of Guardians had reported departures from the Order prohibiting out-relief to able-bodied persons, Sir Alfred Mond, the Minister of Health, replied that from January to May 1921, 204 Boards had reported 224,928 such departures, and that in the exceptional conditions of industry 'it would not have been practicable to refuse such departures, but the Guardians have been instructed to exercise proper discrimination.'[3] A few Boards of Guardians avoided the necessity of reporting to the Minister by instructing their Relieving Officers to treat all unemployed as cases of 'sudden or urgent necessity' even though the same cases were classified this way week after week and month after month.

The Minister accepted the situation very reluctantly, and continued to urge the desirability of reverting to the workhouse test or the labour test. Out-relief for the unemployed was mounting willy-nilly and many Boards of Guardians found themselves obliged to adopt special scales for the purpose instead of treating each case individually as they were supposed to do. In September 1921 the Minister temporarily accepted the inevitable and sent a circular to the Boards of Guardians emphasizing the principles which should govern their administration:

(1) that the amount of relief 'must of necessity be calculated on a lower scale than the earnings of the independent workman who is maintaining himself by his labour . . . a fundamental principle any departure from which must in the end prove disastrous to the recipient of relief as well as to the community at large';

(2) that 'relief should not be given without full investigation of the circumstances of each applicant' and that the applicant should be required to 'sign a form containing a complete statement as to the income of his household from all sources';

(3) that 'the greater proportion of the relief given in the case of able-bodied applicants should be given in specified articles of kind'.[4]

Most Boards of Guardians did not disagree with these principles. The idea that out-relief must be on a lower scale than the earnings of an independent workman appeared to them to be unassailable. If a man could get as much when not working as when working, then clearly he would not work. Even if below the lowest earnings, there was much risk attached to unconditional out-relief; if a man became habituated to it he might become demoralized and workshy. There were plenty of indignant voices claiming to represent the ratepayers who talked of the moral dangers.

However the theory was by no means easy to implement in practice. Some Guardians gave out-relief on a level equal to, or even below, unemployment benefit, which meant that only those who had exhausted their entitlement to benefit or were subject to a periodic 'gap' were eligible. But others argued that unemployment benefit was not, and was not intended to be, enough to live on, particularly where there were dependent children. So they allocated between 3s and 6s for each child in the family, and couples with children got their unemployment benefit supplemented by poor relief.

Children's allowances created a problem for the Guardians in the case of large families, however; if there were a great many children it could mean that the total allowed would bring the income of the family above the earnings of the 'independent workman', thus violating the Minister's first 'fundamental principle'. The Minister's own solution was to suggest a maximum for any family whatever its size, and some Guardians did indeed fix a family maximum of 50s or perhaps 40s.

But the large family was only one of the difficulties encountered when settling the relation between relief and wages. There were innumerable people, particularly in mining and engineering, who were working short time and trying to support families on half their normal wages. Should those with no work at all be better off than those employed three days a week? Alternatively should relief be given to those who were underemployed? Again, among those on relief were many who had never been in regular jobs but who had formerly hung around the fringes of industry, picking up an hour's work or a couple of days' work when available. Such people had supported families in the past, no one knew how. Now the odd jobs had all disappeared, and the men and their families could hardly be refused relief. But the usual scale of relief might well make such people better off than in their normal times. That did not seem right.

As wages and prices were driven down, the Guardians were continually urged by the Ministry to reduce their scales of relief. At the 1922 Trade Union Congress the representative of an unemployed deputation described the endeavours of the Manchester Board of Guardians to keep relief lower than wage packets at a time when some miners with large families were actually working for less money than they would get from the Guardians, and said: 'If we are going to allow that, by their organized force they will lower our standard of living until it is lower than that of the outdoor pauper, which in itself is less than that allowed to the indoor pauper, which also is less than necessary for the maintenance of a criminal. Where then, in the name of God, are we coming to? Let us make a stand, fellow delegates.'[5]

The giving of relief in kind was another of the principles enjoined upon the Guardians by the Ministry. It stemmed partly from a conviction that relief should be concentrated solely on articles of absolute necessity; it was also a defence against those who argued that if you gave the poor money they spent it on drink. But these again were attitudes appropriate to the nineteenth rather than the twentieth century.

Before the war, every Board of Guardians had been accustomed to the 'problem' cases: the 'unemployables', the shiftless, the drunks, the petty thieves, and all those so exhausted by the struggle for existence that they were submerged in a hopeless morass of squalor and want. But the unemployed who were now applying for relief were of a different calibre. They included highly-trained craftsmen, skilled men who had served long apprenticeships and who had never been out of work before except for short periods. They included labourers and other workers classed as unskilled who since 1914 had experienced a great change in their standards of living and their expectations – who had, in the words of the dockworkers, acquired 'status'. They included young ex-servicemen who had gone out to the front in their teens and had been promised a land fit for heroes.

To this generation, relief in kind came as an affront. In particular it was resented by the women, since it was normally given in the form of vouchers to be exchanged for goods at the shops, which meant that shopkeepers and neighbours knew how low you had fallen.

Meanwhile relief in kind was itself in process of change. It had formerly involved loaves of bread doled out to people collapsing from starvation. Now some of the Guardians were busying themselves with medical advice on calories and nutritional standards. The Birmingham Guardians had a carefully measured diet planned as a result of such advice. For a man, wife and three children food vouchers were given for the following items: tea, 9oz; sugar, 3½lb; rice, tapioca or sago, ¾lb; rolled oats or dried fruit, 2lb; cheese or bacon, 1¾lb; sweetened condensed milk, two 14oz tins; margarine or lard, 2lb; cocoa, 8oz; golden syrup, 2lb; blue peas or split peas, 1½lb; soap, 1lb; bread, 22lb; plain flour, 2½lb. 'These goods are supplied by means of food tickets, negotiable at practically all grocers' shops,' runs a contemporary account of the Birmingham scheme. 'When the scheme was started some difficulty arose in the substitution by tradesmen of articles other than those authorized by the Guardians. A threat to strike such offenders off the list, and the institution of surprise visits both to shops and to the homes, have put an end to most of the abuse, and less than half a dozen offenders have been detected.'[6]

In other and less efficient areas than Birmingham, the overwhelming desire of the applicant for something a little different – perhaps a bottle of tomato ketchup or a tin of fruit – was often surreptitiously met by the tradespeople particularly in the mining villages. Some Guardians did not even try; they gave vouchers for stated amounts, leaving the choice of food to the applicant.

The flood of unemployed in 1921 and 1922 so overwhelmed the Guardians' staffs in some areas that the normal processes of visiting, cross-questioning, form signing, summoning to subcommittees etc was much whittled down. But the Minister's instruction that *all* resources must be taken into account when fixing relief was resisted by a number of Boards of Guardians. Birmingham ignored one quarter of the earnings of members of the family other than the head; the object was to provide an incentive to accept any kind of work that was available. Birmingham indeed came into conflict with the Minister on this question. It was one example of the contradictions inherent in the system. The rule that those on relief must be worse off than those at work could not be applied if every time a man's son or daughter earned a few shillings on some odd job the family's relief was reduced by an equivalent amount.

'Poplarism'

Within the Labour and trade union movements a body of opinion was growing up which challenged all the fundamental assumptions upon which the treatment of the unemployed was based. It was argued that a man for whom there was no work should be entitled to 'full maintenance' and moreover, that the responsibility for maintenance should be borne centrally by the state and not by the Guardians out of the local rates. Some Boards of Guardians now had Labour groups on them for the first time, and a few even had Labour majorities. But the new view was not confined to Labour members. Here and there Boards of Guardians began deliberately to push up scales of relief, and to declare that no one should be ashamed to ask for relief as a right.

In such areas the numbers on relief rose faster than in others. The Minister expressed his strong disapproval of the Guardians concerned, and published statistics for June 1922 which showed that although for England and Wales as a whole not more than one person in 21 was receiving Poor Law relief, in certain areas it was one in five. These were Poplar (in the East End of London), Sheffield, Bootle, Middlesbrough, Crickhowell (in South Wales) and Guisborough (in the North Riding). The two last named were mining areas. One person in six was on relief in Barrow-in-Furness and in Bedwellty and Redruth (the last two again being mining areas). Not all the people on relief in these areas were unemployed of course; the figures included the normal categories of old and sick. But there was no doubt that the relatively generous treatment of the unemployed had pushed the numbers up. There were, apart from this, 30 areas where at least one person in ten was on relief.

The most dramatic confrontation on the issue arose between the Ministry and the Poplar Guardians. Poplar was a borough which formed part of London's dockland. To the south it was bounded by the East and West India Docks and by riverside engineering and ship repair works; its chief thoroughfare was the East India Dock Road. The mean streets of two-storied houses were huddled between great railway goods yards and gasworks, and cut across by canals lined with wharves and warehouses. Poplar was full of dockers who, even in good times, went out in the morning not knowing whether they would get work that day. Now bad times had come.*

There was a Labour majority on both the Poplar Board of Guardians and the Poplar Borough Council, and the Labour Group was led by a number of dedicated socialists headed by George Lansbury, who asserted that the unemployed should be entitled to full maintenance 'so that starving men should not blackleg on their fellow workers by taking their work at starvation wages.'⁷ The relief scales fixed by Poplar were above those of most other Boards of Guardians; moreover, there was no maximum for a family, so that in cases of very many children the family's relief could come to more than the wages of the breadwinner when in full-time work.

As the numbers on relief rose so did the cost to the local rates. Roughly two thirds of the rates were contributed by the industrial and commercial premises in the area, and only about one third were paid by the residents. However, the residents were very poor, and their share of the rate burden fell heavily on them. The London Labour Parties had long held the view that the poor rate, instead of being levied borough by borough, should be pooled for the 28 London boroughs so that wealthy West End boroughs like Westminster should contribute to the impoverished East End. On 21 March 1921 the Poplar Borough Council decided to bring the issue to a head. While continuing to levy local rates for their own purposes and those of the local Board of Guardians, they would refuse in their area to levy the rates on behalf of other precepting bodies such as the London County Council, the Metropolitan Police and the Metropolitan Asylums Board.

Legal proceedings were begun against the Poplar councillors, who marched to the High Court on 29 July behind a drum and fife band, followed by a procession carrying trade union banners and emblems with slogans such as 'Let Justice Prevail though the Heavens Fall'. The councillors were ordered by the Court to levy the rates but continued

* In the London docks there were 62,000 registered dockworkers in August 1921 but the maximum number employed on any one day throughout that month was 29,000, Ernest Bevin told the 1921 TUC.

to defy the law, and in the first week of September 30 of them were arrested and sent to prison for contempt of court, the men to Brixton, the women to Holloway. There were scenes of great excitement in Poplar in the days before their arrest, particularly at the final meeting of the Council on 31 August, when councillors addressed the crowds outside the hall to wild applause, and again on 5 September, when the five women councillors were arrested and driven slowly along the East India Dock Road in the Sheriff's car, escorted by a procession of 10,000.

The councillors were in jail for six weeks, during which they were denounced by organs of Conservative opinion* while the leaders of the Labour Party were saying behind the scenes that this sort of thing did harm to the Labour cause. But the prisoners rapidly became a source of acute embarrassment to the government. They had high-lighted the injustice of the rating system, had become popular martyrs, and were, apart from anything else, causing a lot of trouble to the prison authorities. The unemployed and others came and sang outside the prison walls and the prisoners made speeches to them through their cell windows. The London Labour mayors went on a deputation all the way to Gairloch in Scotland to see the Prime Minister, Lloyd George, and though the London Labour Party issued a circular advising local Labour Parties against taking similar action, Bethnal Green and Stepney Borough Councils both decided to follow Poplar's lead, and refuse to levy rates for the outside precepting bodies.

In the end the government gave in. The councillors were released on 12 October without having 'purged their contempt', and legislation was hastily passed to put the main part of the cost of outdoor relief onto a pooled Metropolitan Common Poor Fund. Poplar rates were thus relieved by 6s in the pound, while an extra 1s in the pound fell on Westminster.

But the numbers on outdoor relief went on rising in Poplar, reaching 29,000 by April 1922, and the struggle between the Poplar Guardians and the government also continued. The Minister of Health, Sir

---

* 'The unlawful cause for which some of the Poplar Borough Councillors have gone to prison has confessedly been followed, not with the sole object of relieving distress – other and more temperate methods would better have served that end – but in order to vindicate the Communist doctrine of "full maintenance" for the unemployed' (*Times* 3 September 1921).

Alfred Mond, laid down a maximum scale of relief which could be chargeable to the Metropolitan Common Poor Fund; the Poplar Guardians insisted on going above this scale, and paying for the addition out of their own local rates. Sir Alfred Mond then appointed an inspector, H.I. Cooper, who was the Clerk to the Bolton Guardians, to make an inquiry into the Poplar Guardians' expenditure. Lansbury later observed that Cooper was 'a very violent disciple of the great fundamental principle of the 1834 Poor Law Act, and he was sent to investigate, in an impartial manner, the doings of men who, it was well known, were not disciples of the gospel according to 1834.'[8]

Cooper, whose report was dated 10 May 1922, found indeed that the policy of the Guardians was 'in many instances foreign to the spirit and intention of the Poor Law statutes'.* No attempt had been made, he said, to put into force any labour test for the able-bodied unemployed 'or to discriminate in the granting of relief between those of the unemployed who were deserving and those who were undeserving'.

He pointed out that the Guardians had disregarded the rule that the amount of relief must be calculated on a lower scale than the earnings of an independent workman. The maximum chargeable to the Metropolitan Poor Fund for any family was supposed to be £2 14s a week; the Poplar Guardians, however, gave a man with wife and five children £2 19s 6d and added another 5s for every subsequent child. Thus a dock labourer with seven dependent children was getting £3 8s in relief and unemployment benefit combined, though when working a full week his wages would not come to more than £3 6s.

Under the regulations any income received by a member of the household had to be taken into account when fixing relief. The Poplar rules, however, disregarded the first 15s of a child's earnings, and if they exceeded this amount only a small portion would be calculated as part of the family's income. Thus the Guardians were in numerous instances 'granting relief in cases in which there appears to be no destitution'. In addition to the weekly allowances, boots and clothing could be provided at the discretion of the Relief Committee, and during 12 months 13,245 pairs of boots had been so issued. Second-

---

* *Parish of Poplar Borough. Report of Special Inquiry held under the Direction of the Ministry of Health into the Expenditure of the Guardians,* 1922 HMSO. The subsequent quotations are all from this document.

hand clothing had also been given; 'the clothing is not marked and could be pawned or sold without chance of detection.'

Cooper went on to report that the Guardians had refrained from prosecuting various people who had concealed the fact that they were earning while drawing relief. Such people had merely been cautioned and their relief cancelled. He also reported that about 140 children of people on relief had been sent for a fortnight's summer holiday to the Guardians poor law schools at Shenfield. The children had all been nominated by the Medical Officers, who had been asked to select those who would benefit from a holiday. In addition to maintaining them at Shenfield the Guardians had spent £18 transporting them there and back. Out-relief to their parents was not reduced while the children were away. Cooper observed: 'The sending away of children of out-door relief recipients for a summer holiday at the expense of the rates is, I think, a new departure in the poor law. . . . I think that the ratepayers should not be called upon to bear this expenditure.'

In general, Cooper said, 'The Guardians' policy has a tendency to demoralize recipients and is calculated to destroy incentive to thrift, self-reliance and industry.' And he reproduced the text of a letter sent to the Guardians by a firm on the Isle of Dogs: 'Dear Sir, Our employees who live in Poplar have pointed out to us that they can get more money by being unemployed than working for us, and as we have no wish to prevent them from getting as much as possible, we propose to dismiss them so that they can take advantage of your relief.'

Cooper criticized the treatment of the 800 inmates of the Poplar Workhouse which, he said, was 'regarded more as an almshouse than a workhouse'. The diet was 'too liberal'.* Among other things the Guardians had substituted butter for margarine at an extra annual cost of £600.

Cooper concluded that out of a total of £229,000 spent by Poplar on both indoor and outdoor relief, at least £100,000 a year could be saved.

---

* *Breakfast:* ¾ pint tea, 3oz bread, ½oz butter, ¾ pint porridge, ¼ pint milk.
  Dinner: (for men) 3oz meat, 12oz potatoes etc, 4oz rice or treacle pudding (this was varied with meat pudding, or cheese, or fish instead of meat on certain days).
  Tea: 6 to 8oz bread, 1 pint tea, ½oz butter and either cake or jam or cured fish, or cheese according to the day of the week.

The Guardians replied with a pamphlet entitled 'Guilty and Proud of It', which said:

> The people of Poplar have steadily supported the view that the duty of members of the Board of Guardians is to be Guardians of the POOR and not Guardians of the interests of property. In Poplar there is no cringing or whining on the part of those who apply for public assistance ... Relief is accepted without shame or regrets – in fact in exactly the same spirit as that in which ex-Cabinet Ministers, Royalties, and others accept their pensions and allowances from the Government. In Poplar it is well understood that the poor are poor because they are robbed, and are robbed because they are poor ... [9]

In June 1922 the Minister of Health issued an Order (under Section 52 of the 1834 Poor Law Amendment Act) prohibiting the Poplar Guardians by law from giving relief in excess of the scale laid down for the Metropolitan Common Poor Fund, which had become known as the 'Mond scale'. The Poplar Guardians defied this Order and continued with their own scales. This meant spending £2000 a week above the Mond limit, and by the end of 12 months the Guardians were facing a surcharge of £110,000. The government, however, had other things to think about than Poplar. The coalition had gone; a general election in November 1922 had produced a Conservative majority much divided on economic policy; three Ministers of Health followed one another in close succession, and no attempt was made to enforce the Order or exact payment of any surcharge.

The First Labour Government and After

At last, in December 1923, another general election resulted in a Labour government taking office for the first time. For Poplar it meant triumph. Early in 1924 John Wheatley, the new Labour Minister of Health, cancelled the Mond Order and any surcharge arising from it.

That summer the new government took certain steps towards implementing the Labour pledge of 'full maintenance' for the unemployed as of right. Benefits were raised considerably (see Tables 6 and 7, p. 90), but more fundamental, the conditions were so relaxed that instead of 'gaps' an unemployed person might draw what was now to be known as 'extended benefit' for what seemed like an indefinite period. The object, as the Minister of Labour, Tom Shaw, made clear, was to ensure that 'no genuine workman or workwoman willing and able to work should be submitted either to a policy of gaps or to recourse to the Guardians'.[10]

A new stage had been reached, but it was not, of course, the end of the story. Shaw's formula turned out to be far from watertight. Almost inadvertently the 1924 Act introduced a new obstacle over which the unemployed had to climb, and in 1925 140,000 people were disallowed benefit on the grounds that they were 'not genuinely seeking work'. Thereafter the unemployed began to complain of a special kind of harassment. They were expected to trudge daily from workplace to workplace, and even from town to town, asking for work which they well knew was not to be had; in subsequent interviews with insurance officials they were cross-examined on where they had been, whether they had been further than the work gates, whether they had been content with the word of a foreman or had interviewed a manager and so on. Failure to give the right answers could mean you were refused benefit.

The insurance officials' behaviour reflected the hostility of a great section of middle-class opinion to the unemployment insurance scheme. A government committee appointed in 1925, known as the Blanesburgh Committee, observed that 'public opinion outside the insured classes' was still 'predominantly unfavourable to unemployment insurance'.[11] There was an almost obsessive conviction that unemployment benefit was subject to widespread abuses. The Blanesburgh Committee tried to find evidence of this but did not succeed. Among others the secretary of the Charity Organization Society admitted that he had begun by thinking the abuses serious, but on inquiry he had been unable to find them. 'More than one of our secretaries said that they quite expected to find from our case papers numerous examples of abuses, but when they came to look they found very few.' His people, he said, had been 'much disappointed' when the evidence from among them had been put together. And he said: 'What all of us who have spent our daily lives for many years in industrial portions of London cannot banish from our minds is our observation of gangs of young men hanging round the same public house or bookie's headquarters every day of the week for years.' One COS Committee said: 'There is much evidence that payment of full benefit to single youths of 18 and over is demoralizing to a certain class.' Another said: 'Cases have been known of young men getting food and shelter from their parents and having the whole of their benefit as pocket money.'[12]

Unemployment benefit continued to be a cause of conflict and controversy. So did the issue of 'Poplarism', which had raised once more in an acute form the problem of tactics within the Labour movement. It was not the goal of 'work or maintenance' that was in dispute, but the 'unconstitutional' methods adopted by Poplar to achieve its aim. It seemed to some that if Labour were ever going to win a majority government, it was necessary to show that it would act responsibly and respectably. Herbert Morrison in particular, then Labour Mayor of Hackney, disagreed with the Poplar tactic, believing that in local government it was important to show that you were better administrators than your opponents, and that you would be careful with the ratepayers' money.

There were other and more numerous Labour members of Boards of Guardians who, whatever their views, in practice preferred to avoid a conflict with the central authority and do what they could for their applicants on the quiet. And this attitude was not confined to Labour Guardians, but was to be found on many Boards where the Guardians had begun to feel increasingly identified with the poor who had elected them. Just after the 1924 Labour government had fallen, Neville Chamberlain as the new Minister of Health began an unremitting campaign to bring back labour tests for the unemployed and to reduce the scale and scope of outdoor relief to the able-bodied. He met, however, with widespread passive resistance. After 1926 he took powers to replace rebellious Boards of Guardians with his own nominees, and these powers were actually used to get rid of the Guardians of West Ham in London, Chester-le-Street in Durham and Bedwellty in South Wales.

The tangled struggle only ended when the 620 Boards of Guardians were abolished under the Local Government Act of 1928; it was, however, to begin all over again with their successors in the Thirties, the Public Assistance Committees.

Meanwhile the attitudes of 1834 continued to be fought over – the 'deterrent' argument versus the 'help in need' argument; 'less eligibility' versus 'full maintenance'; the responsibility of the individual versus the obligations of the community towards the individual.

Table 6   Unemployment Benefit Rates

	Adult man	Dependent wife	Each child	Total for man, wife & 2 children	Single adult woman
	s d	s d	s d	s d	s d
November 1920	15 0	—	—	15 0	12 0
March 1921	20 0	—	—	20 0	16 0
June 1921	15 0	—	—	15 0	12 0
November 1921	15 0	5 0	1 0	22 0	12 0
August 1924	18 0	5 0	2 0	27 0	15 0
April 1928	17 0	7 0	2 0	28 0	15 0
March 1930	17 0	9 0	2 0	30 0	15 0
October 1931	15 3	8 0	2 0	27 3	13 6

(Source: Royal Commission on Unemployment Insurance 1931. Final Report. Cmd. 4185, p. 20.)

Table 7   Numbers and Percentages of Insured Workers Unemployed

December	000	per cent males	per cent females	per cent all
1921	2,038	19·4	14·0	17·9
1922	1,464	14·5	8·1	12·8
1923	1,229	11·2	8·9	10·6
1924	1,263	11·5	8·7	10·7
1925	1,243	11·5	7·3	10·4
1926	1,432	13·1	8·4	11·9
1927	1,194	11·3	5·8	9·8
1928	1,334	12·5	7·4	11·1
1929	1,344	12·2	7·9	11·0
1930	2,500	20·4	18·5	19·9

(Source: *Statistical Abstract for the United Kingdom*, No. 78, Table 91)

5
Upper and Lower Middle

The war losses among the middle and upper classes had been devastating. Young men from the universities had volunteered in overwhelming numbers in 1914. Boys from public schools had joined up in a spirit of adventure and heroic self-sacrifice. They went to the front, as they thought, to fight for a noble cause; they were filled with a sense of high purpose. It was from such young men that the junior officers were largely recruited, and the casualties among them were proportionately heavier than in other ranks. At the end of the four years, it seemed that many of the most gifted and promising had been killed.

Some of those who came back tried to obliterate their memories in aimless dissipation. There was a new craze for dancing which lasted throughout the decade. Hotels and restaurants hired bands and made ballroom space. Dance clubs and dance halls sprang up. People danced in the afternoon and throughout the night. Beneath the gaiety many were still suffering from shock.

Some 26,000 young men took advantage of a special government grant enabling them to go to university. This temporary post-war scheme gave many an opportunity they would never have had in normal times. But many ex-officers had difficulty in finding jobs. Some were reduced to door-to-door selling, others invested their gratuities in chicken farming.

While they had been fighting, others had been prospering. During the years immediately after the war profiteering was rampant, and businessmen were making spectacular fortunes. The inflationary boom was accompanied by vast sales of land, indeed it was estimated that in the four years 1918–21 one quarter of England changed hands.[1] Among those who sold were the old landed nobility. The Duke of Sutherland put most of his 1¼ million acres on the market in these years. The sales were attributed to the pressure of death duties, which bore particularly heavily on estates where the owner's death had been quickly followed by that of his heir, killed in action. Other owners, whose sons had been killed, had lost the incentive to hold the estate together. But the most important factor was the emergence of willing buyers. The process of breaking up large estates both in town and country and investing elsewhere, which had been going on slowly for half a century, was suddenly accelerated in these post-war years. At the same time, ownership of a landed estate was ceasing to be the hall-mark of great social prestige and power. Whereas in 1918, 305 peers had owned 10 million acres, by 1929, 210 peers owned 5½ million acres.[2]

While the economic base of the old aristocracy was changing, a new titled class was rising up. During the Lloyd George administration more peers were created annually than at any time before or since.[3] And it was widely rumoured that the newly affluent were buying their titles, particularly knighthoods. In July 1922 Parliament was forced to take note of what the Marquess of Salisbury described as 'scandals of the crudest kind . . . the scandals of honours which are said to be put into the market and sold, in order to obtain money for Party funds'.[4] According to the Duke of Northumberland, a knighthood cost £10,000, a baronetcy £40,000.[5] On the fringe were tricksters who persuaded the naive to part with cash in return for titles which they never in fact received. One such, a Colonel Parkinson of the building firm of Lindsay Parkinson, was persuaded to pay £3000 for a knighthood which failed to materialize. He sued those who had made him false promises, and there was a sensational court case in July 1924.

Rather lower down the social scale, there was a big expansion in what are sometimes thought of as middle-class occupations. The numbers in professional, managerial or clerical jobs rose from 2·4 million to 3·4 million between 1911 and 1931, an increase over the 20 years of 41 per cent. Most of the expansion took place between 1911 and 1921 and some though not all of it was attributable to the war. But after 1921 the trend continued, though more gradually. The changes in the occupational structure are shown in Table 8 (p. 101).

An occupational analysis can serve only as a very partial guide to the structure of society, for it leaves out of account a fundamental element: the distribution of property and ownership of capital. In the period just after the war, 5 per cent of the adult population owned 84 per cent of the capital[6] and this 5 per cent were in a commanding position. They formed, together with their relatives and associates, an upper class whose influence was decisive on everything from affairs of state to social behaviour. No occupational tables can convey the existence of such a class, part of whose wealth is inherited and part in process of replenishment. Thus in Table 8 those from the upper class who are big industrialists will appear in Category 1 as employers. Those who are judges or generals – most commonly though not invariably people of 'good family' – will be found in Category 2 as 'professionals'. Those who are rentiers and simply 'live by owning' will fail to appear in the table at all.

Apart from this, occupational tables often put people in very diverse circumstances into the same group. Thus in Category 1, 'employers', steel barons and shipping magnates are included with the owners of backstreet engineering shops and with the landladies of seaside boarding houses. Category 2 contains both the manager of a firm and his typist.

With all these reservations it is none the less significant that over the 20 years the proportion in Category 1, 'employers', remained more or less stagnant, and the proportion in Category 3, 'manual', was falling. Only the proportion in Category 2, the middle section, was rising, though still vastly outnumbered by the manual workers who at the end of the period represented more than three quarters of the total working population.

In Table 9 the middle section, Category 2, is broken down into groups. Here it can be seen that the greatest rise took place at the lower end of the social scale. Thus the numbers in relatively humble clerical jobs or working as insurance agents rose by no less than 69 per cent over the two decades, whereas those in higher and lower professional work increased by only 30 per cent. (Table 9, p. 102.)

The rise in the numbers of 'white-collar' workers was a trend of some political and social importance. The clerical workers who formed much the largest single group among them were for the most part initially recruited from manual workers' families. Getting an office job was one of the main ways in which young people from such families could better themselves. It was not just that their work was clean and carried out in relatively congenial surroundings; office workers, even of the humblest kind, had a different social standing from manual workers. Despite the fact that the male clerk's pay was often very similar to that of the skilled manual worker, office workers were looked on by themselves, and by others, as 'lower middle-class'. And they tended to identify with those in more affluent circumstances rather than with the manual workers from among whom they had struggled up. This influenced their political attitudes, and in particular their behaviour during the General Strike of 1926.

Although the increase in numbers was most marked among the lower ranges of white-collar occupations, the number of professional people was also expanding. The 'higher professionals' (b) included many who were self-employed rather than salaried. Most doctors, lawyers and architects were still in the position of small businessmen. These professions had been traditionally the ones into which, together with the church, the landed families and squirearchy had sent their younger sons. Up to a point this was still happening. The fashionable doctors and wealthy city lawyers were often people already well-off in their own right, their incomes supplemented by the return on private investments. On the other hand, the harassed and impecunious general practitioners in working-class districts were in a very different situation; they were thankful for the money from the state which came for 'panel' patients insured under the National Health Insurance scheme, and which saved many of them from a life of bad debts and patients who could not afford to pay. Among higher professionals as a whole, the proportion of the self-employed was slowly going down, and the proportion of the salaried was rising.

In the boom years that followed the war, small businessmen, people with investments, and the self-employed were in many cases doing quite well. On the other hand, life for salaried people was less comfortable than it had been before 1914. The post-war inflation hit them hard, particularly those in professional and administrative jobs, since on the whole their salaries failed to keep pace with the rise in prices. At a time when manual workers were successfully winning wage increases by a show of determination and solidarity, white-collar salaries were not showing the same elasticity, and some professional families found themselves pinching and scraping in ways to which they were unaccustomed. There were new discomforts. Before the war many such families had employed a resident domestic servant. Now there was an acute shortage of servants; the number of female domestics had fallen from 1·4 million in 1911 to just over 1 million in 1921. Inevitably a high proportion of those still available were absorbed by the really well-to-do with large establishments. The lower middle class found themselves making do with a 'daily'.

But after the slump came a change for the better. Incomes which had not kept pace with the rise in prices were not reduced to match the fall in prices either. Unlike wages, which were being driven down, salaries remained relatively stable, or fell only slightly. Middle income groups found that the situation was easing and, after 1923, as prices went on falling, they enjoyed a gentle rise in living standards and a new degree of modest affluence.

This relatively favourable position arose because the demand for administrative, teaching, technical and clerical skills was rising with the changing pattern of industry and commerce. While older industries which had made Britain great in the nineteenth century – shipbuilding, iron and steel, cotton – seemed unable to shake off the depression after the 1921 slump, newer industries were surging forward. The war had proved a forcing house for some of them, and they were now looking for a peacetime market for their products. Developing industries included electricity supply and electrical engineering, motors, cycles and everything connected with road transport, aircraft, the artificial silk industry and many branches of the chemical industry. All these needed more scientists, professional engineers, draughtsmen, designers and technicians. Printing and publishing were expanding, involving more writers and journalists as well as other skills connected with book publishing. A building boom beginning after 1923 created a demand for surveyors and architects. The steady growth of banking, commerce and insurance meant a parallel increase in office jobs. The numbers in the Civil Service, hugely expanded during the war, fell a little, but showed no signs of reverting to pre-war levels, since state activities were now branching out in new directions. All industries were employing larger office staffs, needing more people to fill managerial and administrative posts, as well as typists. Selling and advertising skills were in growing demand. So were the services of accountants. This need for more trained people led in turn to a growth in secondary schooling and an increase in the number of teachers.

It was these middle income groups which were the first to benefit directly from the manifold technological changes. Indeed it was their increased spending power which helped to stimulate many of the changes. These could be observed in the new houses for owner-occupiers which, after 1923, were springing up on the outskirts of towns. They were labour-saving houses with running water in bedrooms instead of the old jug-and-bowl washstand. They had gas or electric fires, though not yet in the main living room, where the open coal fire still seemed essential if home was to seem like home. But the shortage of domestics was being compensated for by houses that were much easier to run. Electric light was replacing gas, and all kinds of electrical consumer goods were appearing: irons, vacuum cleaners, kettles, heaters, cookers. The number of electricity consumers rose from ¾ million in 1920 to 3 million in 1930. Housekeeping became easier in innumerable ways. Rustless plate and cutlery eliminated much drudgery, while tinned and bottled foods and ready-prepared ingredients made lighter work of cooking. Ready-made clothes reduced the need for sewing and mending.

By the end of 1923 the radio was bringing a new form of entertainment into the home. Gramophones and records were of a quality previously unknown. Outside the home, the music hall was giving way to the cinema. More cars were coming onto the roads every year, and with them a new species, the owner-driver. Even more popular than the car in the early twenties was the motor-cycle with sidecar. Both offered unprecedented freedom of movement. On every side there were innovations and new experiences. On summer evenings city workers could see aeroplanes sign-writing the words 'Daily Mail' in the sky in giant letters of orange and silver. Though only a few thousand people had so far ventured on air travel – scheduled flights were not very reliable except in calm weather – ten-minute trips in an aeroplane were being offered to holidaymakers off the cliffs at Brighton for five shillings a time.

Many of the new delights came from America: jazz music and dances like the Charleston and the Black Bottom; ice cream sodas; the new cocktail habit (dry martinis, Manhattans, Side Cars, White Ladies); the most popular films; the ubiquitous Ford car. It was customary to talk of the Americans in patronizing tones – they had come into the war only right at the end, and then claimed to have won it. Yet it had to be admitted that most of the trimmings which now embellished everyday life were American. And the enjoyments were many. Looking back, life before the war seemed in comparison incredibly slow-moving, cramped and staid.

The newspapers reported with shocked relish the doings of the Bright Young Things, their 'wild' parties, their fast cars, their midnight bathing, their outrageous behaviour. The Bright Young Things were peculiar to Mayfair society, and since many of them were titled they provided useful copy for the popular press. They drank a lot and experimented here and there with drugs; they were rich, noisy, dissipated and enjoyed shocking their elders.

The urge to defy convention was shared by others less affluent. The sudden realization that something they have been taught by their elders is untrue comes to many people as they leave childhood behind. The event can be shattering or it can be exhilarating. Now numbers of young people appeared to be collectively experiencing such a revelation. They had been brought up in a society which had surrounded sex with taboos and was still under the sway of what D.H.Lawrence described as the 'grey mealy-mouthed canting lie' of the nineteenth century, pretending purity and hugging the 'dirty little secret'.[7] But now the taboos were disappearing, and works like those of Dr Marie Stopes were spreading knowledge and understanding.

The stability of the Edwardian era had gone and with it the assured viewpoint, the confident certainties about right and wrong. In such an atmosphere the teachings of Freud began to assume a new significance. Essentially a product of the nineteenth century, the revolution in psychology associated with his works had made little impact in Britain before the war except in those circles professionally concerned with the treatment of mental illness. Now the new psycho-analysis assumed an importance far beyond the restricted medical objectives which had brought it into being. The exploration of the workings of the mind, it seemed, could provide the clue to the mysteries of human nature.

The concept of an unconscious which governed man's actions to a far greater extent than his conscious mind, the idea that much individual behaviour could be traced back to the repression of some childhood experience, the notion that seemingly irrational anxieties could often be shown to have unconscious origins, all this seemed to shake if not topple the rigid structure of belief – both religious and moral – with which young people had been brought up.

Moreover, the new psychology shed light on many of the trivialities of everyday life. Dreams, for example, had been looked upon as meaningless except by a few religious or superstitious people who believed that they had a prophetic or supernatural significance. Now, according to Freudian theory, dreams could be interpreted as the hidden fulfilment of a repressed wish. Even ordinary slips of the tongue or a tendency to forget the name of a familiar person or place were not accidents. They too could be traced back to the suppression of a disagreeable or painful association.

Superficially the most immediate impact of the new psychoanalysis was a change in vocabulary. Suddenly words like 'fixation', 'complex', 'repression', 'frustration', 'inhibition', 'phobia', and phrases like 'love/hate relationship', 'inferiority complex', 'wish fulfilment', 'persecution mania', which were rarely heard before the war, became commonplace and were scattered about in conversation by people who hardly knew Freud's name, let alone his theories. In the long term, the new psychological approach was to have a pronounced influence on ways of bringing up children and on teaching methods. These however were already marked by a less authoritarian and more relaxed approach than before.

The new attempts to understand human behaviour went hand in hand with changed ideas about the universe. Einstein had completed the general theory of relativity in 1915. The scientific content of Einstein's work remained a mystery to all but mathematicians, despite the flow of magazine articles and books intended to explain its significance to the layman. However its existence encouraged the assumption that everything was relative and nothing was absolute. One contemporary writer recalled: 'Everyone felt that the old notions of the universe order had crashed and that somehow all philosophic values must be recast. The adoption of the theory gave a vague but powerful stimulus to the iconoclasts in every department of life.'[8] Einstein's authority was invoked to support sociological, political and even artistic ideas of which he had probably never heard.

Ideas about world affairs were changing too. Young people became aware that they had been taught history, as H. G. Wells put it, 'in nationalist blinkers, ignoring every country but their own',[9] that the uninspiring lists of kings which had formed the basis of their school history lessons did not help to explain the causes of the war or indeed anything else. Wells himself helped to widen horizons; his massive *Outline of History*, first published in 1920 and later revised, was one of the decade's best-sellers.

Writers of the period – particularly D. H. Lawrence, Aldous Huxley, James Joyce – were tearing away layers of hypocrisy which had been deposited in preceding decades. Literature was not just exploring personal relations more frankly. It was assaulting romantic and pretti-fied views of life.* It was demolishing myths about the war, and reflecting disillusionment with the peace. 'One half of Europe having knocked the other half down, is trying to kick it to death', wrote Bernard Shaw in the preface to *Back to Methuselah*, a play published in 1921 with the theme that men – particularly statesmen – do not live long enough to grow out of behaving like children. The most influen-tial poet for the younger intellectuals was T. S. Eliot who produced *The Waste Land* in 1922, followed in 1925 by *The Hollow Men* with the closing lines: 'This is the way the world ends, Not with a bang but a whimper.' Hitherto the leading writer to treat the theme of English-men in India had been Rudyard Kipling. Now in *Passage to India* (1924) E. M. Forster shed a different and disturbing light on relations between human beings in a colonial society.

There were new trends in the visual arts, some of which aroused hostility from a public which expected a painting to look like a coloured photograph. HYDE PARK ATROCITY: TAKE IT AWAY was the *Daily Mail*'s headline when the Epstein memorial to W. H. Hudson – 'Rima'–was unveiled.[10] A little later paint was thrown over it. The artist most widely esteemed was John Sargent who, when he died, was described by Sir William Orpen as 'one of the greatest portrait painters the world has ever known'.[11]

Many people, particularly among the older generation, were of course resisting the new ideas and trying desperately to preserve intact their old beliefs. Meanwhile the erosion of settled values was accom-panied by a deepening sense of insecurity widespread among the middle class. This post-war unease was reflected in novels of the period,

---

* In Aldous Huxley's *Antic Hay* (1923) an unsuccessful painter recites one of his poems. At the line 'Land of your golden dream' he is interrupted by his younger friends. 'Not "dream" ... you can't possibly say "dream", you know'. ... Not in this year of grace, nineteen twenty-two ... it's altogether *too* late in the day ... After you've accepted the war, swallowed the Russian famine. ... In the age of Rostand, well and good. But now ... the word merely connotes Freud.'

including the last of Galsworthy's Forsyte trilogies, so different from the first Forsyte story, *A Man of Property* (1906), the only volume of the Saga to be published before the war. The new insecurity found expression, too, in a best-selling novel, Warwick Deeping's *Sorrell and Son*, first published in 1925. This was the story of a middle-class man forced to take a menial job and obsessed with a dread of being finally submerged in the working class. The fear, and indeed dislike, of working-class people emerged in nearly every chapter of this long book* and appeared to reflect something which was hardly noticeable in pre-1914 popular literature, a conscious resentment of the working man, who now appeared so much less docile than before and whose increased organizational strength gave grounds for uneasiness, not only among the securely prosperous upper middle class, but also among those recently risen from more humble backgrounds who wished to preserve their new found status. At the time there were many such; people who had fought their way up by their own endeavours to a white-collar job, a suburban house, and a degree of modest comfort unknown to their parents.

* For example in the first chapter, Sorrell is thinking about his son Kit: 'The boy had had to go to a Council school. He had hated it, and so had Sorrell, but for quite different reasons. With the man it had been a matter of resentful pride, but for the boy it had meant contact with common children, and Kit was not a common child. He had all the fastidious nauseas of a boy who has learnt to wash and to use a handkerchief, and not to yell "cheat" at everybody in the heat of a game'. Claud Cockburn in *Bestseller* (1972) suggests that the explanation for the book's immense success in the twenties and thirties must have been that it dramatised the actual feelings of the middle class about their general situation.

Table 8   Major Occupational Groups

	1911	1921	1931
Numbers			
	000	000	000
1 Employers, proprietors, self-employed*	1,232	1,318	1,407
2 Professional, managerial, clerical	2,444	3,114	3,465
3 Manual workers	14,674	14,900	16,152
Percentage			
1 Employers, proprietors, self-employed*	6·7	6·8	6·7
2 Professional, managerial, clerical	13·3	16·1	16·5
3 Manual workers	80·0	77·1	76·8

(Source: G. S. Bain, *The Growth of White Collar Unionism* (1970). The table has been revised to group shop assistants as manual workers.)

* Excluding self-employed professional people, who are in Category 2.

Table 9   Details of Category 2, 'White-Collar'

	1911	1921	1931	Per cent increase 10 yrs 1911 –1921	10 yrs 1921 –1931	20 yrs 1911 –1931
	000	000	000	%	%	%
(a) Managers and administrators	631	704	770	12	9	22
(b) Higher professionals	184	196	240	7	22	30
(c) Lower professionals and technicians	560	679	728	21	7	30
(d) Clerical, insurance agents	832	1,256	1,404	51	12	69
(e) Foremen etc	237	279	323	18	16	36
Total professional, managerial, clerical	2,444	3,114	3,465	27	11	41
Manual workers	14,674	14,900	16,152	2	8	10

(a) Includes higher Civil Service, managers in industry, advertising agents, estate agents, auctioneers and commercial travellers, bank managers, insurance executives.

(b) Includes doctors, lawyers, professional engineers, accountants, editors, journalists, surveyors, architects, clergymen, scientists, statisticians, economists, commissioned officers in the armed forces.

(c) Includes teachers, nurses, draughtsmen, painters, actors, musicians, laboratory technicians, vets, pharmacists, opticians.

(Source: As for Table 8.)

6
Housing: the State Moves In

During the decade 1920 to 1930 two new species of householder were
coming into existence. One was the suburban owner-occupier, buying
a new house on a mortgage. The other was the council tenant. True,
there had been some owner-occupiers before the war, and in one or
two places there had even been small clusters of council tenants. But
the majority of families had always rented their homes from private
landlords, and at the beginning of the decade it was still widely assumed
that this was the natural state of affairs. It was believed that as soon as
the exceptional conditions following the war came to an end, the
building industry would revert to its normal peacetime role of putting
up houses for private investors to buy and let. Yet by 1924 decisions
had been taken which made it certain that the owner-occupier and
the council tenant would jointly dominate new housebuilding for the
next half century.

When the war ended the housing shortage was acute. The 1921
census showed that 9·7 million families were living in 8·8 million
dwellings. The deficit was larger than it had been in 1911. The census
also revealed that 14 per cent of the population were living more than
two to a room. In the south-east of England only 9·4 per cent were
overcrowded to this extent, but in Northumberland and Durham it
was 29·9 per cent; in Scotland, where one and two-roomed dwellings
were common, it was 43 per cent.

Overcrowding was superimposed on more deep-seated problems.
Houses are usually expected to last 70 or 80 years, and many last
longer, so that at any given moment most people will be living in
a dwelling which is the product of an earlier technological period, and
designed for a style of living now outdated. To provide tolerable
conditions, such a house has not only to be kept in repair but to be
modernized, otherwise the inhabitants will find it inconvenient and

uncomfortable. Just after the war people were faced with such discomforts in an acute form. They were twentieth-century people living in a nineteenth-century environment.

To some extent the contradiction affected all classes. The houses of the middle and upper classes had been built on the assumption that there would be plenty of maids to run up and down stairs. Coals had to be carried to living rooms, ashes taken away, hot-water cans brought to bedrooms, slop pails emptied. Meals had to be conveyed from the kitchen in the basement to the dining room on the ground floor. The shortage of servants after the war disturbed this pattern. Even the really well-to-do had to make do with a smaller domestic staff. Gas and electric fires and running water in bedrooms, a service lift from kitchen to dining room, saved labour; even more was saved if the kitchen could be brought to the same floor as the dining room.

In the houses of the better-paid working class, there was a widespread absence of certain amenities which the middle class took for granted. For example, more and more middle-class homes had electric light and were equipped with gas or electric cookers. The majority of working-class houses were still gas-lit and cooking was on a coal range. Most middle-class homes had bathrooms, sometimes created out of other rooms, or added on after the house had been built. But the majority of working-class dwellings had no baths.

Many houses had been built before the days of sewage, drainage, plumbing, indoor water supply and water-borne sanitation. Drains, sinks, piped water and water closets had often been installed at a later date. But such facilities were by no means universal, nor were they always satisfactory. A standard guide to household management gave this advice in the early Twenties to those intending to move house:

> Be especially careful in the matter of drainage ... It is vital to see that all drains are properly trapped; and that there is no direct connection between those carrying away sewage and those emptying the bath, basins and sinks. They must be water-tight so that no bad fumes may escape, and well flushed that they may be kept in thorough working order ... Of equal importance is the water supply. No house, however suitable in other respects, should be taken if the water supply is uncertain or impure.[1]

The introduction of w Cs into the one- and two-room dwellings built for the poor and humble in the nineteenth century was sometimes impossible for sheer lack of space. A special survey conducted just before the first world war showed that out of 175,000 Birmingham houses, 40,000, or over one fifth, had no indoor water supply, sink or waste pipe, while 58,000, or nearly one third, had no separate water closets. Usually such conveniences had been installed in courts for use in common by several families.

Communal water closets and even shared sinks and taps were often to be found in London working-class blocks of flats. Some of these had originally been built by philanthropic societies to rehouse families from rat-infested cellars who had never seen a water closet and (it was thought) would not know how to use a sink without stopping it up. The twentieth-century families now living in such flats might have come from another planet, so different were they in education and behaviour from their predecessors. But they were imprisoned in an environment designed for their grandparents.

In the Scottish cities there were great gloomy stone tenements to which clusters of w cs had been added later. They were installed on the stairs, or built out in stacks, each w c for use in common by several families. Experts had told a Scottish Royal Commission (which had reported in 1917) that the tenements had been built to last too long. 'Thus lasting they become cumberers of the ground . . . since they can only be brought up to modern standards with difficulty.'² Members of this Commission inspected big houses which had come down in the world, particularly in Edinburgh, where large well-proportioned rooms, 'sometimes with remains of beautiful artistic workmanship in the plaster work of ceilings', had been partitioned and were now occupied by many families for whom sanitary accommodation had been added 'in a haphazard fashion, where possible'.³ They were told by the Medical Officer for Dundee that the minimum standard aimed at was one w c to not more than four families. In the mining villages where one- and two-roomed cottages were common, the Commission found a 'widespread absence of decent sanitary conveniences' and 'the persistence of the inspeakably filthy privy midden'.⁴

The importance of sunlight, fresh air and adequate ventilation was by now fully recognized. It had not been so at the time when many of the houses had been built; indeed they might almost have been designed with the intention of excluding just those virtues. Notorious among them were the thousands of 'back-to-backs' in Leeds, Nottingham, and other industrial cities.

Many individually sound and reasonably planned houses were made dark and airless by the proximity of other buildings. This was partly because there had been no law to prevent a builder squeezing as many houses onto a plot of land as he could, but it was also because in the nineteenth century it had been essential for the workman to live as near as possible to his place of employment. Now that hours of work were shorter, and there were trams and bicycles, such close proximity was less necessary. But houses remained huddled up together with workshops, crouched under tall factory chimneys, or stayed squeezed up next to goods yards, foundries, chemical works, gasworks, tanneries. The smoke from open coal fires mingled with fumes and smells from industrial processes; the air was so dirty that the houseproud shut their windows to keep out the 'blacks'.

The best working-class houses were those built in the late Victorian or Edwardian period after building by-laws had been introduced. They had damp courses and an indoor water supply and many were of sound construction. But they too tended to exclude sunlight and fresh air. Built in terraces 30 or 40 to the acre they were often narrow-fronted with long rear extensions so that the main kitchen-living room had a window in one corner overlooking the flank wall of scullery, coalhouse and w c and with a close-up rear view of someone else's scullery, coalhouse and w c. Hardly any of these houses had baths.

The condition of the houses was bound up with the system of ownership. The owner-occupier has a strong personal incentive to repair his house and also to modernize it if and when he can afford to do so. His own standard of comfort depends on the constant improvement of his home. But in the early Twenties there were few owner-occupiers; most houses were rented. The man who does not live in his house but lets it to others and regards it as a source of income has no such personal incentive to modernize. Theoretically he may have a long-term financial interest in maintaining and improving his property if it is to retain or even increase its value. But this prospect conflicts with a short-term desire to spend as little as possible on the property, and to take what rent is forthcoming. In the Twenties most landlords appeared to have taken the second course of action, except in the case of better-class property which could be let on a repairing lease.

The landlords themselves were of many kinds. They included

property companies and financial institutions, family trusts and charitable trusts. There were coalowners and railway companies who let houses to their employees. There were numerous individual landlords, some of whom owned hundreds of houses and some only a pair of houses. Many had mortgages on their property and were paying interest out of the rents they received. Individual landlords both large and small habitually used agents (known as factors in Scotland) to collect the rent, and the tenant often had no idea who his actual landlord was. This absence of personal dealing between tenant and landlord contributed to the neglect of repairs and the deterioration of the property. The agent knew that if the owner was not satisfied he could take his business elsewhere. So he ignored complaints from tenants about repairs, but threatened them with court proceedings if they got into arrears. In the poorer districts relations between the tenant and the agent were usually bad, each side filled with resentment against the other.

It was against this background of shortage, squalor and discontent that a government committee, the Tudor Walters Committee, made proposals for the future in 1918.[5] The Committee knew that for many decades the better off had been abandoning smoky town centres for leafier surroundings. They also knew that to many housing reformers the words 'town planning' were synonymous with 'garden suburb'. The Committee's proposals reflected such influences. Tramway extensions were urgent, they said, so that the new houses could be built on undeveloped land on the outskirts of towns. The houses should not be more than 12 to the acre (8 in rural districts) each with its own garden. The typical narrow working-class terrace house must give place to one with a wide frontage and windows that let in sunshine. Rear additions to the house should be avoided, and the coalhouse and w c should be within the main walls of the building.

The Committee were aware that life in the normal working-class family centred round a kitchen-living room in which a coal range did double duty as a stove for cooking and a fire for warmth. They were anxious that the preparation of food and the washing up should be removed from this room. So they recommended that the sink, the tap, and the copper for washing clothes should be put in a separate scullery and, if possible, cooking arrangements moved there too. If cooking was done on coal, this would mean two fires in winter, but it was suggested that in areas where gas was available at a reasonable cost, this problem could be solved by a gas cooker in the scullery.

The Committee found that 'the desire for the parlour or third room is remarkably widespread'.[6] The front parlour, where there was one, normally housed the best furniture, including the piano. It was used for visitors and special occasions, and gave members of the family a chance not to be always on top of one another.

The clearest sign that times were changing was the discussion about baths. In working-class houses these, where they existed, were usually placed in the scullery since water was already laid on there. The Committee thought the bath could continue to be placed there 'if no other arrangement is practicable', in which case it should be fitted with a hinged top as cover. 'The bath, however, is better in a small apartment off the scullery, planned to serve the double purpose of bathroom and wash-house; in the latter case being made a little larger to include the copper as well as the bath; an arrangement which is both economical and convenient for the small type of house, in that water for the bath can be heated in the copper, while the bath itself may be made use of in washing operations.'[7]

While the Tudor Walters Committee deliberated, the Local Government Board commissioned the Royal Institute of British Architects to procure designs for the new cottages. Two stories high, they were to consist of living room and scullery and two or three bedrooms, some with and some without parlour, and were to have an indoor w c and a fuel store large enough to house one ton of coal. All were to have a fixed bath, but not necessarily in a bathroom.

The designs went ahead. But the big problem was how to get the houses built. The great housing boom at the turn of the century had been largely one of houses built for investment purposes. They had proved an attraction to the smaller investors, such as retiring tradesmen, who had felt that their savings would be safer in bricks and mortar than in less tangible stocks and shares. The boom had come to an end because, it was often said, Lloyd George's People's Budget of 1909–10 had frightened the small investor away from land and property. Whatever the reason, the government in 1919 faced the problem of stimulating output in an industry which had been in the doldrums for many years. Now building costs had soared and there was a serious shortage of labour. It seemed clear that the 'normal' method of providing houses was not going to be commercially-attractive until conditions were more settled.

The Local Government Board went into consultation with local authorities, and the upshot was the Housing and Town Planning Act of 1919 (commonly known as the Addison Act) which for the first time made it an obligation on local councils to provide houses. Their rents were to be comparable with the controlled rents of privately rented houses, which meant that, until building costs fell, they would be produced at a substantial loss. But any loss in excess of a penny rate borne by any local authority was to be offset entirely by an Exchequer grant.

Only an unprecedented emergency could have permitted an arrangement which guaranteed that the Exchequer would foot a bill of unknown size for an operation which it could not control. However Major Astor, Parliamentary Secretary to the Local Government Board, made clear when the Bill was debated that apprehension about the conditions of unrest in the country overrode other considerations. 'When we talk of expense and cost let us realize that everything is comparative, and let us measure the cost of our housing proposals by the cost of Bolshevism to the country and the cost of revolution,' he said to his critics. 'The money we propose to spend on housing is an insurance against Bolshevism and revolution.'[8]

So began the first nationwide programme of council houses, and those built, even if they did not always quite reach the best Tudor Walters standard, were a great improvement on what had gone before. But the programme was only pushed through in the face of great difficulties; materials and skilled building labour continued to be scarce; moreover some local authorities were reluctant to shoulder this new obligation, so that it was not until 1921 that the houses began to appear in any considerable numbers.

Ironically they did so just as the hopes and dreams of a wonderful new world were collapsing. Industry was in the worst depression it had ever known, Black Friday had come and gone, fears like those of Major Astor of 'Bolshevik revolution' had long since evaporated, and with them the sense of urgency which had brought the Addison Act into being. Retrenchment was the new perspective, and before the Geddes Committee had even been appointed the decision was taken to halt local authority house-building. It was announced in June 1921 that when those houses already approved were finished, no more would be built. Dr Addison, the Minister of Health, resigned in protest, and the final number completed under his Act in the end was 170,000 in England and Wales.

Meanwhile, however, the housing shortage seemed as bad as ever. And there was little sign that private enterprise was going to do what was expected of it and resume 'normal' building. A half-hearted attempt to encourage it with a special subsidy had been made, and nearly 40,000 houses built with this help, but the arrangement was discontinued when the Addison Act was abandoned.

The reasons for the failure of private enterprise to get going were much discussed after 1921. It was said that though building costs were now falling, they were still too high to permit houses to be built at rents which could compete with those charged for existing houses, which were still controlled under the Rent Acts. These Rent Acts became the subject of much dispute. They had originated in 1915 after considerable unrest, particularly on the Clyde, where house-owners were taking advantage of the wartime shortage of accommodation to put up rents. The owners at that time complained that they too were being squeezed, because where the property was mortgaged the mortgagee was raising the rate of interest or calling in his money to invest it more profitably elsewhere. The government had been obliged to step in and freeze rents at their 1914 level by law; simultaneously the mortgagee was prohibited from calling in his money or raising interest rates. In 1920, to compensate for the change in the value of money, owners were permitted to add 40 per cent to the 1914 rent, some of which was intended to pay for repairs. And the mortgagee was permitted to add ½ per cent to the rate of interest.

In 1920 nobody, not even the property owners, had advocated all-out decontrol. But after the slump considerable agitation began. The Rent Acts had had to be imposed because of the housing shortage, it was said. But now their very existence was helping to prolong this shortage. It was admitted that houses built after the war were not subject to the Rent Acts – indeed the owner could let them at whatever rent he could get. But, it was contended, this did not alter the fact that the Rent Acts had made housebuilding for letting unattractive to the investor.

In front of a government committee later known as the Onslow

Committee,[9] set up to consider the future of the Rent Acts in 1922, the property owners deployed their case. 'Housing is a business proposition, and unless it can be made remunerative, unless a builder and investor can get a reasonable and adequate return out of it he will never have anything whatever to do with it again,' declared Alderman Cheverton-Brown, the secretary of the National Federation of Property Owners. 'These restrictions have set up a state of anxiety, worry and unrest amongst everyone who was accustomed either to build or deal in or invest money in house property. It is not so much what is actually done, perhaps, as what it causes us to fear may be done in the future . . . if the Government wants housing to be restored to former conditions of free production it can only be by the removal of restrictions.'[10]

The Rent Acts were a source of great grievance and ill-feeling among the existing owners. '80 per cent of the owners of small working-class property are themselves working-class people, or they spring from working-class people,' asserted Cheverton-Brown. 'They have acquired their property with a view to living out of it in their old age; they have never had enough money; they have never saved enough money to speculate in stocks and shares or to send it abroad in mining ventures and so on; they have put it into bricks and mortar, believing that it will be sure and that the return, however small, will be safe.'[11]* He stressed how difficult it was for landlords to persuade courts to evict people who were in arrears of rent and the tendency of the courts merely to make orders for the repayment of arrears over a long period.

Mr Arthur Moore of the Improved Industrial Dwelling Co, and representing the Conference of Owners of Industrial Property and

---

* The property owners continually stressed that most landlords were small men. Tenants' representatives and Labour movement spokesmen continually argued that most houses were owned by rich men. Indignantly repudiating the alleged suggestions of his political opponents that most houses were owned by widows and orphans, the Clydeside ILP member of Parliament David Kirkwood said on one occasion: 'The biggest property owner on the Clyde is Lord Glenconner. There is a fine widow and orphan for you' (4 April 1924). There is no contemporary survey on who the landlords were, but it could have been that the pattern of ownership in the big cities was not unlike that revealed 40 years later in the Milner-Holland report on London housing. This showed that 60 per cent of all landlords owned only a single letting. But only 14 per cent of the houses fell into this category. 5 per cent of the landlords owned 57 per cent of the houses. In other words the contention of each side may have been right. Most landlords were 'small' men; most houses were owned by 'big' men.

Trust Property, complained that the Rent Acts had had 'a most demoralizing effect upon the ethics of the working classes'.[12] 'The tenant in 1914 used to regard his rent as a contractual liability,' he said. But now 'a good many come to regard it as a sort of act of grace to pay rent'.[13] And he said that in one block of dwellings, where there was a lot of unemployment, the owners had treated the tenants kindly, and let the arrears go on. 'That did not prevent the whole of that building organizing a charabanc trip to the Derby and the whole of the rent was left unpaid that week.'[14]

Landlords' grievances were reinforced on 3 November 1922, by a House of Lords decision in a test case known as Kerr *v.* Bride which held that a landlord who increased the rent by 40 per cent under the 1920 Act was first obliged to give a preliminary notice to quit. A large number of landlords, particularly in Scotland, had failed to comply with this technicality. It meant that their tenants could legally withhold all further rent until the 40 per cent increase which they had been paying for a twelvemonth or more had been recovered. Under the guidance of the Scottish Labour Housing Association (an organization which claimed to have about 200,000 members), many thousands of tenants in Glasgow and elsewhere began a glorious, rent-free existence.

The House of Lords decision came right in the middle of the 1922 general election campaign, and spectacular advances made by the Labour candidates in Scotland were widely attributed to this rent situation. The new Conservative government which took office after the 1922 election was not inclined to permit it to continue and hastily passed a new law which enabled the landlords to turn the tables on their tenants. 'Creeping decontrol' was introduced, which meant that any house of which the landlord gained vacant possession became forthwith decontrolled, and the owner could charge what rent he liked. At the same time it was made easier for an owner to get possession. It was not long before there were urgent complaints that evictions were mounting.

In 1923 private enterprise at last showed signs of starting to build again. But not houses to rent; houses for sale to owner-occupiers. This was a new development, and it grew up alongside the improvement in living standards now being experienced by the middle class. One of the people who recognized its significance and welcomed it was Neville Chamberlain, the Minister of Health in the new Conservative government. It was the beginning of a whole new approach – one which suggested that the satisfaction of the desire for home ownership among the lower middle class and more highly-paid manual workers would pave the way to stability.

Chamberlain was in any case convinced that the way to solve the housing shortage was for the middle classes to provide themselves with new homes. The houses they vacated would in turn be occupied by the less well-off. The bigger the pool of houses, the more filtering up there would be, so that ultimately even the poorest of the poor would benefit. The natural thing, he believed, was to add to the pool at the better-off end.

That was one of the objects of his 1923 Housing Act. It offered a subsidy to private enterprise for every house built provided it was of standard dimensions. It could be either let or sold, and most in fact were sold to owner-occupiers. The Act gave local authorities power to advance money to people who wanted to become owner-occupiers but could not manage the initial deposit. It also gave a subsidy to local authorities for council house building, but this was only to take place where the Minister was convinced that it would be better done by municipal enterprise than left to the private sector.

Thus local authorities were to be confined to housing the poorest classes for whom no one else would build for the time being. The subsidy to private enterprise and the arrangements for borrowing were intended to spur private building into action in every direction. Once housebuilding had got properly under way, the subsidy could be withdrawn.

Under this stimulus the output of private enterprise houses, both subsidized and unsubsidized, began significantly to rise at last. After 1925 output was maintained at a continuously high level and by the beginning of 1930 a million new houses had been built, mainly for owner-occupiers. Most of them were small two-storey houses of red brick. They had no basements or attics, and in comparison with their predecessors were convenient and labour-saving. They sprawled out on the outskirts of towns, the tramway extensions envisaged by Tudor Walters having come to pass, while in London big tube extensions to Hendon in the North and Morden in the South were taking place.

This private enterprise building boom was only in its early stages when a Labour government took office for the first time at the beginning of 1924. It held office but not power, a minority government doomed to be brought down amid much recrimination only nine months later. Meanwhile in place of the measures of socialist change which some Labour supporters had hoped for had come a modest little list of such minor reforms as the Liberals in the House could be persuaded to support. It looked at first as though the housing front would be no different from the rest. John Wheatley, one of the radical group of ILP members from the Clydeside, was Minister of Health, and his first important move – a Bill to stop evictions of unemployed people who were in arrears of rent – failed to get Liberal support and was withdrawn, with David Kirkwood, another Clydesider, angrily asserting that the new Labour government was no different from the Tories.

But Wheatley's Housing Bill, which was designed to promote a 15-year programme of subsidized municipal housebuilding, was carried through and later came to be recognized as the major – indeed almost the only – achievement of Britain's first Labour government. The subsidies were, like those under the Chamberlain Act, at a fixed rate per house built, but they were very much larger.* Simultaneously, on the promise of continuous work, Wheatley was able to get the cooperation of the building unions in expanding the labour force.

When the Wheatley Housing Bill was introduced, little was said to signify that a fundamental change was coming to pass. In not very precise terms, the Labour movement had for some years made clear its belief that housing should be a public service rather than a field for private profit. No such challenge was thrown down by Wheatley when he introduced his Bill; he merely pointed out that no private investment was taking place in working-class houses to rent and asked: 'Are we to remain without houses merely because people who have money to invest refuse to invest that money directly in working-class houses?'[15] He made only one important change in the quality of the houses to be built; it was laid down that the controversial bath must be 'in a bathroom'; baths in sculleries were to be ended.

* In both cases the houses were financed by borrowing, the capital sum being borrowed and paid back with interest over a long period. The subsidies were a yearly sum to help offset these annual loan charges. The Wheatley subsidy was £9 per house per year for 40 years provided £4 10s was allocated per year from the rates over the same period. The Chamberlain subsidy was £6 per house for 20 years with no compulsory contribution from the rates.

A significant feature of the Wheatley Act was that it abolished the conditional status of local authority buildings – the rule which said that councils could only build if, and where, and when, nobody else would. Henceforth local authorities were going to be seen as the main providers of working-class houses. The Act was enough to release pent-up energy in the localities. The local authorities got into their stride once more, this time in earnest. In the end they built over half a million houses under the Wheatley Act alone. It was not finally repealed until 1932, by which time new slum-clearance activities had been set in train.

Most of the Wheatley houses were built 12 to the acre. A high proportion of them were, like those of owner-occupiers, put down on the outskirts of towns in what came to be known as 'dormitory' estates. These created a new set of problems: they meant long journeys to work, and housewives suffered from a new isolation. And in spite of the desire expressed to the Tudor Walters Committee for a parlour, many of them were 'non-parlour' houses. Moreover it soon became clear that the Tudor Walters Committee had only half comprehended the revolution in cooking habits that was coming. It was not long before all cooking had been transferred to the scullery, which became known as the 'kitchen', and which was grumbled about because it was too small to eat in. The problems, such as they were, however, served to underline the magnitude of the revolution in housing standards which was taking place. The vast new council estates created a new style of living, with new opportunities and new hobbies, not the least important of which was gardening. Young couples whose parents and grandparents had lost all contact with the soil returned to it once more, cultivating their own vegetables and taking pride in displays of flowers.

Municipal housebuilding became meanwhile a normal part of local government activity. It gave an opportunity to innumerable councillors of every political colour to participate in something more rewarding, it seemed, than the administration of the poor law. Even the most intellectually limited among them could contribute ideas about the design of a fireplace or the height of a sink, and could retire from public life in the knowledge that they had helped to achieve something tangible which would still stand long after their day was over. It was ironical that all this enormously respectable activity should have been given its initial impetus by John Wheatley, a 'revolutionary' who died a disappointed man in 1930.

'The days of private capital-owners investing their capital in houses to rent to the working classes have gone for ever,' he had told the Commons.[16] His opponents had not believed him, but he had been quite right. The future lay with the owner-occupiers and the council tenants. The investors in cheap houses to rent, the private owners of the great monotonous grimy working-class streets, had had their day. Very slowly, without realizing it, they were on their way out.

1 A miner's wife drying her husband's pit clothes in front of the fire. There were as yet few pithead baths where the miner could wash and change and leave his pit clothes to be dried out.

2. The railways ran on coal-fired steam engines. Here a footplate man is at work preparing for a run.

3 Unloading wheat at the London docks. Mechanical aids were few and dockers commonly carried loads of up to 2½ cwt on their backs.

4 A queue of unemployed outside an employment exchange in 1924. Note the small stature of some of the men. Under-feeding during a childhood passed in the Victorian era had left its mark on many adults.

5 Narrow Marsh, Nottingham. A picture taken in 1919 showing back-to-back and blind-back houses, one of the legacies of an earlier century.

6 New council houses. The Roehampton estate, Wandsworth, was built by the London County Council 1922–1927. Set in green surroundings, it was the kind of thing people envisaged when they talked of 'homes for heroes'.

7 The front room of a new council house on the Roehampton estate in 1924. Note the gas lighting and coal grate; also the patterned lino, patterned rug and patterned table-cloth. Though the better-off, in revolt against Victorian clutter, were going over to plain walls, floors and fabrics, most working class families clung to the styles fashionable in an earlier epoch.

8 The new generation had somehow to be taught in old schools which often consisted of one very large class room only. This picture, taken in Warrington in 1928, shows several classes at work in one classroom.

9 An outdoor meeting on Clapham Common on Sunday, 9 May 1926, the sixth day of the General Strike. Meetings like this were going on all over the country.

10 Armoured cars escort food wagons from the docks to Hyde Park on the fifth day of the General Strike.

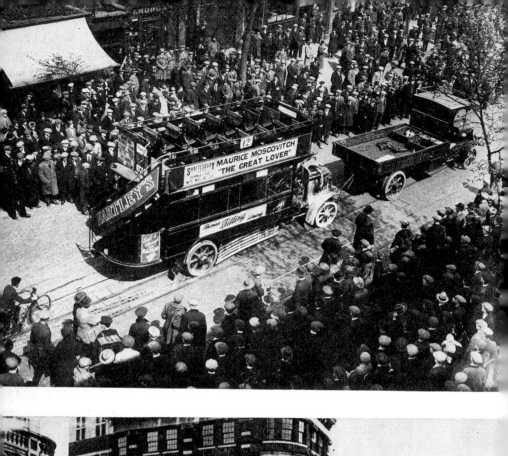

13 A Government volunteer in the General Strike acting as conductor on a bus in central London. Note the college scarf and plus fours.

11 A London bus is towed away after being put out of action by strikers on the third day of the General Strike.

12 Mounted police disperse a crowd at Elephant and Castle during the General Strike.

14 1928: A London traffic jam.

15 Outside a polling station in the 1929 general election. Women under thirty had the vote for the first time.

Table 10 Housebuilding

England and Wales	Local authorities	Private enterprise subsidized	Private enterprise without state assistance	Total
Year ended March				
1920	576	139		
1921	15,585	12,964	30,000	160,335
1922	80,783	20,288		
1923	57,535	10,318	23,800	91,653
1924	14,353	4,311	67,546	86,210
1925	20,624	47,045	69,220	136,889
1926	44,218	62,769	66,439	173,426
1927	74,093	79,686	63,950	217,629
1928	104,034	74,548	60,332	238,914
1929	55,723	49,069	64,740	169,532
1930	60,245	50,124	91,691	202,060
	527,769	401,261	567,648	1,476,648
Scotland				
1920	—	—	—	—
1921	1,201	364		
1922	5,796	1,289	5,000	23,942
1923	9,527	765		
1924	5,233	223	1,850	7,306
1925	3,238	1,785	1,852	6,875
1926	5,290	3,800	1,815	10,905
1927	9,621	3,995	2,017	17,285
1928	16,460	3,177	2,147	22,674
1929	13,954	3,087	1,275	18,326
1930	13,023	3,701	1,408	18,132
	83,343	22,186	17,364	125,445*

* Including some not in the previous columns built by the Second Scottish National Housing Co. for the government.

(Source: *Statistical Abstract for the United Kingdom*, No. 78, Table 32.)

7
Education: 'Elementary' or 'Advanced'?

Most industrial workers could look back only on rudimentary school-ing. This was as true of the trade union leaders as of the rank-and-file trade unionists. Ernest Bevin, General Secretary of the Transport and General Workers' Union, had left school at the age of eleven to become a farm boy. J. H. Thomas, General Secretary of the National Union of Railwaymen, had been an errand boy at the age of eight. Ben Turner, the textile workers' leader, had started in a cotton mill as a 'half-timer' when he was ten. Many of the Labour MPs who were elected to the House of Commons for the first time in 1923 were manual workers in origin, and were deeply conscious of their lack of formal schooling which, they believed, put them at a disadvantage when confronting Conservative MPs who had been to Eton.*

Since 1900 local education authorities had been able to compel attendance at school up to the age of 14, but to allow certain exemp-tions. These depended on local by-laws which varied from one area to another, but were so widely granted that, at the outbreak of war, about 40 per cent of all children were leaving school before reaching the age

---

* J.R. Clynes described in his memoirs his feelings when attempting to persuade his Conservative opponents to help the regions of high unemployment. 'They had been educated to polished periods of histrionic eloquence; we were forced to plead human necessity in rough voices, using such broken and inadequate words as our home-made vocabularies could with mental agony discover.' (*Memoirs 1924–37*, p. 71). Many Labour MPs apparently had these sensations, though there was in fact little justification for them, for as a whole they were not lacking in eloquence, and some displayed much verbal agility and wit. But that they sounded very different from their opponents could not be denied. It was before the days when a grammar school background was to become reasonably common to members of both Conservative and Labour parliamentary parties, so blurring differences of speech.

of 14. In the textile areas the 'half-time' system still prevailed under which children spent part of each day at work and part at school. Those with no exemption often worked long hours before and after school and at weekends. During the war, pressure for child workers greatly increased. H. A. L. Fisher, Liberal President of the Board of Education in the Lloyd George government, told the House of Commons on 10 August 1917 that in three years of war some 600,000 children had been withdrawn prematurely from school to work in munitions, the fields and the mines.

Under the Fisher Education Act of 1918 exemptions from school attendance under the age of 14 were at last abolished. But the operation of this reform had to be delayed until some years after the war, and it was not until 1922 that full-time schooling to the end of the term when the child had its 14th birthday became universal and compulsory. Other new legislation prohibited the employment of children under 14 in factories, which meant they were debarred from such work even on Saturdays or during the school holidays. At the same time the hours that a child could work before or after school were legally restricted, so that employment was much reduced in miscellaneous occupations – for example on milk rounds, as van or messenger boys, or in shops. The reduction in child labour had come about gradually over many decades. The final raising of the school leaving age to 14 forced the authorities to face up to a problem hitherto shelved: what kind of schooling was appropriate for the older child?

The educational system fell into three broad categories. Much the largest of these was the free public elementary sector. Small in comparison was the secondary education sector, which catered for a minority of children on a partly fee-paying and partly free-place basis. Both these categories were now incorporated in the state system of education. Thirdly there were fee-paying schools, entirely independent of the state. Included in this third category were the boys' preparatory boarding and day schools and the public schools to which the ruling elite sent their sons. The annual fee at Eton was £210 in the mid-Twenties, more than a skilled worker earned in a year. Boys normally stayed at their public school until they were 18 or 19, going on to Oxford or Cambridge if desired. Except for women's colleges there was little competition to go to university, and most boys whose parents could pay the fees could get to Oxford or Cambridge. Only

1·5 per cent of young people aged 18, 19 and 20 were in universities in 1919–20.

The mass of children began and ended their education in public elementary schools. Roughly two thirds of these were owned and controlled by the local education authorities. About one third were voluntary schools, usually Church of England or Roman Catholic, in which the local authority had control over secular instruction, but religious teaching was controlled by the voluntary body. The elementary schools were not 'primary' or junior schools; they were for the most part all-age schools and, as their name implied, were neither staffed nor equipped to provide more than a very limited education.

Each year a handful of particularly clever or fortunate elementary school children managed to qualify for a free place at a secondary school, usually at the age of 11. Here they would find themselves outnumbered by fee-paying children, some of whom, like themselves, had started their schooling in an elementary school while others had been to a fee-paying preparatory establishment.* In 1922–3 less than 9 per cent of all children aged 13–14 were in secondary schools, including the fee-paying pupils.

Some of the secondary schools had been built and were owned by the local education authorities (now the County Councils and the County Boroughs). Others had been grammar schools established before the days of state education, and which carried endowments of ancient origin. Since 1907 all these schools had been obliged to allocate a minimum of 25 per cent of their school places to the local education authority for non-fee-paying pupils, as a condition for grant aid. Some local authorities had managed to expand the number of free places well above this minimum. For children who did not win a free place the average fee in 1923 was between £12 and £13 a year. This covered less than half the cost. Most of the rest of the money was found from the Exchequer and the local rates.

The secondary schools provided a five-year course leading up to school certificate, normally taken at the age of 16. To an increasing extent they were also developing sixth form work and preparing pupils for university entrance, though less than 5 per cent of secondary

---

* In 1920, 67 per cent of secondary school pupils were fee-paying. 33 per cent had come from schools other than elementary schools, i.e. presumably fee-paying junior schools.

school pupils went on to university. Secondary school education was commonly looked on as preparation for a lower professional or commercial job, or for entry into the lower and middle grades of the Civil Service or local government, or into teaching. The free place system provided the manual worker's child with an opportunity to put his foot on the first rung of the educational ladder which in theory could lead to the very top. In practice it usually gave such a child a chance to qualify for a white-collar job.

Despite the free place system, the secondary schools continued to draw the majority of their pupils from among the children of the middle strata, from teachers and the less affluent professions, from shopkeepers and small proprietors, and people in white-collar jobs. Indeed many of the free places were won by children from the middle strata. The children of manual workers, whether skilled or unskilled, made up less than one third of the still very small secondary school population.*

In origin, secondary and elementary education were not two stages of education, but two alternative and separate systems, one small and fee-paying, one free for the mass. The free place system in secondary schools had thrown a bridge between the two, a narrow bridge – or, as some put it, a slender hand rail – which only the most gifted children were expected to cross. Or indeed to want to cross. Their numbers had always been limited by the desire of the poorest parents for their children to start earning their bread as soon as possible.

But during the war a sudden and quite unprecedented demand for school places developed. It came not only from the rapidly growing white-collar sections of the population but also from among industrial workers for whom in some cases increased wages during the war made payment of fees a possibility. The secondary school population nearly doubled from 174,000 in 1913 to 308,000 in 1920. Even so the number of secondary school places was far too low to satisfy demand, either for free or for fee-paying places. In 1919–20 over 11,000 children who

* In *Social Progress and Educational Waste* (1926), Kenneth Lindsay examined the social origins of secondary school children. At a time when free places had risen to 39 per cent of the total, skilled and unskilled workmen, together with postmen, policemen, seamen, soldiers, and domestic servants comprised 31 per cent of the parents. Clergymen, teachers, members of other professions, farmers, traders, traders' assistants, contractors, minor officials, clerks and commercial travellers made up 67 per cent. A similar survey carried out in 1913 showed the proportions to be 23 and 76 respectively (see *Statistics of Public Education in England and Wales*, Cd 7674, Table 43).

had passed the qualifying examination were refused free places because there were not enough to go round. Another 10,000 were denied admission as fee-payers, again for lack of accommodation. What had originally been conceived as a simple qualifying entrance examination, making available secondary schooling to all those elementary school children who could reach a desired standard, had now become a highly competitive affair. It was clear that a system which offered secondary schooling to not more than 9 per cent of all children was inadequate to meet the demand.

This pressure for secondary school places was so new as to be still the cause of astonishment in the middle Twenties. The Report of the Board of Education for 1923–4 devoted several pages to comment on this unexpected development and to speculation as to whether the pressure would continue and if so to what it would lead.[1]

Simultaneously ideas concerning educational advance had begun to change. Before the war, those who had been keenest, including many in the trade union movement, had thought in terms of enlarging the secondary sector, so that greater numbers could participate. But they still looked on secondary schooling as something for a minority of clever children with the ability to profit from an advanced type of education. They simply believed that this minority could be considerably enlarged. Such views, however, were now being submerged in a much more radical climate of opinion. Should not all children be given an educational opportunity equal to that now granted to only a few? The wealthy sent their sons to school until the age of 18 quite regardless of their natural ability. The less affluent middle strata kept their children at school at least until the age of 16, whether they were stupid or clever. If it was good for them, why wasn't it good for all children? In such a climate of opinion the Labour Party's programme in 1918 for a system of education 'which shall get rid of all class distinctions and privileges' and bring to every boy and girl 'all the training, physical, mental and moral, literary, technical and artistic, of which he is capable' corresponded to the desires of millions of parents who knew themselves to have been educationally deprived, and were determined that their children should have something better.

The ideas behind this generalization were developed and forcibly expressed in a booklet, *Secondary Education for All*, edited by R.H. Tawney and published by the Labour Party in 1922. It pointed out that those who could afford to pay received a secondary education as a matter of course, but that for the working class such an education was commonly regarded as a privilege to be conceded only to the exceptionally brilliant or fortunate.

The organization of education on lines of class . . . has been at once a symptom, an effect and a cause of the control of the lives of the mass of men and women by a privileged minority. The very assumption on which it is based, that all that the child of the worker needs is 'elementary education' – as though the mass of the people, like anthropoid apes, had fewer convolutions in their brains than the rich – is in itself a piece of insolence.[2]

Asserting that 'the so-called "educational ladder" is not a ladder but a greasy pole',[3] it declared its aim as free secondary education for all children and the raising of the school leaving age, initially to 15, ultimately to 16.

Secondary Education for All came out at a time when hopes for educational expansion had been dimmed. Earlier the 1918 Fisher Act had appeared to offer an opportunity for great educational advance. Not only did it provide for a minimum universal leaving age of 14; it permitted local authorities to make by-laws raising it to 15. For the age groups 11 to 15, Section 2 (later Section 20 of the Education Act of 1921) expressly charged education authorities with the duty of 'organizing in public elementary schools, courses of advanced instruction for the older or more intelligent children . . . including children who stay at such schools beyond the age of 14.' What exactly was intended by 'courses of advanced instruction' was not at that stage clearly formulated. But the promise was there. The Act also provided for nursery schools, and for day continuation schools to which young workers under the age of 18 would be released for eight hours a week.

The 1921 economic crisis dispelled the climate of hope. In circular 1190, issued at the beginning of the year, the Board of Education put a ban on new school building unless the circumstances were quite exceptional. By May 1921, H. A. L. Fisher, still President of the Board of Education, was talking about the necessity for postponing the operation of parts of the 1918 Act.[4] By August 1921 the Lloyd George government had appointed the Geddes Committee to advise the Cabinet on economies and in its first report, published early in 1922, the Committee made elementary education one of its chief targets. Its proposals included raising the age of entry to six and reducing teachers' salaries. Neither of these two drastic recommendations was accepted by the government. But the Chancellor of the Exchequer announced on 1 March 1922 that he was in favour of increasing the number of children per teacher in so far as it was practicable. And this was done; certain areas were told their standards of staffing were too high, and between 1922 and 1932 the number of elementary school teachers was reduced by over 4000. The number of pupils per teacher rose from 30·8 to 31·4. Nearly a third of the teachers were uncertificated, that is to say they were not properly qualified. Over one fifth of the classes had more than 50 pupils.

Secondary education did not escape the economy drive. Local authorities were told that the number of free places was not to exceed that of the year before. The number of secondary school pupils and teachers fell slightly during the year 1922–3. It was announced that no new awards of state scholarships to universities would be made in the next two years.[5] Meanwhile the Geddes axe, as it was called, put an end to certain things promised under the Fisher Act altogether. These included the nursery schools and the continuation schools, neither of which materialized except in one or two areas.

It was not until 1924, when the first Labour government took office, that the Geddes restrictions were entirely withdrawn. The virtual ban on new elementary school building was lifted, and local authorities were told to make a drive to get rid of classes of over 50, beginning with those of over 60. The problem of what to do with the great mass of older children in the elementary schools was however referred to a consultative committee known as the Hadow Committee. It was made clear that the Labour government would give priority to secondary education.

Charles Trevelyan, President of the Board of Education, told the Commons that in his government's view 'the central need is a great expansion of secondary education'. He pointed out that in many districts the secondary schools were overfull and still turning applicants away. His object, he said, was to double the number of pupils in such schools and to set a minimum of at least 40 per cent of free places instead of the existing 25 per cent. He placed this emphasis on secondary education 'because everything cannot be done at once and this is what is most needed'.[6]

In choosing to concentrate on the secondary schools, the Labour government was doing the one thing which could be expected to command support not only from its own followers, but from its Liberal colleagues and indeed its Conservative opponents. The demand for more white-collar workers was marked. This need could only be met by an increase in the number of young people with a suitable educational background. The children of the middle class could not alone fill the gap. They had to be supplemented by additional recruits from among the more intelligent working-class children. In practice, however, the expansionist policy inaugurated by the short-lived Labour government in 1924 took the form of extending the average length of school life so that children were staying on longer. As a result the number of secondary school pupils, which had been 308,000 in 1920 and 349,000 in 1924, rose to 411,000 by 1931. But the annual intake of children hardly rose at all. The most significant aspect of the expansionist policy was the rise in free places. The percentage of non-fee-paying pupils went up from 33 to 47. Some local education authorities began to abolish fees altogether in the secondary schools they owned themselves, including Bradford, Halifax, Manchester, Oldham, Salford, Sheffield, Smethwick and Wallasey in England and Glamorgan, Rhondda, Swansea, Merthyr, Newport and Cardiff in Wales.

This still left 80 per cent of children over 11 in elementary schools. Here the rise in numbers of 12- and 13-year-olds following the raising of the leaving age had produced near-crisis conditions in some areas. The school buildings alone made progress difficult. Many were like fortresses designed, as one critic put it, 'to resist both the ravages and the improvements of time'.[7] Intended for the mass instruction of very young children in the three Rs, they frequently consisted of one large room which could accommodate 100 or more children, and perhaps two or three smaller rooms. They had been built at a time when one qualified teacher was expected to keep an eye on several inexperienced pupil teachers each in charge of a separate group in the same room.

The new generation had somehow to be taught in these nineteenth-century buildings which now had to accommodate children of 13, 14 and even 15 supposed to be having the 'advanced instruction' laid down in the Fisher Act. The large rooms were partitioned, sometimes not unsuccessfully, to provide smaller classrooms. But as late as 1924 one fifth of all pupils were being taught in rooms in which more than one teacher and more than one class had simultaneously to be accommodated.[8]

Despite these environmental disadvantages, which would take decades to overcome, certain other developments were helping to ease the situation. The fall in the birth-rate meant that fewer children were entering school each year. This made it less hard to achieve a gradual fall in the proportion of classes with over 50, which came down to 6·6 per cent by 1930. Equally important, the schools were benefiting from a gradual improvement in the quality of teaching staff. The struggle of the teachers for adequate pay and professional status had borne fruit. A committee under the chairmanship of Lord Burnham established standard scales of salary for teachers after the war which later became obligatory on local education authorities. Initially below the level demanded by the National Union of Teachers, the scales did not fall when prices fell during and after 1921,* so that teachers' remuneration became much more adequate than it had ever been. Recruitment of properly trained teaching staff became easier. As the years passed there were fewer and fewer untrained teachers employed in the elementary schools.

The Hadow Committee had meanwhile been asked to consider what kind of education should be given to those children who did not get into secondary school, but who stayed on at elementary school up to the age of 15. At the time there were powerful voices raised in opposition to any educational expansion for the mass of working-class children. Certain groups of employers had always resisted any further raising of the school leaving age. The Federation of British Industries, in a memorandum published in January 1918, had observed that 'in selecting children for higher education, care should be taken to avoid creating, as was done, for example, in India, a large class of persons whose education is unsuitable for the employment which they eventually enter.'[9]

There was a substantial body of middle-class opinion which held that the sort of thing the Labour Party stood for – secondary education for all – was a luxury which the taxpayer should not be asked to pay for. In the debate on 22 July 1924, Fisher himself argued that full-time

---

* Though a certain reduction in the cost of teachers' salaries was brought about by making teachers' superannuation contributory instead of noncontributory.

secondary education should be limited to those children able to receive and profit by it. Sir Martin Conway M P voiced an opinion which was not unusual when he said:

There are plenty of children who cannot learn from teachers at all ... They can learn only from life. Now our system of education is built up on the basis of reading, writing and arithmetic and abstractions of that sort. There are people with definite concrete minds who cannot profit by any abstract teaching at all ... All abstract teaching is wasted on large numbers of children whom you hold back from the great school of life where they can learn, in order to keep them in a trammelled school ... There are many children who are far better removed from school at a very early age.[10]

Sir Martin had been educated at a public school and was M P for the United Universities.

The Hadow Committee surveyed the efforts made by local authorities to provide 'courses of advanced instruction' for the children who were not in secondary schools.[11] It found that some attempts had been made, particularly in London and Manchester, to set up 'central' schools on a selective basis for those who just failed entry into a secondary school. These central schools however were still classed as part of the elementary school system, attracting similar grants, but they were aimed at giving an improved general education to the older children. There were also some junior technical schools with a pronounced vocational bias. Other local authorities were trying to develop separate senior departments within elementary schools. A questionnaire to local authorities from the Board of Education in 1925 revealed that out of 1,987,000 children over the age of 11 in elementary schools, only 107,000 or 5·4 per cent were definitely in 'courses of advanced instruction'.[12] This number included all those in central schools and separate senior departments. Meanwhile some local authorities were trying to introduce into their all-age schools new courses suited to the needs of the older pupils. However for most of the children it was still as Tawney had described it: 'like the rope which the Indian juggler throws into the air to end in vacancy'.[13] 13-year-olds were marking time, it was said, under teachers who had not been trained to cope with them and in schools which had not been intended to accommodate them.

The Hadow Committee produced its report in 1926. It urged that education should be seen in two stages, primary and post-primary, and that all children at the age of 11 or 12 should be transferred to new surroundings. For this purpose it proposed to abolish the term 'elementary' with its all-age implications, and to substitute the term 'primary' for the first stage, and to give to the next stage of education, to which all children would move on, the name of 'secondary'. The existing secondary schools would be renamed 'grammar' schools, and would form one type of secondary education only. The others would be called 'modern' schools. Alternatively they could be organized as 'senior departments' of existing elementary schools. 'Between the age of eleven and (if possible) that of fifteen all the children of the country who do not go forward to "secondary education" in the present and narrow sense of the word, should go forward none the less to what is, in our view, a form of secondary education, in the truer and broader sense of the word,' observed the Committee.[14]

The Committee wanted the pupil-teacher ratio to be as favourable in the 'modern' schools as in the existing secondary (grammar) schools, and thought that the qualifications of the teachers should be as high and the standard of equipment the same. It believed that the courses of study at its modern schools should have a less academic bias than those of the grammar schools; indeed it observed in passing that 'some of the pupils in existing secondary schools would profit by a less academic curriculum'.[15] Though it urged that the subjects included in the modern school's curriculum should be much the same as those in a grammar school, it suggested that more time should be given to handwork, and a practical bias should be introduced in the third or fourth year of the course. Unlike the grammar schools, whose courses were planned for a period of five years (i.e. up to 16), the modern school's courses would be limited by the earlier school-leaving age. But the Committee recommended that the minimum leaving age should be raised to 15 by 1932, so that four-year courses could become general.

The curriculum recommended by the Committee for its modern schools was beyond the horizon of the average elementary school. It included some subjects which hitherto had been virtually confined to the secondary schools. For other subjects, nominally common to both, a changed approach was proposed involving new standards of teaching, equipment and accommodation. Thus a course in a modern foreign language, such as French, was recommended. Hitherto such courses had been confined to grammar schools, central schools and a few elementary schools attempting advanced work. It was suggested that the teaching of a foreign language should be carried on in one room, equipped with lending library, newspapers and, possibly, a gramophone with language records. It admitted that the supply of teachers qualified to give instruction in a foreign language was quite inadequate, and spent part of its report discussing how the need could be met.

The Committee suggested the outline of a science syllabus, but observed that: 'the special equipment required for the teaching of science hardly exists in many schools.' All the same, science courses were considered essential. The prevailing approach to the teaching of mathematics was heavily criticized. For this, as for literature, geography and history it was clear that not only specialist teachers would be required but adequate school libraries. The Committee wanted courses for boys in woodwork and metalwork, which again required special rooms and equipment. It wanted physical training to be part of the course, but faced the fact that elementary schools did not on the whole possess gymnasia or apparatus, nor did they employ teachers trained in the subject.

In general the Committee observed that 'the education of children over the age of 11 in Modern schools or in Senior class is one species of the genus "secondary education." It is not an inferior species, and it ought not to be hampered by conditions of accommodation and equipment inferior to those of the schools now described as "secondary".'[16]

After the Hadow report, reorganization of the schools made certain progress. The building restrictions had to a great extent been lifted, and the new schools seemed full of light, with their large windows and cheerful decorations. They had sufficient class space to allow for more flexible grouping of children. Some even had gymnasia and dining halls. They were in marked contrast to the gloomy nineteenth-century buildings still in use for the majority. Most of them were opened either as senior or as junior schools, instead of as all-age schools. At the same time local education authorities were able to turn some all-age schools into senior schools, redistributing the younger children among the remainder and classifying them as primary schools. By 1931 one quarter of the older children were in separate senior schools or departments (they were never called 'modern' schools until after the second world war).

Reorganization was not helped by the existence of the 'non-provided' or church schools. Most of them were all-age and many, particularly the Roman Catholic ones, were reluctant to lose their older pupils, yet were in no financial position to provide their own senior schools. The Hadow Committee had foreseen these difficulties: 'We admit we are here walking on difficult ground, and that there are fires burning beneath the thin crust on which we tread'.[17]

The fires burst through when the second Labour government in 1930 tried to raise the school leaving age to 15. Its Bill was partially wrecked over the religious issue before the House of Lords finally threw it out in 1931. The leaving age remained at 14, though more and more children were voluntarily staying on beyond the minimum leaving age. Meanwhile the modern schools (or 'senior' schools as they continued to be called) never reached parity with the grammar schools in standards of staffing, accommodation or equipment as the Hadow Committee had intended; indeed they were kept firmly under the regulations for Public Elementary Schools, which provided for standards much below those accorded to secondary schools. Thus in 1930 when the Exchequer and rates contribution per pupil in secondary schools was £20 8s, in the elementary schools (of which the senior schools still formed a part) it was £12 16s.

In spite of the Hadow Committee's insistence that modern schools should not be regarded as an 'inferior species' as compared with the secondary schools, the Report led in practice to the continued division of schools into inferior and superior. The Hadow assumption that children could be typed at an early age according to estimates of their suitability for one kind of school or another helped to reinforce the belief that some children were worthy of high-quality schooling and others not. It set the stage for the acute post-war controversy over the 11-plus exam, intelligence testing, the discrepancy in standards between the grammar and secondary modern schools and the merits of a comprehensive system.

Table 11   Public Elementary Schools: England and Wales

	1913	1920	1930
Number of children in average attendance *000*	5,365	5,187	4,941
Number of full-time teachers *000*	163	165	168
Percentage of certificated teachers	65·4	68·2	74·1
Number of children in average attendance per full-time teacher	33·0	31·3	29·4
Percentages of classes with more than 50 children	N.A.	25·4	6·6
Expenditure per child	£4. 13s	£9	£12. 16s

(Source: *Statistical Abstract for the United Kingdom*, No. 78, Tables 40, 49.)

Table 12   Secondary Schools: England and Wales

	1913	1920	1930
Number of pupils *000*	174	308	394
Percentage non-fee-paying	36·2	32·9	45·0
Percentage ex-elementary	64·1	66·8	71·2
Number of full-time teachers *000*	10	16	21
Number of pupils per teacher	16·7	19·2	18·6
Expenditure per child	£15. 2s	£19. 13s	£28. 15s
Average fee paid by fee-paying pupils	£7. 9s	£8. 9s	£12. 19s

(Source: *Statistical Abstract for the United Kingdom*, No. 78, Table 43.)

8

Old Age Pensions: Means Test or Insurance?

In 1925 the Conservative government introduced the first state contributory pension scheme. Thus old age pensions would be tied to a weekly insurance stamp. It was the culmination of several years of argument and indecision. At the time there seemed to be two other possibilities. One was to carry on with the existing pensions scheme started by Lloyd George in 1908, which gave 10s a week to people of 70 after a means test. Another alternative would have been to bring in a universal pension without a means test, making age the only qualification. This had been recommended by a government committee, known as the Ryland Adkins Committee, in 1919. It was also the programme of the Labour Party and the TUC.

However, the 1924 Labour government failed to implement a universal scheme and Neville Chamberlain, who became once more Minister of Health in the Baldwin government which followed, made clear in the Commons that he adhered to the view of his father. Joseph Chamberlain had believed in the 'necessity of enabling the industrious working people to make a better provision for old age' but thought that a universal pension was 'impracticable from the point of view of expense and . . . immoral and undesirable from the point of view of its influence upon thrift and industry'.[1] In the years that followed, state pensions became so tangled up with the insurance concept that it became difficult to visualize any other kind of scheme and hard to remember that in earlier years a contributory pension had not seemed at all natural or inevitable. Indeed, the 1925 Act marked a sharp break with the past.

In 1921 there were 2½ million people over the age of 65, or about 6 per cent of the population. Of these about 1·1 million were over 70.

Among them women greatly outnumbered men. It was already realized that the proportion of old people in the population was growing, and the statesmen who resisted a universal pension on grounds of expense were already using an argument which would be heard for the next 40 years. It is not so much the cost now, they said, as the cost in the future.

The war had deprived a significant group of the elderly of their natural support. In 1922 the number of war pensions drawn by parents for sons who had been killed was 368,000 – more than double those drawn by war widows. The Lloyd George pension of 10s a week was not enough to live on by itself, even though you had to undergo a means test to get it. On the other hand Poor Law applicants were specifically debarred from receiving it. The result was that if you were starving and forced to go on relief you got no pension, but neither did you if you had an income above a certain limit. However, between 50 and 60 per cent of all people over 70 negotiated the narrow path between having too little and having too much and managed to qualify for the pension in the years just after the war. Unlike Poor Law relief it was not regarded as anything to be ashamed of, indeed to some extent the pension conferred status. Despite this, the means test was much resented because it often cut down or extinguished the pensions of those who had worked hardest and saved most, while it penalized those whose children tried to support them.

All this had emerged at the sessions of the Ryland Adkins Committee in 1919 from the evidence of the members of local pensions committees who were appointed by local authorities and were involved in the administration of the scheme. It was said that when the old people lived with married sons or daughters, the pensions officers would assess the value of the board and lodging provided, count this as the pensioner's income and use it to reduce the pension. A witness from Portsmouth spoke of men who took in their mothers-in-law, often 'without a penny' but 'the officer goes and finds the place nice and clean and he says it is worth 8s or 10s a week and the applicant is supposed to have that amount of money coming in'.[2] A Manchester councillor spoke of the couples whose parents had been disallowed because they had given them financial help. A councillor from Sheffield said that children took their parents to live with them, but if it was a decent class of home the pensions officer would estimate the value of the board and lodging at 15s or 16s a week, which meant that the right to the pension was forfeit. The same thing happened when people got pensions or grants from employers for long service, or Friendly Society superannuation: they were set against the pension and used to scale it down or to refuse it altogether. 'We have found the Old Age Pensions Acts work absolutely against the thrifty and the honest, upright people,' he said. 'You can understand that it is a very painful position for myself, a working man, to have to sit in the chair and tell people that you cannot help them, though you recognize that they have done everything they possibly can to lead a respectable honest life, and have been thrifty and saving.'[3]

A Labour MP, C.W.Bowerman, spoke of his experience on a pensions committee: 'There is nothing more painful to my mind than to have to sit and hear the Pensions Officer weigh up the value of this or that – food, lighting, rooms and so on. You hear that month after month discussed in connection with some cases and sometimes it has been repulsive to me to listen to it. You have to form a judgment or try to form a judgment as to whether you will give a man a shilling extra or deprive him of a shilling.'[4] A woman member of the Stockton-on-Tees Board of Guardians said: 'I am a Guardian and I am under the impression that the questioning is worse than the questioning of the relieving officers that we have heard so much about lately.'[5] Later she said: 'If a son allows his father an ounce of tobacco a week, that is put down as income and a certain percentage on the value of the furniture, which is most absurd. They cannot possibly eat the furniture and they do not want to part with household goods they have had for 50 years, perhaps.'[6]

The upshot was an uncompromising recommendation from the majority on the Ryland Adkins Committee: 'We have ... been irresistibly forced to advocate that the means limit be abolished altogether, and that the Old Age Pension be given to all citizens at the age of 70.'[7] The means test was retained in the Act which followed, however, although it was to some extent revised, the income limits being raised, while new regulations allowed the value of furniture to be ignored.

Another question discussed by the Ryland Adkins Committee was the pension age. Many witnesses wanted it lowered. The TUC spokesmen said their aim was a universal pension at 60. The chairman of the East Riding of Yorkshire pensions committee wanted 65. He said that by that age many agricultural workers 'by being exposed in their early years to very inclement weather in the winter time are bent up with rheumatism and that kind of thing. Their hands are crippled though their general health is good.'[8] A witness from St Helens said that 'the heavy work at the glass and the chemical works particularly makes a man old quickly. The gases turn the hair a peculiar colour and he gets quite washed-out looking and certainly at 55 many of the men who have worked in chemical works appear to be 70 ... In the mining industry men keep fit fairly well; it is astonishing.'[9] The witness from Sheffield said that most men were not capable of earning a living after 65 because Sheffield trades were 'very arduous'.[10]

The Deputy Lord Mayor of Cardiff also wanted a lowering of the age, although, he said, there were many very strong and healthy men of 70 who had led active outdoor lives and were still able to get work at Cardiff docks where the labourers worked in gangs. And he personally knew of men between 65 and 70 earning excellent money as boilermakers.[11] But the representative from Huntingdonshire wanted the pension age kept at 70. He argued that in agriculture some of the old men were more valuable than the young ones because of their experience.[12]

The Ryland Adkins Committee failed to recommend a lowering of the pension age because of the cost. They wanted the pension to be raised from 7/6d as it then was to 10s, and this was done in the Act of 1919. Their proposal to make the pension universal without means limit was rejected.

In 1921, 1922 and 1923 the Labour opposition tabled motions that the means limit be abolished. These motions were all rejected on the grounds of cost, and indeed by this time widespread unemployment and industrial stagnation had led to a conviction that retrenchment in public spending must be paramount. Yet it was clear that the relaxation in the means test under the 1919 Act had been no more than marginal. An income of more than 10s a week was set off against the pension; if it reached 19s a week, the pension was extinguished. Help from sons and daughters was still being valued and used to reduce the pension. If a pensioner tried to keep chickens in his backyard or grow vegetables in his garden patch, he had to make a return of the eggs or vegetables produced so that their commercial value could be assessed and counted as income.

At last when the Labour government took office at the beginning of 1924 the King's speech included the promise of a Bill 'to deal with the discouragement of thrift involved in the present means limitation to the grant of Old Age Pensions.' The Bill was still awaited in May when a deputation from the TUC went to see the Prime Minister Ramsay MacDonald to ask, among other things, that 'all qualified may receive the full pension irrespective of any income received from any other source.'[13] The TUC spokesmen said they knew they were pushing at an open door; in reply MacDonald was reassuring.

However when the Bill was at last published in June 1924 it became clear that, for the time being, at any rate, the door to a pension without means test had been closed. Instead a very substantial increase in the means limit was proposed, so that the pension would not be reduced if the personal income from sources other than earnings was below 25s (50s for married couples). Above this figure the pension was scaled down, and extinguished if the income per pensioner exceeded 34s or 68s for married couples.

But the means test was to be applied in the old way to earnings. In treating these differently from other kinds of income such as savings and gifts, the Labour government was introducing for the first time a retirement condition. It was not one which had been asked for by the TUC, and the Ryland Adkins Committee had specifically argued that it was good for those old people who could earn a little to continue to do so. But Philip Snowden, Labour Chancellor of the Exchequer, suggested that in times of unemployment they wanted the old to retire. 'I do not think it right to do anything to encourage earnings by individuals above 70 years of age . . . I do not want to subsidize wages.'[14]

Snowden argued a case against a universal pension without a means test, though it had formed part of the programme of the Labour movement:

It means of course that pensions would be given to millionaires and dukes. They would be given to persons who do not need them, who do not want them, and I might add in some cases, who do not deserve them. The case of universal old age pensions is not really logical . . . If the country had means to squander and it knew of no other purpose to which they could be devoted, then it might give old age pensions to these dukes and millionaires.[15]*

* Snowden was interrupted at this point in his speech by a Liberal MP, Wedgwood Benn, who said: 'How many dukes are there?' Snowden: 'Twenty-two.' Benn: 'Over seventy?' Snowden: 'I should think the longevity among Dukes is very high.'

The change in the means limit brought in by the 1924 Labour government was however substantial, and in the following year the number receiving the pension topped a million for the first time, or more than 60 per cent of those over 70.

The failure of the Labour government to introduce a universal pension without a means test gave the Conservative government in 1925 an opportunity to change the whole approach to the question and, on the basis of plans drawn up and discussed over the previous two years with the civil servants, to bring in a contributory pension linked to the existing National Health Insurance scheme. One of the objections to a contributory scheme had always been that if the individual was really going to pay for his own pension in an actuarial sense he would need 20 years or more to do it in, so any existing generation of old people would have to be left out. The 1925 Conservative government made no attempt to deal with this objection; they by-passed it. Their plan was to award a pension at the age of 65 to anyone who had been insured for National Health Insurance for the previous five years. Those who qualified at 65 would get the 10s pension free of means test. The pensions were to be financed initially by the contributions of employers and employees who had not yet reached pension age, and not by the pensioners themselves: the current weekly payments would however earn employees the right to a pension when their turn came. So employers and employees began to contribute 9d a week between them to the new scheme. In addition there would be a government grant which would grow as the years passed. There was no retirement condition attached to the pension.

All this marked a turning-point of great significance. It started the process whereby the major cost of pensions was put onto employers and employees instead of on general taxation. There were protests against this at the time, both from the employers and from the Labour opposition, who contended that it was no moment to add to the burdens of industry; their objections were overridden.

It was the end of aspirations for a universal citizen's pension given as a right at a certain age. For though the TUC continued to pass resolutions asking for universal pensions at 60, the demand became more and more formal; by the mid-Thirties a contributory basis had in practice been accepted.

Since the pension was linked with National Health Insurance, about

30 per cent of the population were left out of it, including non-manual workers earning more than £250 a year, casual workers, and people working on their own account. And although the scheme gave 10s to a man's wife when she reached the age of 65 and 10s to his widow, many women, one way or another, failed to qualify, although they greatly outnumbered men at pension age. Those left out continued for many decades to fall back on the Lloyd George pension still granted subject to a means test. Nevertheless from 1928 onwards a growing number of old people began to receive their 10s a week without a means test; they acquired as a result a new status and a new self-respect.

Meanwhile the new pension was not, and was not intended to be, enough to live on without other resources. Indeed Neville Chamberlain made a virtue out of this:

It is not the function of any system of state insurance to supersede every other kind of thrift. We rather regard the function of a state scheme as being to provide a basis so substantial that it will encourage people to try and add to it and thus achieve complete independence for themselves . . . In that way we shall encourage those virtues of thrift which have done so much for the country in the past . . . It is not perhaps a policy which would command the enthusiasm of the thriftless or the ne'er-do-well . . . Our policy is to use the great resources of the State, not for the distribution of an indiscriminate largesse, but to help those who have the will and desire to raise themselves to higher and better things.[16]

9
Industrial Change

Initially most of the leaders of British industry thought that the economic crisis of 1921 would prove transient. The slump seemed to them a manifestation of the normal trade cycle. Its unusual severity was attributed to dislocation caused by the war and the boom that had followed. By 1923 and 1924, after unemployment had fallen considerably, company chairmen were prophesying that recovery was round the corner. However, in contrast to the United States which, after a brief recession in 1921, was now launched on an eight-year boom, the return to prosperity in Britain was very partial.

True, some newer industries like electricity and electrical engineering, motors and everything connected with road transport, were forging ahead. But the major heavy industries which before the war had contributed most to Britain's exports – coalmining, shipbuilding, iron and steel, cotton – remained in difficulties. This in turn led to significant shifts in the industrial pattern during the decade (see Table 13, p. 148). Many manual workers found that their old jobs were disappearing. The work to which they were accustomed, for which they might have been trained when young, was no longer available.

Most fundamental was the changing position of coalmining, in terms of employment Britain's biggest industry. The almost uninterrupted rise in demand for British coal which had characterized previous decades went into reverse, and the industry faced a shrinking market. Between 1920 and 1929 the workforce in the coalfields declined by 22 per cent.[1]

The same thing was happening to other industries which had once caused Britain to be referred to as the 'workshop of the world'. In shipbuilding, employment fell by 50 per cent between 1920 and 1929; in iron and steel by 36 per cent; in mechanical engineering by 43 per cent. And though the decline in the textile industry appeared on the surface to be more moderate at this stage, cotton workers suffered much from various forms of underemployment.

In the same period employment in agriculture, which had been in decline for many decades, fell by an estimated 14 per cent.

In contrast to this dismal picture, employment in road passenger and goods transport rose by one third, and in vehicle manufacture by over one quarter. The building and building materials industries were expanding, partly as a result of the big housebuilding programmes. Increasing literacy and longer leisure hours contributed to the rise in printing and publishing (see Table 13). Numerically most important was the growth in the distributive trades which, incidentally, persisted after 1929 when most other industries were caught up in the downward swing of depression.

Long before this happened it was clear that British industry was suffering from some chronic sickness. Even in the years of comparative prosperity from 1923 to 1929, the number of unemployed never fell below a million. And to a growing extent, unemployment was concentrated in the old staple industries where the labour force was in decline. In July 1927, a relatively good month for the period since the average number of unemployed through the country was less than 10 per cent of all insured workers, the proportion out of work in coal-mining was 21, in shipbuilding 22, in iron and steel 18 (see Table 14, p. 149).

The Regional Impact

During the 1921–2 recession, unemployment had been general throughout the country, and although particularly heavy in Scotland, did not appear to have a pronounced geographical nature. This was partly because after the mining lockout ended in August 1921 the coal industry was temporarily less hard hit than, for example, engineering or building. Thus the proportion out of work in London and the south-east was as high as that in Wales, while there was little difference between the unemployment rate in the north-east and that of the Midlands. It was only after the general slump was over that a new regional pattern in unemployment began to emerge (see Table 15, p. 149).

The coalfields, together with the older basic industries, were concentrated geographically in Wales, in the north of England and in parts of Scotland. In the second half of the Twenties unemployment in these regions was markedly heavier than in the south. It was not only those employed in the older industries who were affected. The stagnation here had repercussions on innumerable subsidiary trades in the same areas. By 1927, 5·8 per cent of insured workers in London were unemployed, but in the north-eastern region (which included the Durham and Yorkshire coalfields) it was 13·7 per cent, in Wales 19·5 per cent.

Within these depressed regions were certain parts so stricken by unemployment that by 1927 they were being referred to as 'distressed areas'. In 1928 the government set up an Industrial Transference Board which estimated that there was a permanent surplus of labour of 200,000 in the coalmining industry, as well as 450,000 on short time. There was also a permanent surplus of 100,000 men in the shipbuilding, iron and steel and heavy engineering trades, and an unascertained number in the textile industry. The unemployment, commented the Board, 'is concentrated in areas where almost the whole community has depended on one or two industries, and whole communities therefore are involved in the slow paralysis it brings with it.'[2] The Board could think of only one solution: 'the permanent removal of as many workers as possible away from the depressed industries and areas to other areas where the prospect of employment – notwithstanding a certain amount of unemployment – is more favourable'.

The Board expressed disappointment at the slow rate of emigration overseas to Australia and Canada in comparison with previous decades and suggested ways in which it could be assisted and speeded up. But its main hope lay in migration to other parts of Britain where unemployment was relatively low and employment was expanding.

In fact the Board was only seeking to speed a movement already taking place. For just as striking as the stagnation of the depressed regions was the expansion of light industries in London, the south-east of England and, to a lesser extent, the Midlands. Throughout the decade the chance of work in these regions was acting like a magnet, drawing workers and their families away from the old industrial areas into the new.

A characteristic of the new industrial developments was the movement out of congested central districts onto the outskirts of towns. In London the old workshops in the centre were closing down while new factories were springing up in the suburbs and further out in the surrounding countryside. Existing concerns were reestablishing themselves on a larger scale where there was room to expand. They were joined by new businesses which, freed from dependence on steam power by the use of electricity, were settling near their largest market. In 1925 the Chief Inspector of Factories reported that recently-opened factories in areas surrounding London included ones making electrical appliances, artificial limbs, bedsteads, quilts, motor-bodies, electrical fittings, pencils, wireless apparatus, pickles, ice, artificial silk stockings. In 1927 he reported that in addition to new works in North London, several large furniture factories had been set up in Buckinghamshire, and new factories in the Reading district included ones making patent medicines, silk robes, chewing gum, soap, and water heaters. In 1928 he observed that the number of factories had increased by over 3000 in the Southern Division in eight years, and that some of the new works were 'of great size'. Between Acton and Slough there were now 150,000 factory workers compared with only 60,000 five years ago.

The same outward movement was taking place in Birmingham. New factories were built on the outskirts, and their old premises were taken over and modernized by other firms.

Between 1923 and 1929, the insured working population rose by 8 per cent. But in London it rose by 13·6 per cent and in the south-eastern region outside London by 22 per cent. On the other hand the working population in Wales declined by 2½ per cent.

When the 1931 census figures became available the great change in the regional pattern became clear. The growth in population for Great Britain as a whole between 1921 and 1931 had been 4·8 per cent, but the increase in London and the south-east had been 10·8 per cent, whereas the population of South Wales and of Scotland had declined (see Table 16, p. 150).

In some ways the trends of the previous decade had been put into reverse. Thus in the period 1911 to 1921 South Wales, Northumberland and Durham had seen the greatest rate of increase in the population. But these were now the regions hardest hit. Though the natural growth – i.e. the excess of births over deaths – was high, migration had offset it in Northumberland and Durham, and overtaken it in South Wales.

Though there are no figures to prove it, the evidence suggests that the migration started in the Twenties was much accelerated in the early Thirties, when the distress in the depressed areas became intensified. Only in the late Thirties, after the drift to the south had been under way and officially encouraged for many years, did the realization dawn that it was damaging to the economy, the environment, and to living standards as a whole. By that time it was too late to reverse the trend.*

Small Workshops Decline

All through the decade the small workshop was making way for something bigger (see Table 17, p. 150). The trend was not new, but it was given impetus both by the fast developing use of electric power, and by the growing flexibility of road transport, which made local communities less dependent on local supplies. Since the turn of the century electricity had been slowly replacing steam for driving machinery and other processes. In 1921 there were 135,000 factories registered with the factory inspectorate in Great Britain. It was estimated that in rather more than half of them, electricity was used for driving machinery. In addition there were 148,000 workshops which had no power-driven machinery of any kind.

Ten years later the position had greatly changed. The number of factories had risen by nearly 20,000; the number of workshops had fallen by over 50,000. According to the official definition, installation of mechanical power transformed a 'workshop' into a 'factory', and undoubtedly a proportion of the additional factories which had grown up were simply former workshops in which power-driven machinery had been installed. But over 30,000 workshops had vanished altogether.

The small employers were finding it increasingly hard to keep afloat. It was above all in the villages that the decline was taking place. Here

* The effects of the drift to the prosperous areas of the south and Midlands and the changing policies towards the depressed areas is dealt with in greater detail in *Britain in the Nineteen Thirties*, particularly Chapters 4 and 5.

the blacksmiths and saddlers were disappearing; so were the van and cart builders whose customers were fading away as horse-drawn traffic declined. The little local dressmakers, tailors and milliners found they could no longer compete with the mass-produced, ready-to-wear clothes on sale in nearby towns. Small carpenters' and joiners' shops, clogmakers' establishments, even village bakeries, were closing down. Local brewing and flour milling concerns were doing the same. The decline in rural industry was offset to only a small extent by the rise in motor repair works in the countryside.

Many of the new so-called 'factories' were relatively small affairs. According to the first analysis made of their size by the Chief Inspector of Factories in 1930, over three quarters of all factories employed less than 25 workers. (See Table 18, p. 151.) Though the majority of factories were small, over two thirds of all factory workers were in firms employing more than 100, and nearly 30 per cent worked for concerns employing over 500.

Unification and Concentration

In the most modern factories the single-drive steam engine with its network of overhead shafts and transmission belts was gradually being replaced with machines driven individually or in groups by electricity. It made a great difference to comfort, cleanliness and safety. But Britain was much behind her continental neighbours in the development of electric power. In the mid-Twenties over 600 separate electricity undertakings (some municipal, some private) were operating at very varying levels of efficiency, and selling current at many different frequencies and voltages. An electric light bulb which would work in one area could not be used in the next. Apart from those supplying the public, there were more than 100 non-statutory undertakings, and much electricity used by industry was generated by the firms concerned.* However in 1926 Parliament set up a Central Electricity Board, and charged it with the job of constructing a national grid

---

* In 1930 the Census of Production found that over half the electricity used by industrial concerns was generated by their own plant.

which would link together the more efficient power stations in which, ultimately, all output would be concentrated. The Board was not to own the power stations; it was to promote unification and coordination among the numerous enterprises. After the grid came into being, electrification speeded up.

The railways also were subject to rationalization soon after the war. Over 100 railway companies were merged into four giants: the Great Western, the London Midland and Scottish, the London and North Eastern, and the Southern. Parliament, which had resisted railway amalgamations throughout the nineteenth century, now intervened to enforce them.

In almost every industry concentration of ownership was taking place. Indeed the climate of opinion which had distrusted monopoly and favoured free competition was changing. Nowadays large-scale ownership was equated – not always accurately – with efficiency. In shipping, about one half of liner tonnage came under the control of five groups: P & O, Royal Mail, Cunard, Ellerman and Furness-Withy. In chemicals, four big firms – United Alkali, Brunner Mond, Nobel Industries and British Dyestuffs – came together in 1926 to form Imperial Chemical Industries.

Some combinations were 'vertical' ones joining up firms whose products dovetailed. For example, iron and steel manufacturers were buying up coal and iron properties. The Balfour Committee reporting in 1927[3] estimated that the pig-iron manufacturers controlled 70 per cent of their ore supply and 60 per cent of their coal supply. More and more industries came under the domination of very large firms. Thus the output of 'artificial silk' (later known as rayon) was in the hands of two concerns, Courtaulds and British Celanese. Sewing cotton was dominated by J & P Coats; 75 per cent of all soap was produced by Lever Brothers, a company which was on the way to owning everything involved in the process, including plantations, shipping, whaling, seed crushing, oil refining and fisheries.

Some big groups were not concerned merely with products which dovetailed; they comprised firms whose products had no connection with one another but which had come together for financial reasons. Other companies were linked not by any formal ties but by interlocking directorships.

The impulse for this drive to larger units was in part technological.

A small company could not raise capital for purposes of modernization, whereas a large firm could. Sometimes the considerations were marketing ones. And it was argued that it was easier for a large unit to ride out a slump. But some of the motives for concentration were more negative, and these showed themselves in particular towards the end of the decade, when the object might be to buy up a competing firm and close it down.

Neglect of the Old Industries

The modernization and reequipment which was taking place tended to be directed towards the new industries rather than the old – a trend already noticeable before the war. The failure of Britain's older industries to recover at a time when their rivals in other countries appeared to be prospering had its roots in the economic pattern which had prevailed before 1914, when Britain had neglected to modernize her older industries while in some cases simultaneously supplying the rest of the world with the means to outstrip them.[4] Thus textiles, which before the war had accounted for over half Britain's exports, were now suffering competition from factories in Europe and the Far East, which had been equipped with the latest British textile machinery. The degree of mechanization in the British coalfields was well behind that of their chief foreign rivals. While Britain's shipbuilding industry had supplied 60 per cent of the world's mercantile tonnage before the war, the oil-fired marine engine, to which shipping was increasingly turning, had been neglected. Investment in home industries had lagged because the yield from investment abroad was higher. There had been a marked rise in new investment overseas both in the Empire and elsewhere. The City of London, the centre of the world's money market, had concentrated on this rather than on investment in industry at home.

This unbalanced position was exacerbated during the war. Shipbuilding capacity was much enlarged, but at the same time, countries which had formerly been Britain's main customers – Japan, Holland, Scandinavia – were now deprived of their normal source of supply and began to build up their own capacity. Thus Britain emerged from the war with an enlarged industry and her major customers gone.

In the long run, the way out of this dilemma was twofold. First, a restructuring of industry so that dependence on the older ones would be modified while new ones took their place. Second, modernization and reequipment. Some modernization did take place. But on the whole the owners saw price-cutting as the best method of competing with their newly formidable foreign rivals. This, they believed, could be brought about in three main ways. Firstly, by reduction in the wages of their own labour force. Secondly, by all-round wage and price cuts in what were known as the 'sheltered industries', a term that had come into use to denote industries dependent only on the home market, such as building and railways, whose price level had a marked effect on everyone else's costs. Thirdly, by lower taxation which would facilitate price cuts. A further much-discussed remedy was protection, or 'safeguarding' as it was called. The arguments around free trade versus safeguarding raged throughout the decade.

The bankers and City interests were meanwhile preoccupied with the need to restore London to its former position as the world's financial centre. This was the motive for the deflationary monetary policy pursued by every British government after 1920 in preparation for the return of Britain to the gold standard, a goal achieved at pre-war parity in April 1925. The bankers argued that it would pave the way to international currency stability, without which Britain could not regain her former prosperity. But in the short term the return to the gold standard was a further blow to all the old export industries, since it overvalued the pound, and so made British export prices even less competitive than they had been before, inevitably increasing the pressure by British exporters to force down prices, and therefore wages, even further than before. Moreover it involved the maintenance of high interest rates, which in turn were a discouragement to expansion.

J. M. Keynes was one of those who attacked the decision to return to the gold standard at pre-war parity, claiming that it overvalued the pound by 10 per cent and was 'a policy of reducing everyone's wages by 2s in the £. He who wills the end wills the means. What now faces the Government is the ticklish task of carrying out their own dangerous and unnecessary decision.'[5] But Keynes' voice was a minority one, and his pleas for an easy credit policy to encourage businessmen to enter on new enterprises were in direct conflict with orthodox policies of sound finance and a tight hold on credit.

The owners of the export industries looked back nostalgically to the wages and prices of 1914, and spoke as though Britain's problems would only be solved when both had returned to their pre-war relationship.

Table 13   Numbers of Wage-earners Employed in Certain Industries

	1920	1929	Increase or decrease	Per cent increase or decrease
	000	000	000	
Coalmining*	1,203	932	−271	−22%
Iron and steel	488	313	−175	−36%
Shipbuilding	259	129	−130	−50%
Mechanical engineering	784	441	−343	−43%
Cotton	520	464	−56	−11%
Woollen and worsted	261	246	−15	−6%
Docks	142	109	−33	−23%
Agriculture	1,048	899	−149	−14%
Railways†	575	500	−75	−15%
Building, bricks, cement	841	964	+123	+14%
Printing and publishing	263	293	+30	+11%
Electrical engineering	139	157	+18	+13%
Vehicle manuf., motors etc	186	238	+52	+28%
Tram, omnibus service and other road transport	261	349	+88	+33%
Distributive trades†	1,773	2,039	+266	+15%

* Wage earners on colliery books.
† Including salaried staff.

(Source: Agatha Chapman, *Wages and Salaries in the United Kingdom, 1920–1938.*)
    In this table the salaried sections, which were increasing in numbers in most industries, have been omitted, so as to show the impact on manual workers alone. However, for the railways the salaried staffs which comprised about one fifth of the total have been included. For the distributive trades salaried staffs have also been included, since shop assistants who comprised nearly half the total were classed as salaried. The figures are estimates.

Table 14   Percentage Unemployed in Certain Major Industries

	July 1923	July 1927	July 1929	July 1930
Average for whole country	11·6	9·2	9·7	16·7
Coalmining	3·0	21·5	18·9	28·3
Shipbuilding	43·6	22·3	23·0	31·7
Steel melting, iron puddling iron and steel rolling etc	21·2	18·2	19·9	32·6
Cotton spinning and weaving	21·6	9·4	14·4	44·7
Woollen and worsted	9·5	9·5	15·8	26·1

(Source: *Statistical Abstract for the United Kingdom*, No. 78.)

Table 15   Percentage Rates of Unemployment: Regional Analysis

Region	(*August 1922*)	1927	1929
London	13	5·8	5·6
South-east	12	5·0	5·6
South-west	15	7·3	8·1
Midlands	18	8·4	9·3
North-east	18	13·7	13·7
North-west	16	10·6	13·3
Scotland	21	10·6	12·1
Wales	12	19·5	19·3
Great Britain		9·6	10·4

(Source for the second two columns is the *Report of the Ministry of Labour* for 1929. The first column is compiled by the authors of *The Third Winter of Unemployment* (1923), based on examination of the Ministry's figures at the time. The Ministry did not begin publishing regional unemployment percentages until 1926.)

F

Table 16   Regional Population Changes

	1911	1921	1931	Per cent increase 1911 −1921	Per cent increase 1921 −1931
Region	000	000	000		
London and South-east	11,703	12,190	13,502	4·2	10·8
South-west counties	1,993	1,970	2,057	−1·2	4·4
Eastern counties	1,731	1,763	1,822	1·8	3·3
West Midlands	4,012	4,307	4,540	7·4	5·4
East Midlands	2,113	2,222	2,377	5·2	7·0
West Riding	3,128	3,305	3,443	5·7	4·2
Northern rural belt*	1,182	1,230	1,281	4·1	4·1
Lancashire and Cheshire	5,722	6,003	6,128	4·9	2·1
Northumberland and Durham	2,067	2,238	2,248	8·3	0·5
North and Central Wales	685	691	691	0·9	0·0
South Wales	1,736	1,967	1,899	13·3	−3·4
England and Wales	36,070	37,885	39,988	5·0	5·6
Scotland	4,761	4,882	4,843	2·5	−0·8
Great Britain	40,831	42,767	44,831	4·7	4·8

* Cumberland, Westmorland, Yorkshire East Riding, Yorkshire North Riding.

(Sources: Census of England & Wales, General Report, p. 33. Statistical Abstract for the UK for Scottish figures.)

Table 17   Factories and Workshops registered with the Factory Inspectorate

	1921	1931	Increase or decrease
Factories	135,356	155,354	+19,998
Workshops	148,226	95,714	−52,552
Total workplaces	283,582	251,068	−32,554

(Source: this table is compiled from the Reports of the Chief Inspector of Factories for 1921 and 1931. The 'workplaces' of course exclude mines and docks and other premises for which the Factory Inspector was not responsible.)

Table 18 Size of Factories in 1930

Numbers employed	Factories Number	per cent	Persons Employed Number	per cent
1–25	97,463	76·3	648,601	13·0
26–50	11,571	9·1	416,087	8·4
51–100	8,113	6·4	573,645	11·5
101–250	6,830	5·3	1,074,295	21·5
251–500	2,421	1·9	828,006	16·6
501–1,000	949	0·7	634,957	12·7
1,000 and over	421	0·3	813,130	16·3
Total	127,768	100·0	4,988,721	100·0

(Source: Annual Report of Chief Inspector of Factories 1931, Cmd. 4098, Table 14.)

10
Hours, Wages and Organization

Among the changes which industrial workers were experiencing, the most significant was the reduction in hours of work. Before the war a 54-hour week had been normal and one of 60 hours common. The war itself brought a still longer working week.

But in 1919 and 1920 the overwhelming desire for shorter hours resulted in the rapid spread of a 47- or 48-hour week with wages adjusted so that there should be no loss of pay. In this respect, at least, the promises of a better world after the war came true.

Trades with continuous processes, such as iron and steel, paper mills, flour mills and others, turned over from the previous two shifts of 11 or 11½ hours to three shifts of 8 hours. The change for other workers was hardly less dramatic. Previously a normal starting time for factories had been 6 a.m. After a couple of hours' work there would be a pause for breakfast, followed by a morning spell, a dinner break and then an afternoon spell. Some workers might live close enough to go home for dinner. For the others the actual time spent on factory premises for a nominal 10½-hour day had been at least 12 hours.

The new shorter working week meant that the breakfast break was done away with and the working day organized in two spells instead of three. The workers clocked on at 7.30 or 8 am so that for much of the year they got to work in daylight instead of in darkness, and were no longer obliged to get up at 5 or 5.30 in the morning. There was a drawback. The new arrangements meant longer spells of work at a stretch, perhaps five hours continuous work from 8 am to 1 pm. This however led gradually to the introduction of 10-minute breaks for tea or cocoa in the middle of the morning and afternoon spells.

Some factories kept to the old working day but went over to a 5-day week. This, however, was not as popular as the 5½-day week, which meant shorter weekday hours, with work for half a day on

Saturdays. The new hours transformed life for those with long journeys to work. 'It used to be all work and bed,' remarked a Bristol woman who walked four miles there and four miles back every day.[1]

Any proposal to revert to pre-war hours met with much more opposition than wage reductions. And though work above the standard hours was paid at a higher rate, there was often a strong objection to overtime.

Meanwhile it was discovered, rather to the surprise of some, that the reduction in hours taken as a whole had a beneficial effect on output. In many cases it rose fairly quickly up to the level attained when the working week was longer.[2]

The shorter hours remained for working people a permanent irreversible gain at a time when the other advances made in the years after the war were not being maintained. 1920 was the only year between the wars when there was virtually full employment. Temporarily the bargaining power of the wage earner was enhanced, and though prices were rising, wages rose faster.

With the onset of the 1921 slump prices fell heavily, particularly those of imported foods from the Empire. By 1923 the official Cost of Living Index showed a reduction of 30 per cent as compared with 1920. It can be argued that food was overweighted in this index. If a more balanced pattern of expenditure is assumed, as in the estimates compiled by R. Stone,[3] the drop in the price level appears smaller, about 26 per cent between 1920 and 1923. Wages, however, fell more than prices in this period whichever way the price level is calculated. Wage-rates showed a reduction of 38 per cent. (See Tables 19 and 20 (graph) p. 159–60).

After 1923 prices continued to fall but much more slowly. The wages experience thereafter was more mixed. Some sections, particularly in the expanding industries, were able to win increases in wages so that by 1927 in relation to the new price level they were better off than in 1920 though in money terms getting much less. Others were able to keep wage levels steady, so that as prices fell their standards showed a marginal improvement. Others again, particularly in the older industries, were unable to resist continuing wage reductions. The employers soon looked on 1920 as a freak year, and the prosperity of wage earners then as abnormal. They habitually used 1914 standards as the yardstick, contending that where wages were higher in real terms than in 1914, a wage cut should, if necessary, be acceptable. In fact, so great had been the collapse that real wages for many miners and some engineers were already lower than in 1914. This, however, was not the case for the majority of workers, who were immeasurably better off than they had been before the war. But their expectations were no longer based on pre-war standards; they were based on the immediate post-war years.

A wage cut, even if paralleled by price falls, is a very painful process, and particularly so for those whose circumstances are not eased by savings. Suddenly, between one week and the next, the individual suffers an abrupt cut in spending power, perhaps making it difficult for him to meet normal commitments such as rent. In such circumstances it is cold comfort to be told that since prices are falling you are now getting as much in real terms as you were some months ago. This was, however, the experience of large groups of workers throughout the decade. And added to it was the fact that their jobs were precarious and they suffered much from short time even when not actually unemployed.

Trade Unions

For the trade unions the period of confidence was over by 1921. The next two years saw a slow defensive war, a falling back from one position to another. The object was to cling to what you had gained earlier; it was seldom possible to contemplate going forward. Funds were eroded by payment of union benefits to unemployed members. The number in trade unions dropped from over 8 million in 1920 to 5·4 million in 1923. In the same period, membership affiliated to the TUC fell from 6·5 million to 4·4 million. After 1923 trade union membership remained steady for about three years, wages became more stable and, as we have seen, some improvements were achieved. But nearly two thirds of all manual workers were unorganized.

Though the original object of the trade unions affiliated to the TUC had been primarily the defence or improvement of the wages and working conditions of their members, the Trades Union Congress had long been concerned with wider questions. The Hull Congress in 1924 had adopted an Industrial Workers' Charter which included such aims as public ownership of land, coalmines and railways, as well as 'proper provision for the adequate participation of the workers in control and management'. At the same Congress, trade union structure was discussed, and the TUC General Council was instructed to draw up a scheme for 'organization by industry'. 'Time after time in industrial conflicts defects in trade union structure have been revealed,' observed Walter Citrine, then Assistant Secretary to the TUC, in a memorandum published the following year.[4] He listed the objects of the trade unions as not just 'betterment of wages and working conditions' but 'control of industry' and 'scientific functioning against capitalism'.[5] He suggested that 'underlying the reasoning of those who support improved trade union organization is the ever-present realization, partially articulate though it may be, of the wider destiny which the movement is to fulfil.'[6]

It was generally accepted that there were too many trade unions and the Hull resolution stipulated that their number should be 'reduced to an absolute minimum'. At the time, the $4\frac{1}{2}$ million members affiliated to the TUC were organized in about 200 separate unions. Another million trade unionists were in unions outside the TUC, and these organizations numbered nearly a thousand. Some of those not in the TUC were societies for white-collar or professional workers who did not care to be associated with manual workers. Others were small organizations for manual workers.

A reduction in numbers was not the only issue, however. The structure of trade unionism was primarily a product of the nineteenth century. First in the field had been the craft unions, which had been narrowly exclusive and to some extent remained so, seeing it as part of their function to preserve the status of their members in relation to other workers. On the other hand, the general workers' unions, in origin products of the 'new unionism' of the 1880s, were open to all in theory, but in practice organized the less skilled and the labourers in most industries.

The number of different unions into which the employees of even a single firm could be organized made negotiations complicated, if not divisive. For example, in the building trade, there would be carpenters, bricklayers, painters, plumbers, plasterers and others all working on a single housing site, perhaps employed by a single building contractor, yet all in separate craft unions. They would work side by side with labourers who might be in a society intended for builders' labourers or in a general workers 'union, but were likely to be in no union at all. The multiplicity of organizations in most industries had led to competition between unions, 'poaching' of members by one union from another, and demarcation disputes, particularly in shipbuilding.

The pre-war syndicalists had preached the need to move towards industrial unionism (or, as the Hull resolution put it, 'organization by industry'), so that all who worked in one industry, from the most highly-paid craftsman to the most lowly unskilled, would be in one organization. Industrial unionism was seen not only as a method of eliminating inter-union disputes and establishing a wider unity, but as a necessary step towards workers' control of industry.

In the post-war period active trade unionists attached to the Minority Movement held the same belief. The National Minority Movement, which had been formed in 1924 on the initiative of the Communist Party, was a broad alliance of left-wing trade unionists. It had powerful support among the miners and a certain following among the active rank and file in the AEU, the Electrical Trades Union, the Furnishing Trades Association and the Woodworkers Society. Convinced since the slump that capitalism was breaking down the spokesmen of the Minority Movement continually urged the workers to unite to overthrow it. Organization by industry, together with the development of powerful workshop organization, was seen as essential to this struggle. 'A multiplicity of unions, each with its own particular little nest of officials, constitute an obstacle which would damn any prospect of success in any movement,' declared MM's New Year message in 1925.[7]

In practice the movement towards industrial unionism had already before the war come up against formidable obstacles. The National Union of Railwaymen, for instance, which aimed to be an industrial union and to organize every grade of person employed by the railway companies, had found itself compelled to exist side by side with the Associated Society of Locomotive Engineers and Firemen (a craft union confined to railway drivers and other footplatemen) and with the Railway Clerks Association. The nearest thing to industrial unionism in practice was the Miners Federation of Great Britain, which had succeeded in combining all the major district miners' associations for the purposes of national wage negotiations, though even here the clerks, certain of the craftsmen, and in some areas the surface workers, were not in unions attached to the MFGB.

Though the 1924 Hull Congress declared in favour of organization by industry, and the General Council spent three years investigating and compiling reports on the matter which were annually discussed, the actual movements towards amalgamation which took place during the Twenties were not on the whole in the direction of industrial union-ism. Rather they tended to repeat an older pattern, so that what emerged from the period was larger craft unions than before, and larger general workers' unions. In the building trade the bricklayers' unions joined with the stonemasons in 1921 to form the Amalgamated Union of Building Trade Workers. In the same year, the two major carpenters' unions merged into the Amalgamated Society of Woodworkers. The Amalgamated Engineering Union came into existence in 1920 as a result of a fusion between the old Amalgamated Society of Engineers and a number of smaller craft unions. The AEU was dominated by skilled men, particularly fitters and turners. In 1926 it tried to move towards 'organization by industry' by opening its ranks to all male workers in engineering, whether skilled or not. However, this attempt was inhibited not only by the reluctance of some branch officials to recruit semi-skilled and unskilled workers, but by the fact that the general workers' unions were already established among these workers. Moreover the general workers' unions took in women, who were being increasingly employed in a semi-skilled capacity in engineering, but whom the AEU still refused to admit.

The general workers' unions were meanwhile consolidating their position in a series of moves which were to have a profound effect on the later development of trade unionism in Britain, and which were to become a major obstacle to the further spread of industrial unions. The Transport and General Workers' Union was formed in 1922 by a merger of 23 separate unions. Although the TGWU was intended as an organization for transport workers of every kind except railwaymen, and embraced dockers, busmen, tramwaymen, lorry-drivers, and taxi-drivers, it also had a general workers' section, which was later on much enlarged when in 1929 it took in the old Workers' Union, with a membership of some 100,000 scattered throughout numerous trades, particularly engineering. The general secretary of the TGWU and one of the leading men involved in its formation, was Ernest Bevin, who had already earned a reputation as 'the dockers' KC'. Even before the accession of the Workers' Union, the TGWU had a membership of 300,000, and was thus one of the largest unions affiliated to the TUC. Equal in size was the National Union of General and Municipal Workers, which came into being in 1924 by means of a merger between the old NUGW (formerly the gasworkers), the National Amalgamated Union of Labour and the Municipal Employees Association. The union included workers in gas, engineering, shipbuilding, chemicals, food, drink and tobacco, and other trades. Because of their size the voice of these two unions became increasingly powerful in the councils of the Trades Union Congress throughout the Twenties and later on into the Thirties.

The TUC itself reflected the diverse and confused structure of the unions affiliated to it. It had begun in the previous century as an annual gathering of delegates from different unions who spent a week discussing resolutions. It was then headed by a Parliamentary Committee, whose job was to keep the views of the unions before the government. This had been replaced in 1921 by a General Council, whose special function was to 'coordinate industrial action', 'to promote common action by the trade union movement' on any matter of general concern. This General Council consisted of 32 members, representing each of 17 industrial categories into which the unions were grouped, and it had no powers to insist on any particular course of action by any individual union. It was really a consultative body, the result of two warring tendencies: the need of unions for mutual support, and the fear of each union of domination by another whose interests might not coincide with its own.

Within the movement there was wide divergence in tactical approach towards the determined wage-cutting by sections of the employers which had been experienced since 1921. Those in the Minority Movement believed that the function of the unions was to mobilize the members for a determined stand against the employers' attacks, and that in such a stand one section should go to the help of another. With this in view they wanted the General Council to have more power to call on unions for active support of one another.

But most of the leaders were nervous of giving more power to the General Council. In any case, many of them looked on the approach of the Minority Movement to the wages struggle as unrealistic, if not dangerous. They thought that the way to safeguard their members' interests was to cooperate in moves to promote the prosperity of their industry, and if, in times of bad trade, wage cuts appeared inevitable, to try and achieve some compromise which would moderate the severity of their impact.

This, then, was the picture in 1925. On the face of it the trade union movement was ill-equipped, both ideologically and organizationally, for the kind of struggle thrust upon it in 1926.

Table 19   Wage Standards Compared with 1914

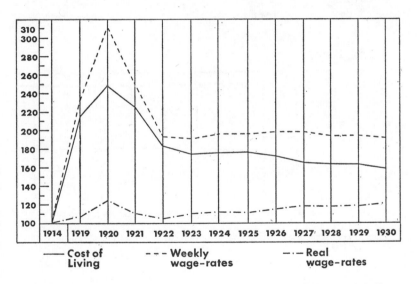

(Sources: The Cost of Living Index is the official one taken from the *Statistical Abstract for the United Kingdom* No. 78. The weekly wage-rates are taken from *Trends in British Society since 1900* edited by E.H.Halsey, based on E.H.Phelps Brown and S.V.Hopkins, *Wage Rates in Five Countries 1860–1939* (OUP 1950). The wage-rates index is reworked to present 1914 as 100.)

Table 20 Wage Standards Compared with 1920 (see Appendix)

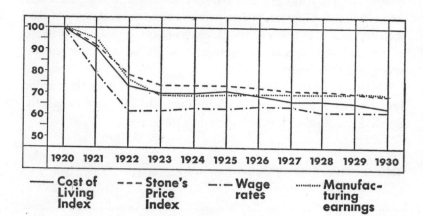

——— Cost of   – – – Stone's   —·— Wage   ·········· Manufac-
Living   Price   rates   turing
Index   Index   earnings

EARNINGS

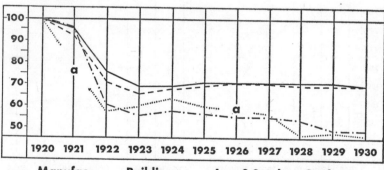

·——— Manufac-   – – – Building   —·— Iron & Steel   :······ Coal
turing   (a - strike
years)

(Sources: The Cost of Living Index is the official one taken from the *Statistical Abstract for the United Kingdom*, No. 78. Stone's Price Index is that compiled by Richard Stone and D.A.Rowe in *Consumer Expenditure and Behaviour in the United Kingdom 1920–38*, vol II, 1966. The Wage-rates Index is taken from *Trends in British Society since 1900*, edited by E.H.Halsey, based on E.H.Phelps Brown and S.V.Hopkins *Wage Rates in Five Countries* (OUP 1950). The earnings are all taken from the yearly earnings tables estimates of Agatha Chapman in *Wages and Salaries in the United Kingdom, 1920–38* (1955). All the indexes concerned are reworked so as to present 1920 as 100.)

Table 21   Weekly Earnings – Some Examples

	1924			1928		
Males	£	s	d	£	s	d
Newspaper printing etc	4	15	4	4	16	5
Tram and omnibus services	3	10	3	3	10	1
Electricity supply	3	5	3	3	8	1
Building	2	19	11	2	19	10
Iron and steel smelting, rolling	3	1	0	3	0	6
Shipbuilding and repair	2	14	6	2	14	0
Engineering	2	13	0	2	16	0
Cotton	2	7	7	2	8	2
Females						
Tobacco	1	12	9	1	15	4
Woollen and worsted	1	10	11	1	10	3
Cotton	1	9	2	1	9	1
Boot and shoe manuf.	1	10	1	1	9	0
Hosiery	1	8	10	1	10	0
Dressmaking	1	8	6	1	9	10
Laundries	1	6	2	1	5	10

(Source: *British Labour Statistics. Historical Abstract 1886–1968* (1971), Table 39.)

Table 22   Stoppages of Work due to Industrial Disputes

Year	Number of working days lost	Year	Number of working days lost
	000		000
1913	9,804	1924	8,424
		1925	7,952
1919	34,969	1926	162,233
1920	26,568	1927	1,174
1921	85,872	1928	1,388
1922	19,850	1929	8,287
1923	10,672	1930	4,399

(Source: *British Labour Statistics. Historical Abstract 1886–1968*, Table 197.)

Table 23   Trade Unions – Numbers and Membership

	All Trade Unions		Affiliated to Trades Union Congress	
Year*	Membership 000	Number of Unions	Membership 000	Number of Unions
1913	4,135	1,269	2,232	207
1918	6,533	1,264	4,532	262
1919	7,926	1,360	5,284	266
1920	8,348	1,384	6,505	215
1921	6,633	1,275	6,417	213
1922	5,625	1,232	5,128	206
1923	5,429	1,192	4,369	194
1924	5,544	1,194	4,328	203
1925	5,506	1,176	4,351	205
1926	5,219	1,164	4,366	207
1927	4,919	1,159	4,164	204
1928	4,806	1,142	3,875	196
1929	4,858	1,133	3,673	202
1930	4,842	1,121	3,744	210
1931	4,624	1,108	3,719	210

* Figures for all Trade Unions are for the end of each year. Those for unions affiliated to TUC are for mid-year.

(Sources: *British Labour Statistics. Historical Abstract 1886–1968*, Table 196. Report of 63rd Annual Trades Union Congress.)

Table 24 Composition of Trades Union Congress 1925–6

Group	Number of Unions	Member- ship	Principal Unions in group	Member- ship
		000		*000*
1 Mining & Quarrying	9	841	Miners Federation of Gt Britain	800
2 Railways	3	455	Nat. Un. Railwaymen	327
			Assoc. Soc. Loco- motive Engineers & Firemen	61
			Railway Clerks Assoc.	66
3 Transport (other than railways)	9	396	Transport & General Workers Un.	300
			Nat. Un. of Seamen	60
4 Shipbuilding	4	115	Boilermakers & Iron & Steel Shipbuilders	76
5 Engineering, founding & vehicle building	24	393	Amalgamated Engineering Un.	205
			Nat. Un. Foundry Workers	35
			Nat. Un. Vehicle Builders	27
			Electrical Trades Un.	25
6 Iron & steel and minor metal trades	21	141	Iron & Steel Trades Confed.	84
7 Building, wood- working & furnishing	15	355	Amal. Soc. Woodworkers	116
			Amal. Un. Building Trade Workers	60
			Nat. Amal. Soc. Painters etc	41
			Plumbers & Domestic Engineers	18

Table 24   *Composition of Trades Union Congress 1925–6 (contd.)*

Group	Number of Unions	Member-ship	Principal Unions in group	Member-ship
		000		000
			Furnishing Trades Assoc.	22
			Altogether Builders' Labourers	30
8 Printing & paper	13	170	Nat. Un. Paper Workers etc	75
			Natsopa	20
			Typographical Assoc.	31
			London Soc. Compositors	15
9 Cotton	38	233	Amal. Weavers Assoc.	163
			Spinners & Twiners	48
10 Textiles (other than cotton)	17	165	Nat. Un. Textile Workers	65
11 Clothing	8	95	Tailors & Garment Workers	56
12 Leather, boot & shoe	5	90	Nat. Un. Boot & Shoe	81
13 Glass, pottery, chemicals, food, drink, tobacco, brushmaking, distribution	17	191	Nat. Un. Distributive & Allied Workers	95
			Shop Assistants etc	36
			Pottery Workers, Nat. Soc.	18
14 Agriculture	1	30	Nat. Un. Agricultural Workers	30

Table 24   Composition of Trades Union Congress 1925-6 (contd.)

Group	Number of Unions	Member- ship	Principal Unions in group	Member- ship
		000		*000*
15 Public employees	11	158	Post Office Workers Un.	85
			Post Office Engineering Un.	18
			Civil Service Clerical Assoc.	19
16 Non-manual workers	8	62	Musicians Un.	20
			Insurance Workers Nat. Fed.	15
			Nat. Amal. Un. Life Assurance etc	10
			Nat. Un. Clerks	6
17 General workers	4	474	Nat. Un. General & Municipal Workers	320
			Workers' Un.	152
Total	207	4,366		

(Source: Report of 58th Annual Trades Union Congress.)

I I
The Mining Crisis

In 1919 the Sankey Commission had taken the view that the 'present system of ownership and working in the coal industry stands condemned,' but nothing had been done in the subsequent six years to change the system, and hardly any of the remedies advocated by the expert witnesses to the Commission had been put into operation. Rational layout of the mines was still inhibited by the system of land ownership. The reorganization of colliery undertakings into larger units which had been suggested as necessary at the time of Sankey had only come about here and there, and the industry was still in the hands of 1400 companies. Some progress had been made towards overcoming technical backwardness, but in 1924 less than 19 per cent of British coal was cut by machinery, as compared with nearly 70 per cent in America.

On the other hand, there had been an increasing tendency for colliery companies to be bought up by, or amalgamated with, non-mining concerns, particularly firms which were big coal users. Shipowners like William France Fenwick, iron and steel groups like Baldwins, engineering concerns like Guest Keen and Nettlefold all owned collieries, and used the coal produced for their own industrial purposes. Indeed about one quarter of all coal dug was absorbed in this way, instead of being put on the market, and the miners' leaders constantly alleged that such coal was transferred below its true market value so that part of the profits made by their employers was concealed.

Ever since Sankey it had been clear that the industry was heading for trouble. In part, its problems arose from the challenge of new forms of power. For example, ships which used to run on coal were going over to oil. But on top of this, British coal exports were facing fierce competition from more up-to-date coalfields abroad, while the demand from those home industries which were heavy users, such as iron and steel, was below normal owing to the continuing depression in these industries. The British coalmines had indeed only escaped a severe depression after 1921 by a series of lucky accidents which had kept the export trade busy; they included an American strike in 1922 and the French occupation of the Ruhr in 1923. During this temporary period of somewhat artificial prosperity the miners, who had endured hard conditions after the 1921 lockout, succeeded in getting an improved wages agreement. Even so, they claimed that they were worse off than they had been in 1914, and it seemed that only one thing of permanent value had been left them from Sankey: the seven-hour day.

By the beginning of 1925 the special conditions which had brought the industry a precarious prosperity had disappeared, and the depression that had been lying in wait closed in. Sales began to decline; miners were put on short time. And just at this moment came a further blow to exports: in April 1925 Britain returned to the gold standard at pre-war parity.

The colliery owners were resentful that a system which had enriched them in the past should no longer do so. As we have seen, they ranged from small men to big industrialists with connections throughout industry. Whichever they were, they saw only one real solution: lower coal prices to be brought about by lower pay for the mineworkers. On 30 June 1925, they gave a month's notice to the miners to end the existing wages agreement and replace it with one which involved immediate and severe reductions.

The Miners Federation rejected these proposals outright. The Conservative government, of which Stanley Baldwin was now Prime Minister, attempted to mediate between the two sides and appointed a Court of Inquiry, but the miners refused to attend it. Instead they turned to the rest of the trade union movement for support. Here there was a widespread conviction that the attack on miners' wages was the prelude to attempts to undermine the standards of other sections. This belief was strengthened when the miners' leaders alleged that Baldwin had told them in the course of an interview that 'all the workers of this country have got to take reductions in wages to help put industry on its feet.'[1] The three railway unions and the Transport and General Workers Union agreed to place an embargo on all movements of coal unless the colliery employers withdrew their notices. On Thursday 30 July a special conference of trade union executives ratified the decision for an embargo and empowered the TUC to give financial support.

The Baldwin government was now faced with a challenge it could not meet. A national coal stoppage with the miners and mineowners fighting it out on their own would be bad enough for the economy, but coupled with the kind of solidarity action now threatened it would bring industrial life to a halt. And indeed such solidarity action would not in practice be directed against the coalowners. Its purpose would be to coerce the government into taking steps to rescue the industry. Not quite prepared for such a crisis, Baldwin decided to buy time. On Friday 31 July he met the TUC and miners' representatives and told them that the coalowners had agreed to suspend the notices, while the government would guarantee a subsidy to the industry until 1 May 1926. Meanwhile, a further Royal Commission would inquire into the industry.

In the trade union movement it went down as 'Red Friday'. To many it was not only a day of victory which seemed to wipe out the shame of 'Black Friday', it was proof that no government could stand up against the united will of the trade union movement. The miners' leaders were less euphoric. A subsidy to prop up the existing system of ownership was not part of their aim; they wanted the industry to be taken into public ownership as recommended by Sankey. And they knew that on 1 May 1926 they might well be faced with exactly the same crisis all over again. They accepted the respite somewhat warily. To them it only meant an armistice.

As for the Baldwin government, its humiliation was great, and there was no lack of voices both inside and outside Parliament to underline that fact. 'Is England to be governed by Parliament and the Cabinet or by a handful of trade union leaders?' asked the Home Secretary.[2] So it was that almost immediately after the crisis was over the government began to organize. Next time – if there was a next time – they were going to meet the challenge.

The Employers and the Samuel Commission

In front of the new Royal Commission on the coal industry which was appointed under the chairmanship of Sir Herbert Samuel on 5 September 1925, the mineowners deployed their arguments. A reduction in the price of coal was essential if coal exports were to be resumed, they said. Moreover lower coal prices were needed by other heavy industries at home. Shipowners and directors of iron and steel companies came to the Commission to explain how vital low-priced coal was to the recovery of their depressed industries.

If coal prices were to be reduced, argued the mineowners, what was needed was firstly a downward adjustment in miners' wages; secondly these must be negotiated on a district basis, not on a national basis, so that account could be taken of differing conditions in different coalfields; thirdly, there should be a longer working day.

The mineowners were not only concerned with the wages of their own workforce. They complained of the high railway charges for transporting coal, and urged that railwaymen's wages should be reduced.[3] They objected to the charges for loading coal at the docks, and said that dockers' and coal-trimmers' wages should come down.[4] They complained that labourers in the building industry were getting more than skilled men in shipbuilding, and spoke of the burden of high local rates which, they said, were 'partly due to the high rates of increase of wages to employees of public authorities'.[5]

The Royal Commission consisted of four men: Sir Herbert Samuel, a former Liberal Cabinet Minister with extensive family connections in banking; Sir William Beveridge, formerly an eminent civil servant and now director of the London School of Economics; Sir Herbert Lawrence, director of insurance companies, railway companies and Vickers Ltd; Kenneth Lee, chairman of Tootal, Broadhurst, Lee, a big cotton firm.

When the Commissioners eventually issued their report on 10 March 1926, it revealed many of the views common to the more up-to-date industrialists. Displaying a certain hostility to the landowners, they advocated state acquisition of all coal royalties. But they were equally firm in turning down proposals of the Miners' Federation, the TUC and the Labour Party for public ownership of the mines. The admitted need for changes in the organization of the colliery companies so as to bring about modernization and greater efficiency could, in their view, best be met by emulating the trend in other industries – amalgamation of small units into large ones. This faced them with the problem of how to coerce those colliery companies which had obstinately refused either to amalgamate or to modernize – a problem which they clearly thought could only be solved over a long period of time. In the immediate situation the Commission was emphatic about one thing. The subsidy had got to stop. It was 'wrong in principle', indefensible, that people in other industries should be taxed in order to subsidize the profits and wages of another industry.[6] This led to one inevitable conclusion: they 'saw no escape' from a reduction in the wages of all but the worst-paid in the coalmining industry as a 'temporary sacrifice'. While recognizing that any material fall in wages would bring real wages below pre-war levels for a proportion of the miners, 'this is a necessity to which other great industries have been driven. In the situation immediately confronting us it cannot be avoided for the coal industry except by making that industry a burden on the rest of the community or by returning to a longer working day.'[7]

The Government Organizes

While the Commission was deliberating, the government was actively engaged in setting up an organization which would enable it to meet the kind of challenge it had faced in July 1925. Emergency machinery was created to keep food and transport services going if there was a railway stoppage. The country was divided into ten regions, each with a Civil Commissioner, and under him officers responsible for food, road haulage, coal, etc. In previous emergencies – as during the railway strike of 1919 – the organization for food distribution had been operated by government administrators with powers to requisition privately-owned lorries. The apparatus surrounding the Civil Commissioners after September 1925 was of a rather different character. In place of official administrators, there was built up a network of 150 voluntary haulage committees composed of businessmen from the food and distributive trades. Serving on the London Haulage Committee, was Major E. G. Monro, representing George Monro Ltd, the most influential of the Covent Garden fruit and vegetable firms; there was a Rudd from E. W. Rudd Ltd, the butchers and meat hauliers; a Rickett associated with Rickett, Cockerell, the big coal merchants; a Paterson from Carter Paterson; a man representing J.Lyons Ltd and another representing Thomas Tillings Ltd, and so on. Some of these individuals were in charge of subcommittees, again consisting of representatives from the firms in the trades concerned. It was thus intended that one of the main components of the emergency organization would be in the hands not of civil servants, or the armed forces, or local government administrators, but of businessmen. The Civil Commissioners were responsible for recruiting and training volunteers as lorry drivers, but these were to be allocated to work for any firm whose regular drivers went on strike. One argument for this arrangement was that it cost the government nothing, since the firms who carried out the distribution would charge commercial rates for whatever they carried. But the main result was that the apparatus was in the hands of people who were identified with the cause of defeating the unions.

Parallel with the government's own organization, a private body, the Organization for the Maintenance of Supplies (OMS), was formed with government blessing. It was nominally led by retired persons distinguished for their services to the Empire; its chairman was Lord Hardinge of Penshurst, a former Viceroy of India, and its council included Admiral Lord Jellicoe, the hero of the battle of Jutland, Lt-General Sir Francis Lloyd, Sir Lynden Macassey (who had represented the dock employers at the 1920 docks inquiry), Sir Rennell Rodd, a diplomat, and others. The object of OMS was to enlist volunteers and train them as drivers or to do other work vacated by strikers, and to provide the government with classified lists of men who would be available for service when the emergency came.

These arrangements meant that the activities of the armed forces could be directed mainly towards protecting strike-breakers rather than acting as strike-breakers, though in the event the armed forces were used in both capacities. The chief role of the armed forces, however, was seen as one of readiness to deal with large-scale civil disorder, should that arise. And the main job of the police was to be 'the maintenance of law and order and the protection of persons and property from violence',[8] for which purpose they were to be augmented by volunteer special constables.

It was noticeable that in all these preparations the local authorities were virtually bypassed. At other moments of national emergency in Britain, the town clerks have been brought in on the ground floor, and made the centre of activity in every locality. But on this occasion, local authorities received their first official instructions from a Ministry of Health Circular 636 sent out on 20 November 1925, which was long after the framework organization had been built. The circular merely informed them what was being done, and more or less told them that they were not expected to take any action unless specifically asked to do so by their local, government-appointed chairman of the volunteer services committee or their local police authority. Clearly the government was uncomfortably aware that there were at least some local authorities who could not be relied on for support.

Side by side with organizational steps came certain political ones, in particular the arrest and trial on a charge of conspiracy to incite to mutiny of 12 leaders of the Communist Party, including Harry Pollitt, the secretary of the National Minority Movement. This move came just after a decision by the Labour Party Annual Conference to expel Communists from the Party. The 12 were all sent to prison.

By April 1926 OMS had, so it claimed, a list of 100,000 volunteers, the emergency transport organization was fully in being, the armed forces and police had their orders, and everything was poised for the big trial of strength. And the machine having been perfected and wound up, it was of course inevitable that some people in key positions should hope that it would be used and not wasted – used to smash the enemy once and for all.

The General Council's Dilemma

The trade unions, against whom all these preparations were in train, were hardly preparing at all. Moreover the TUC leaders seemed anxious to parade their state of unpreparedness, as though fearing the consequences of any appearance of throwing down the gauntlet.

Red Friday had engendered a mood of confidence in the rank and file. It had seemed to show that no government could withstand a united challenge from the movement. Soon after, at the Scarborough Congress in September 1925, a resolution was carried declaring that 'the trade union movement must organize to prepare the trade unions in conjunction with the party of the workers to struggle for the overthrow of capitalism', and which asserted that 'strong well-organized shop committees are indispensable weapons in the struggle to force the capitalists to relinquish their grip on industry.'[9] The mover of the resolution, which had been tabled by the Tailor and Garment Workers Union, said it was of 'a more or less revolutionary character', that trade union activity concerning wages was not sufficient and 'we will now have to definitely set our faces towards the overthrow of the capitalist.' The seconder on behalf of the Boilermakers was Harry Pollitt of the Minority Movement, who was shortly to be arrested. Opposition voices were heard arguing that political rather than trade union action was the way to abolish the capitalist system, but no member of the General Council cared to speak against the resolution, which was carried by 2,456,000 votes to 1,218,000.

But when discussing a proposal to give the TUC General Council the power to call for a stoppage of work by one union in aid of another, and moreover to give it practical powers enabling it to conduct a national stoppage, such as the right to levy funds from affiliated unions and to arrange with the Co-operative Movement for the distribution of food, Congress shied away from the implications. T.E.Naylor, of the London Society of Compositors, opposed 'the substituting of the principle of the general strike' for the normal method of 'each industry proceeding in the way best suited to its own ends and possibilities'.[10] It was not only that unions felt their autonomy might be threatened if the General Council were given such powers. Some union leaders believed that if the TUC had a central strike fund this might encourage irresponsibility, and might increase the pressure of members on their leaders to take strike action when there was little hope of success.[11] The resolution was remitted to the General Council, which later referred it to a Special Industrial Committee, which in turn decided that the existing powers of the General Council were sufficient.

Lack of power for the General Council was not, indeed, a matter which exercised the minds of most of its members. Red Friday had shown that the *threat* of industrial action could be used successfully to coerce the government. They had merely blown their trumpets and the walls of Jericho had fallen. Actually *taking* industrial action on a national scale was a very different matter. They were well aware that if there was a further mining crisis in May 1926, when the subsidy was due to come to an end, with the miners refusing once more to accept wage reductions, the rest of the trade union movement would expect to take action in support. But the government was now openly preparing to defeat them in the event of a general strike; such a perspective filled them with misgiving. What if they blew their trumpets and the walls still stood?

There were matters on which they found it very difficult to get agreement among themselves. For instance, what in any case did they hope to persuade the government to do? In January 1926 Walter Citrine, Acting General Secretary to the TUC, raised an important question with the General Council's Industrial Subcommittee: should the TUC demand continuation of the government subsidy to the mining industry after 1 May? But the Subcommittee decided not to consider this matter. The miners' leaders had never believed that a subsidy was the answer to the industry's problems; it was a temporary expedient which enabled the owners of inefficient mines to make profits and to carry on in the old way. As for the non-miner members of the Subcommittee, they were hoping more and more that the Samuel Commission, when it reported, would provide the basis for a negotiated solution. In that way a showdown with the government could be avoided.

The Samuel Commission did report, as we have seen, on 10 March 1926. It proposed extensive reorganization of the mining industry which, it thought, would bring about ultimate prosperity. But in the meanwhile it 'saw no escape' from a reduction in miners' standards as a 'temporary sacrifice'. The TUC leaders went into consultation with the miners, hoping that some accommodation could be reached on the basis of the Samuel Report. The miners' leaders, however, wanted the TUC to stand by their demands: no reduction in wages, no increase in hours, no departure from national agreements. Most of the TUC leaders had had to agree to wage reductions for their members in the previous few years, and they began to believe that the miners' obdurate refusal to contemplate any further lowering of their standards was unrealistic. They argued, moreover, that the reorganization proposals of the Samuel Report would help get the coal industry on its feet,* and

---

* 'I must confess that the Report had a distinct fascination for me,' wrote Ernest Bevin, Secretary of the Transport and General Workers Union, arguing that the reorganization produced would in the end mean a higher wage standard. 'It may have meant some adjustments in varying forms, but this is nothing new; every one of us has had to face these problems in other industries across the table' (Alan Bullock, *The Life and Times of Ernest Bevin*, vol I, p. 295).

that the miners would be in a strong moral position if they agreed to the Report, so that the onus of obstructing it would fall on the mine-owners.

Throughout March and April the crucial policy decisions were being argued out in the General Council's Special Industrial Committee, of which Arthur Pugh of the Iron and Steel Trades Confederation was chairman, Walter Citrine secretary, and J.H.Thomas, General Secretary of the National Union of Railwaymen, much the most forceful member. On 8 April this Committee rejected a request from the miners for reaffirmation of support for their stand on the grounds that a 'purely negative policy (was) unwise.'[12] Instead, the miners and owners were urged to negotiate on the basis of the Samuel Report, so as to 'reduce points of difference to the smallest possible dimensions'.[13]

The TUC leaders wanted to persuade the miners to move from their position of 'no reduction in wages' to another which suggested 'no reduction in wages, unless . . .' They thought that if the wages question could form part of a general deal containing also reorganization, the attack on wages could be minimized; by this time they clearly doubted whether it could be avoided altogether. They saw themselves as mediators between the government, the coalowners and the miners over what Pugh described as 'issues that have somehow to be settled by negotiation and consent, whether this is before or after a large-scale stoppage of industry'.[14] They spent much time trying to persuade the miners to accept the Report, and trying to persuade the government that the miners could be got to accept the Report.

But they found to their dismay that the government itself was being highly evasive about the Report's reorganization proposals, and was insisting on acceptance by the miners of wage reductions in isolation from the Report's other recommendations. Backward and forward went the negotiations all through April between the miners, the TUC subcommittee, the coalowners, the government. Every time there was deadlock. May the First, the date when the subsidy was due to end, drew nearer.

In the middle of April the mineowners posted notices in most districts ending the miners' contracts on 30 April. They then announced the new terms they were prepared to offer in each district separately. These terms meant very substantial wage reductions, particularly in the chief exporting coalfields of South Wales, Durham and Scotland.

It was clear that unless the new terms were accepted the miners would be locked out.

The TUC leaders now had no option. They were forced to make a stand or publicly abandon all the pledges of support to the miners, and suffer the ignominy they had undergone at the time of Black Friday. This was unthinkable even to those most anxious to avoid a struggle, while to others the prospect of making a stand at last came as a relief.

They summoned a special Conference of Executives of trade unions for 29 April. The Conference heard a report on behalf of the TUC negotiators from the chairman, Arthur Pugh, who said: 'In our view the wages and working conditions of mineworkers are already so depressed as to render it imperative to seek for remedies other than a further degradation in their standards of life, or the abrogation of the present standard hours.'[15] They heard A. J. Cook speak on behalf of the miners:

We are the victims of an industry that private ownership has ruined, as it is ruining the country as well. We are the victims ... in more senses than one – in loss of life and in maiming day after day to the extent of 200,000 a year. We are further victims in having no economic security while toiling for our daily bread ... It is bad enough to face the physical dangers of heat, water, gas and the uncertainty of life, but when, added to that, at the end of the week the miner's wife cannot pay her way, it is intolerable.[16]

The Conference adjourned. The next day they heard that Baldwin had submitted a proposal from the coalowners for a national minimum wage much lower than before, and an increase in the working day to eight hours. The miners had turned the proposal down. Two thirds of them were by this time locked out, and Conference heard that the Cabinet had refused to agree to a suspension of the lockout notices so that negotiations could proceed. They were told by J. H. Thomas that they would be called upon to take 'the most momentous decision that any body of trade unionists was ever called to make up their minds about'.[17] Then they were given a memorandum containing proposals for a national stoppage and asked to come back next day with a decision on whether it should be adopted.

The following day, 1 May, the Conference reassembled knowing that the government had proclaimed a state of emergency. They had examined the hastily-compiled memorandum proposing that a list of trades should cease work 'as and when required by the General Council'. One by one the names of affiliated unions were read out, and they were asked to signify whether they would support the General Council's proposals and would 'place their powers in the hands of the General Council and carry out the instructions which the General Council may issue from time to time concerning necessary action and conduct of the dispute'.[18]

The Executive members were worried people. Some, it is true, were supporters of the Minority Movement who wanted to go into the attack, and believed that if the trade union movement showed sufficient solidarity it would win this battle for the miners and so strengthen the position of other sections of workers. But others feared that the movement might be heading for disaster. They did not believe that their members would respond gladly to such a call. They were conscious of terrible weaknesses in their ranks, and of vast areas of industry where non-unionism prevailed. Many had reached their position because they were good negotiators: good at getting reasonable settlements *without a strike*. They did not want to risk such agreements or to put their carefully hoarded funds in jeopardy. Yet it was true that the threat of a strike, even if unspoken, had always been a potent weapon – the only real sanction – at the back of any successful negotiations. Might it not force Baldwin and the coalowners to back down now? They remembered Black Friday and were conscious that if they did not show solidarity they might never be forgiven.

So it was that when the roll-call was taken, only the seamen's union voted against, representing under 50,000 members. Some unions explained that they could not decide until they had had further consultations, and a number of small unions, representing 319,000, were not present. But those unions who voted a clear 'Yes' to the General Council's proposals represented 3,653,327.

After the roll-call, Ernest Bevin, General Secretary of the Transport and General Workers Union, explained that certain trades listed in the memorandum were to cease work from midnight on Monday 3 May 'if a settlement has not been found.' He roused the Conference to cheers when he said:

We look upon your 'yes' as meaning that you have placed your all upon the altar for this great Movement, and having placed it there, even if every penny goes, if every asset goes, history will ultimately write up that it was a magnificent generation that was prepared to do it rather than see the miners driven down like slaves.[19]

The Executive members dispersed. They had two and half days in which to make all arrangements for the stoppage at midnight on Monday 3 May. Meanwhile the T U C negotiators continued their efforts to find a formula which could be accepted by both government and miners. For some of them, at least, the hope was strong that the decision to call for a national stoppage would produce a more conciliatory attitude in the government, making it possible that the lockout notices would be suspended so that the whole thing could be called off. But more and more they began to fear that this would not happen. 'I picture it as a whirlpool, knowing I cannot help being dragged in, knowing that the State must win on an issue like this,' J. H. Thomas was alleged to have told Baldwin at one session. 'I believe that nothing which my colleagues or myself can do will prevent that plunge with the consequences that I believe are inevitable. That is why I feel it is a desperate state.'[20]

The arguments went on until sometime after midnight on Sunday 2 May, when Baldwin at last delivered an ultimatum. Alleging that 'overt acts' had taken place 'including gross interference with the freedom of the press', he said that before there could be further negotiations there must be unconditional withdrawal of the instructions for the General Strike. The 'overt act' was the refusal by trade unionists on the *Daily Mail* to print a leader which said that a general strike was 'a revolutionary movement intended to inflict suffering upon the great mass of innocent persons in the community'.

In great consternation the T U C negotiators, who had been quite unaware of the unofficial stoppage on the *Daily Mail*, once more sought an interview with Baldwin. But Baldwin had gone to bed. They could not escape the whirlpool after all. The government had pushed them in. 'I felt we had been cruelly let down,' recorded Citrine.[21] The Strike began as planned at midnight on Monday 3 May. It lasted nine days.

12
The General Strike

For many people the words 'general strike' carried revolutionary implications. The syndicalists who had had a certain influence in the trade unions before the war had seen it as the ultimate weapon. 'We shall always do our best to help strikes to be successful,' Tom Mann had written, 'and shall prepare the way as rapidly as possible for THE GENERAL STRIKE of national proportions. This will be the actual Social and Industrial Revolution.'[1] Syndicalism as such had disappeared, and the Communists and near-Communists who were leading the Minority Movement (including Tom Mann himself) had discarded the theory that revolutionary trade unionism alone could bring socialism. Even so, it seemed clear to them that a general strike could force the resignation of the government and begin the process of a fundamental change.

In these circumstances the TUC leaders were anxious to stress that the Strike had a limited and purely industrial object; moreover they tried to avoid use of the term 'general strike' and used instead the words 'national strike'. Government spokesmen, however, insisted on presenting the Strike as a threat to parliamentary government. No doubt this emphasis was mainly born of a desire to frighten the middle class and cause discomfort to the Labour leaders. But to some extent it sprang from a genuine realization that if the trade unions were victorious in this trial of strength, the existing power structure could be shaken to its foundations.

The TUC's plan of action did not in fact envisage a universal and simultaneous stoppage, but stoppages by selected industries in the first week, to be reinforced by further industries later. This strategy was devised by Bevin, who argued that it was important to throw in reserves and reach maximum strength after the first week of strike, at a time when there might be a tendency for the first wave to weaken and begin drifting back to work.

The 'first-line' industries called out on 3 May included transport, printing and the press, iron and steel, electricity, gas and building. But shipyard workers and most engineering workers were classed as 'second-line' and not to come out until told to.

The TUC leaders did not want the Strike to be seen as an attack on the people. So unions involved in electricity and gas were asked to cease the supply of power to industry but to allow lighting to continue. All workers engaged on building were to cease work *except* those definitely employed on housing and hospitals. It was laid down that there must be no interference with health and sanitary services, or with food distribution – 'the trade unions concerned should do everything in their power to organize the distribution of milk and food to the whole population.'

The unions were asked to place their powers in the hands of the General Council, and to carry out its instructions. But the actual call-out of groups of workers was to be left to the unions themselves, who would also be responsible for strike pay, if any, for their members.

As we have seen, the plan had been hastily drawn up with little time for prior consultation. It was not surprising therefore that its inter-pretation was a matter of confusion, while some of it turned out to be unworkable. Thus, the National Union of Foundry Workers, whose headquarters was in Manchester, sent out telegrams on Sunday 2 May calling out its entire membership of 34,000, and sent further telegrams on the Monday cancelling most of the strike notices when it discovered that only part of its membership was involved in the 'first line'.

The railway unions said that the proposal to transport food only was unworkable; they could not run trains for a single commodity. They decided to tell their members to stop all trains. The Electrical Trades Union said their members could not discriminate between light and power and put out instructions to stop the power stations; Citrine sent them an urgent message to prevent this, and there was much ensuing muddle. The decision to close down the *Daily Herald* along with the other national newspapers deprived the TUC itself of any means of communication with the public; this had to be remedied later by production of the *British Worker*, after the government had successfully managed to produce its own newspaper, the *British Gazette*.

The worst confusion arose over the question of food distribution. A TUC offer to the government to cooperate in the distribution of food had been ignored. From 1 May to 4 May a 'Food and Essential Services Committee' was locked in argument. It was composed of representatives of the main unions concerned under the chairmanship of Margaret Bondfield, one of the two women members of the TUC General Council. It was feared that if the road transport workers moved food which the railwaymen had 'blacked' this could lead to antagonism between the two. From time to time the Committee put up propositions to the General Council which were rejected. At last, after the Strike had already begun, the Committee decided to give local transport union representatives responsibility for granting permits for the distribution of essential foods, thus transferring headquarters' biggest problem to the localities, where it immediately became the biggest problem all over again.

The failures in foresight and preparation were not, however, decisive. What mattered most was the response by the workers, and this exceeded all expectations. Within the first 24 hours this was already apparent. No trains ran, the docks were paralysed, most trams and buses had disappeared, the great iron and steel industry was at a standstill, blast furnaces and coke ovens were damped down. Perhaps the greatest shock to a bewildered middle class was the fact that there were no newspapers.

Trade unionists were a minority in the working population, and by no means all trade unionists had been called out – under 3 million, including miners. But this strike was a living demonstration of how strong trade unionism was in the key sectors of the economy. Many who came out were risking jobs at a time of great unemployment and insecurity, and some faced personal calamities such as loss of pension rights. And this was a stoppage on behalf of the miners, not on behalf of themselves. Yet in some industries it was the most complete ever seen. There were of course some workers who refused to participate, and some who came out on strike very unwillingly. But in contrast to this, many non-unionists came out side by side with trade unionists. Such was the feeling that some clerical and supervisory sections were caught up in it, though 'white-collar' workers, of whom few were organized, had always seemed to identify themselves with the management above them rather than the manual workers below.

All these tendencies were visible on the railways, where more men came out than had struck in support of their own demands in 1919.

G

Zero hour was at midnight Monday 3 May but several hours earlier night shifts had failed to come on duty; engine drivers drove the trains to the places nearest their homes and abandoned them; signalmen stayed on only long enough to see the last trains safely to rest. On 8 May a telegram sent from the National Union of Railwaymen to its members read: 'Stoppage 100 per cent efficient. Be sure and maintain our position. You cannot improve it.'[2] Indeed the railwaymen formed the backbone of the strike in many areas, playing the main part in local decisions.

Unlike any previous railway strike, many of the clerical and supervisory staff were out. The 65,000-strong Railway Clerks Association, which organized staff workers, had never before issued a national strike call; moreover a big proportion of the employees in the grades concerned were not in the union. In many places they now joined both the strike and the union. For example it was early on reported from Hull that a hundred new members had been enrolled;[3] in Swindon it was over seventy. Many RCA members had a new experience – their services were much in demand at local strike committee headquarters, and they made friends for the first time with NUR and ASLEF men. Their response caused indignation in management circles, where plans to run trains by volunteer strike breakers were disorganized because the skilled supervision needed for such an operation was largely absent.

Similar straws in the wind showed elsewhere. Everyone had known in advance that the dockers would come out solidly on strike, and so they did in all the main ports. Tumultuous gatherings of strikers entirely immobilized the London docks for several days, until the government moved in troops and forced the unloading of supplies with machine-guns trained on pickets. But what no one had expected was that the Port of London clerical and supervisory staffs would come out with the dockers. They did so; it was their first venture in strike action and, like that of the railway clerks, a cause of astonishment.

In most industries the rank and file of the membership displayed much greater enthusiasm for the strike than their leaders. The print industry was one of these. Print was, like transport, a 'first-line' industry in the TUC strike plan. The editorial in the *Daily Mail* which had provoked the unofficial strike and given Baldwin his pretext for breaking off negotiations on 2 May had in fact been originally set up by the compositors on the newspaper. It was the Natsopa* men in the machine room, backed by members of other unions in the foundry and packing departments, who told the management that if the paper was to come out, the editorial would have to be deleted. George Isaacs, the Natsopa General Secretary, hurried to the scene and tried to persuade his members to go on with their work, but failed. Natsopa had 20,000 members; their enthusiasm was matched by that of the much larger Paper Workers' Union,† which had 75,000 members, over half of them women. When the production of the government's emergency *British Gazette* induced the TUC General Council to publish its own *British Worker* at the *Daily Herald* plant, the Paper Workers' Union members in the warehouse offered to do their share of the work for strike pay only.‡ Their strike pay was 10s per week for men and 5s for women.

The leaders of these unions called their members all out as requested by the TUC; so did the leaders of the Typographical Association, which organized compositors in the provinces. But there was some trouble initially with the London Society of Compositors, which had 14,000 members. The London 'comps' were among the highest paid of all industrial workers. They had an unshakable loyalty to one another, but were not noted for their sense of identity with the wider trade union movement. Their General Secretary, T. E. Naylor, had built up a relationship with the newspaper proprietors which he believed to be beneficial to all parties. He had told the 1925 TUC that he was opposed to 'the principle of the general strike' and at the Memorial Hall meeting on 1 May the Society's representatives had made it clear that they could not cooperate in a general strike until the membership had been consulted. On Monday 3 May the Society's Joint Board decided by a majority vote that the General Strike was a mistake. On 4 May many London 'comps' discovered that they were the only people turning up at their places of work. Some chapels sent deputations to the union's headquarters asking what their position would be if they refused to carry on; others ceased work against their Society's orders. When a

---

* National Society of Operative Printers and Assistants.

† National Union of Printing, Bookbinding, Machine Ruling and Paper Workers.

‡ This offer was refused, since the other unions involved would not agree. Indeed the terms and conditions for those employed on the *British Worker* were the subject of protracted negotiations which initially held up production for some hours.

crowded delegate meeting at last took place in the Memorial Hall on Wednesday 5 May, however, the General Secretary was obliged to say that the Joint Board had been 'driven by the irresistible logic of events' to advise members to cease work. Before he had finished, his words were broken into by loud cheers, which were immediately repeated by the crowd outside in Farringdon Street. The resolution to join the Strike was carried unanimously.

The events in the building trade also showed a diversity of view among the union leaders; it showed moreover how ill-suited the structure of British trade unionism was for such a combined operation as a general strike. Each craft had a separate union, and while unity could be built up at site level, and often was, there was much disunity at the top. The TUC's call to cease work on building *except* housing and hospitals and sanitary services was interpreted differently by each of the unions involved, and the contradictory instructions sent down to the members caused some discord. The leaders of the Amalgamated Union of Building Trade Workers (bricklayers) issued a call to the 60,000 members: 'If in doubt come out.'[4] About 28,000 members came out, and brought with them a number of non-unionists without strike pay; they were offered union membership without entrance fee in recognition of their action. But some other unions had a less radical interpretation of the TUC's instructions, so that on some jobs the bricklayers went on strike while other trades remained at work. The leaders of the National Society of Painters said afterwards that they had not been able to 'give the TUC all they asked'. Their interpretation of the call was a narrow one and caused discontent in the localities, in some of which the painters disregarded their union's orders and came out on strike. In contrast, the Scottish Painters Society called out all members *including* those on housing. The largest building union, the Amalgamated Society of Woodworkers, which organized the joiners and carpenters and had 114,000 members, tried hard to implement the TUC's plan strictly, and later reported that its difficulty was to restrain those not called out from coming out.[5] The frustration felt by members was expressed in resolutions passed just after the Strike: for example one from the Langley Branch: 'That in future when the Executive Council deem it advisable to call a strike, due notice be given of same, and that all members be called out thereby preventing ill-feeling amongst our members who are out on strike, and taunts of members who happen to be on housing schemes.'⁶

The strike headquarters of the building unions was transferred to the National Federation of Building Trades Operatives' office in Clapham, but attempts to reconcile the differences between the unions were not at all successful. Relations were in any case not too good. The AUBTW, for example, did not at the time belong to the NFBTO.

As with the builders, so for most unions, the TUC's call for a stoppage was not clear-cut, and allowed for considerable variation in interpretation. Broadly speaking, the TUC plan split industries into four main categories. First there were 'first-line' industries where everyone was called out, like railways and print. Secondly, 'first-line' industries where some people were to go on working, like building. Thirdly, 'second-line' industries, like general engineering, for which the call-out was postponed until 11 May, by which time the Strike had been on for a week. Fourth, there were some industries which were never called out at all, like textiles and food manufacturing. What nobody had anticipated was that so many trade unionists not called out should be clamouring to come out.

The Amalgamated Engineering Union, one of the 'big six', with over 200,000 members, was particularly affected. About half its members were in the 'first line' and were called out at once; the other half were in the 'second line' and told to stay at work until called out. In practice the union's main difficulty was to prevent those in the 'second line' from going on strike immediately.

The union's district organizing delegates were astonished by the response of the members. After the Strike was over the delegate from Sheffield reported: 'In all districts in this division both members and many non-unionists responded to the instructions of the General Council ... Our greatest difficulty during the dispute was to keep men at work who had not been officially called out, their complaint being that they wanted to be in the fight.'⁷ The report from Manchester said: 'Our members employed in railway workshops and sheds, coalmines, printing offices, and other places involved in the first call responded to a man. Our greatest difficulty was in preventing many of those not called out in the first instance from coming out before they were called out. When the call came, however, to cease work on the 11th inst, the response was unanimous.' From Dundee the report said:

'Here, as elsewhere, our greatest difficulty in the first week was to prevent men ceasing work before being called upon to do so.'

The AEU district delegates were much moved by the behaviour of their members. The Colchester report said: 'When a dispute appeared imminent, I expressed the hope that there would be complete solidarity in our ranks. But it must be confessed that my wildest hopes were surpassed – what a movement!' That from Halifax said: 'Never shall I forget the 12th of May, 1926, when the meeting of members was held and looking across the crowded room in which every member pledged himself to support the miner in the hour of need.' The report from a London division said: 'The response to the call of the TUC was beyond all expectations ... a wonderful inspiration, especially when it is realized that they were not out for themselves on either wages or working conditions, but were streaming out in thousands on behalf of the miners' standard of life. When the millions of men in this country are prepared to do this, it speaks well for the brotherhood of man.'

Like other unions, the AEU found difficulty in interpreting the TUC plan. For instance, did 'transport' which was 'first-line' include motor manufacturing? Coventry settled the matter by calling out all motor-car workers; in Wolverhampton too the motor industry was brought to a standstill; in Derby the AEU District Committee decided to stop Rolls Royce.

The foundry workers who had been initially told to come out and subsequently ordered to stay at work were also behaving awkwardly. Most of them obeyed their union's instruction, but the West Bromwich organizer was obliged to send a wire to headquarters: 'Members disappointed at turn of events; unable to hold the position.' There was trouble too in Wrexham, and in South Leeds the members refused to go back to work. The Sheffield branch complained that since the steel-workers had been called out their members were being required to work with blacklegs. The National Union of Foundry Workers was too poor to provide any strike pay, but the general call to all its members on 11 May came as a relief. One very small union whose members were engaged in similar work, the Central Ironmoulders Association, 8000 strong, was clear that workers in iron castings were not required to strike. But its members in Warrington came out on strike against orders. And a Leeds official reported that the instruction to stay at work 'had not met with the approval of the men'.[8]

The Boilermakers Society, an ancient craft union with 76,000 members, was another which was partly in the 'first line' and partly in the 'second line'. They had suffered much unemployment and the union was providing no strike pay. The Manchester District Committee reported after the Strike: 'When the call came our members answered it immediately in railway shop, running shed, loco contract shop and boiler shop, and persuasion alone kept the engineering shops at work until the call was heard from London. Our members faced the situation with scant financial resources, but convinced that "a good name is rather to be chosen than great riches".'[9]

The National Amalgamated Furnishing Trades Association, with 22,000 members told those employed on aircraft, railway repair work and commercial building to strike, and those making furniture, pianos and gramophones to stay at work; the latter were 'straining at the leash to come out,' reported the General Secretary.[10] The National Union of Distributive and Allied Workers said afterwards that it had difficulty in convincing those who were not subject to the TUC call that 'it was their duty to remain at their posts'.[11] The Transport and General Workers' Union reported that the London taximen who had been excluded from the TUC's initial strike call had 'made strong representations that permission should be given them to withdraw their labour'. This permission was given and they ceased work on 5 May.[12]

Not all workers were filled with this enthusiasm. Though bus- and tram-drivers responded eagerly to the strike call in London and most provincial towns, in one or two they came out unwillingly and later began drifting back to work, the very thing that Bevin had feared. And in Bristol, where the drivers were all non-unionists, they failed to come out at all. The least willing response, however, came from the van- and lorry-drivers, many of whom were non-unionists. The drivers in commercial road transport, still very undeveloped, worked for many employers, often in isolation, so that some of the conditions which predispose workers to combine into a union were lacking. Moreover, this was the one sphere where anti-strike organization was in full swing, and where, if a man refused to work, his place could relatively easily be taken by a government volunteer. The main sanction against road transport during the Strike, indeed, came from other workers who refused to load or unload at the beginning or end of a journey, while in the north-east and in Scotland miners picketed the roads in force, turning back vehicles which had not been given T U C permits and even impounding them.*

᱾ But side by side with the lack of enthusiasm of a few groups of workers, all kinds of people were coming out on strike who had no business to be doing so on a strict interpretation of the T U C call. Thus a thousand workers employed by Messrs Lyons at Cadby Hall, Kensington, struck; Rowntree's cocoa workers came out at York; workers in flour mills stopped at Liverpool and so did workers in oil-cake mills; workers came out at Dunlop rubber in the Midlands, at boot and shoe factories in Northampton. Some of these groups were called out by local union officials and some not. Sometimes the excuse was that employers were using blackleg vans to transport goods, but some had no such pretext; they just couldn't bear to be left out. Groups of textile workers in Yorkshire came out in spite of their union's instructions to the contrary. The employers took the National Union of Textile Workers to court, where it was found that members had acted illegally. 'Their moral passion was greater than their regard for legality,' recorded their President, Ben Turner.[13] In London, Lancashire and the north-east coast, groups of seamen joined the Strike. Their union had officially cast its vote against the Strike, and the strikers were taken to law, not by their employers, but by their union head office.

The local organizations set up to lead the Strike were very diverse. Citrine had wanted the local trades councils, to which local union branches were affiliated, to be the nucleus of the local strike organizations, but others, particularly Bevin, disagreed, and the upshot was that trades councils were given a vague instruction which virtually left them free to take the lead or not. In a few areas the unions directly involved in the Strike set up their own strike committees for their own places of work and held little communication with strikers from other industries. In most areas, however, some sort of central strike committee came into being. In some cases it was a joint strike committee consisting of representatives of all those unions involved in the Strike. In other cases a joint strike committee was formed under the auspices of

---

* In *Strike: A Live History 1887–1971* by R. A. Leeson, a trade unionist who was helping at the Scottish T U C Headquarters, has the following recollections: 'We would have commercial travellers ringing us up, highly indignant at being waylaid on the road by gangs of miners. One day I had an anxious phone call from one of the pickets. "What shall we do? The field's full." "What field?" "We are stopping the cars on the road and turning them into a field." "Well, find another field," I said.'

the local trades council executive. Some trades councils formed 'councils of action', something they had been urged to do by the Minority Movement, and which they remembered doing in 1920 over the 'Hands Off Russia' movement. In the north-east a 'Northumberland and Durham General Council Joint Strike Committee' was formed to coordinate activities for the whole of the region covered by the government's Civil Commissioner for the Northern Division. A conference called by this body in Gateshead on 8 May had representatives from 52 strike committees, 28 councils of action, 4 Labour parties and 3 trades councils.

These local strike organizations were at the receiving end of somewhat conflicting directives. An early difficulty which faced them was deciding who was supposed to be on strike and who not. 'Strike call exceptionally well obeyed. Some confusion owing to ambiguity in general instructions as regards demarcation, but endeavouring to secure uniformity of action,' ran a typical report from West Ham.[14] Another matter which seemed not altogether clear-cut was the degree of responsibility that a local strike organization was entitled to shoulder. A report from Wolverhampton where the trades council had set up an 'Emergency Committee' mentioned this dilemma:

> The impression existed among some members of the Emergency Committee that they, the Emergency Committee, had full power to call out all workers, irrespective of official instructions, but we think the sub-Emergency Committee was quite right in taking the point of view that their duty was not to give instructions to cease work, but that they should only carry out the wishes of the General Council, and endeavour to obtain concerted action in the bringing out of men, but even this was very difficult owing to each union sending down different circular letters to their branches, this being most evident in the building trades.[15]

Not quite all the local strike committees took such a circumspect view of their functions, and indeed there was an uneasy feeling at T U C headquarters that some of them were greatly exceeding their powers. Charles Dukes, a leader of the General and Municipal Workers Union, later commented sourly: 'Immediately the strike commenced the very people who for months, if not for years, had been shouting more power to the General Council, themselves in their respective localities, really thought they were the General Council.'[16]

But even local strike organizations which took the most limited view

of their powers found it difficult to get clarification from TUC headquarters, partly because most of them were physically cut off, since the
trains were not running and the posts were disrupted by the absence of
mail trains. Even if the premises from which they were operating had a
telephone they found the lines to the TUC at Eccleston Square constantly engaged. Telegrams flew backward and forward, but these
hardly gave scope for argument. Moreover, when the TUC leaders
became convinced that their telegrams were being scrutinized by the
authorities, they devised a code which was sent down to the localities
by hand and which, if anything, slowed up communication even more.
The most important method of sending instructions and reporting back
was by dispatch rider. The trade unions had few cars, but there was a
growing number of young workers with motor-cycles and sidecars,
and they came forward in every area to volunteer their services. Some
big towns acted as centres for dissemination of TUC instructions: for
example, Coventry distributed material to Rugby, Warwick, Leaming-
ton, Nuneaton, Hickley and Bedworth, and had the use of 9 cars and
60 motor-cycles with a volunteer force of engineers to keep them in
working order. Smaller towns a long way from London established
links with neighbouring towns; every one of them had its little team of
dispatch riders.

Most local strike organizations found themselves in continuous
session. Subcommittees proliferated and volunteers thronged round,
but still they could not cope with all that had to be done. They were
organizing picketing rotas, granting transport permits, collecting
money for the relief of distress, providing entertainment to keep up
morale. Shopkeepers were relaying BBC news through loudspeakers
which boomed and crackled and often faded away, but which gave the
impression that strikers were drifting back to work and many trains
were running. In this situation it was urgent to tell people what was
really happening. Yet the TUC's *British Worker* was in short supply,
unobtainable in some areas. The answer of the local strike committees
was to issue their own bulletins.

A TUC dispatch rider covering the route from London to Plymouth
in the first week of the Strike made notes on what he saw. His report
read in part as follows:

Reading: Not a tram, few buses, pickets everywhere. Streets full of strikers.

Headquarters seem as well organized and active as Eccleston Square. Splendid service of riders for communication. *Swindon:* like a dead city except for workers standing around . . . No trams or local buses. Very active at headquarters. *Bath:* Not a tram. Few buses. Huge meetings. Town very quiet otherwise. Splendid enthusiasm here. *Bristol:* Trams running but power men to come out at 5 pm Friday. Buses running . . . Town full of people in streets. Pickets everywhere. Terrific activity being displayed at headquarters. *Bridgwater:* Not a tram. Few buses. Very quiet. *Taunton and Exeter:* . . . No trams, few buses. Huge meetings. Very active headquarters. Wonderful spirit, especially at Exeter. *Plymouth:* No trams, few buses. Pickets everywhere. Huge crowds of strikers at all approaches to headquarters. Greatest activity at headquarters and spirit seems excellent . . . Between all towns visited on route 5 in all out of the way villages the one or two pickets were in evidence and I understand that the response from these little places has been wonderful, especially round the Taunton, Exeter and Plymouth Districts. It's true to say that every little village and hamlet had its T U C representative in the shape of pickets.[17]

'Wonderful spirit', 'terrific activity', 'huge meetings', 'splendid enthusiasm' – no doubt this dispatch rider's own enthusiasm coloured his report. But it is also true that such excitement was widespread. What caused it? Feelings of affinity with the miners? Belief that if the miners went down, all would go down? Accumulated resentment against employers at the relentless pressure on standards which had accompanied deflation? Just a wish to be in on a tremendous event? No doubt all these ideas and impulses played some part. But on a long view the General Strike revealed something which had been maturing for decades. The Labour movement, arguing and quarrelling, always talking about the need for a better life but with no agreement on how to achieve it, had brought about a profound change in the outlook of working people; it had given them a new self-respect. The belief that you should be deferential to those in the class above you was being replaced by a belief that if you joined with others you could stand up and feel proud of your working-class status. For years such sentiments had been expressed at trade union conferences and meetings. Now at last they were being put into practice. The call to a general strike came as a great release.

The Strikers' Opponents

While 3 million workers went on strike the government appealed for volunteers to take the strikers' places. They were wanted as train-drivers, signalmen, guards, porters, bus-drivers, tram-drivers, lorry-drivers, for unloading ships, for rough work in power stations and at gasworks, and for any work of which they were capable on the make-shift newspapers which the proprietors were trying to get out, including the government's own *British Gazette*. In addition they were wanted for activities special to the occasion: as car drivers to get people to and from work, as dispatch riders (for the government's own organization needed dispatch riders just as the strikers did), as helpers to run canteens for other volunteers. Above all, they were wanted as special constables, whose job was not only to maintain law and order but, as the Home Secretary put it, to protect 'those who desire to carry on their work notwithstanding the decrees of Trade Unions'.[18] The number of volunteers registering for duty rose rapidly and by 12 May it had reached 323,000, of which, it appeared, 240,000 had been enrolled as special constables. The authorities had difficulty in finding jobs for all these volunteers and THEY ALSO SERVE was a reassuring headline in the *British Gazette*.

The TUC had feared that the unemployed would act as blacklegs, since there were over a million manual workers signing on at the employment exchanges, including one fifth of those normally employed in iron and steel and one quarter of those who usually worked at the docks. They ranged from highly-skilled craftsmen to unskilled and rather shiftless people, many of whom had never been in a union. Some of these unemployed did volunteer for work but their number seems to have been small. Most such workers appear to have been held back either by instincts of solidarity or fear of social ostracism.

The overwhelming majority of strike-breakers and of special constables came from the upper and middle classes, from among professional people, commercial people, from those in managerial posts, from clerical workers, and from among the students. Few of them volunteered because they needed a job – indeed, so far as the government's organization was concerned, a great many refused payment.*

---

* 'In spite of its colossal size and ramifications, the Government's organization has been

Moreover most of those who offered the government the use of their cars paid for their own petrol.[19] Like the strikers, they were true volunteers, giving service in a cause in which they believed.

Most university students accepted the prevailing middle-class assumption that this challenge from the trade unions put their whole way of life at risk. Many of them took it for granted that they were going into battle for a noble purpose: to protect the nation, the liberties of the people, and constitutional government from attack by wicked men. For though few thought that the miners were exactly wicked, they were believed to be misled by wicked men, by leaders who wanted to smash up everything that England stood for, and plunge us into anarchy. So the students volunteered with as deep and sincere a conviction as their elder brothers had volunteered for the front in 1914. They were not deterred by the prospect of a rough-house, indeed it unquestionably attracted some of them. Once into the fray there was the exhilaration of participating in a great contest, the team spirit, the jokes, the tendency of others to treat one like a hero, the excitement of doing something quite out of the ordinary. Even the boredom of sitting in a signal box all day, with no trains going by, gave one something to talk about.

The office workers who responded to the government's call often had an additional motive: loyalty to their own firm. Clerical workers who had struggled to pull themselves up out of the ranks of the industrial workers now volunteered for the kind of dirty jobs which it had been their life's ambition to avoid. The railway clerks and the Port of London staffs who had joined in the Strike were very exceptional. Most office workers valued their special status, their relationship with the management, and now had a deep instinct that the strikers must be defeated if their own position was not to be threatened. So clerks and salesmen descended to the vaults of Smithfield meat market and brought up meat belonging to their respective employers; clerical workers, storekeepers and supervisory staffs employed by trawler owners and fish merchants unloaded fish at Fleetwood; thousands of young men who normally worked in Liverpool shipping offices were

comparatively inexpensive. Its whole basis has been voluntary and a great many people entitled to receive payment have refused to take anything, because they wished to help the country during the crisis to the fullest possible extent' (*British Gazette* 13 May 1926).

organized into squads for work in the docks; they were housed in ships and warehouses so that they did not have to pass the dock gates.

Like the students, the office workers enjoyed the sensation of being part of a patriotic crusade and of doing their bit. They enjoyed also the informality, friendliness and *esprit de corps* that arose, and the flattering appreciation shown by their employers. Girl typists who struggled into work at city offices were made to feel splendid for having got there at all, even though when they arrived there might be little work to do, and much of the day would be spent in talking about the hazards they had overcome on the journey in and speculation about the journey home again.

Meanwhile many employers whose firms were not engaged in vital work encouraged their non-manual staffs to volunteer for government service. The managing director of Harrods announced that any employees enrolling for national work would have their wages made up to the sums they ordinarily received.

Car-owners made a spectacular contribution to the government cause. Private cars still numbered no more than 600,000 for the whole of Great Britain, and nearly all of them were owned by middle- and upper-class people. Driving was a new skill which the younger generation were acquiring, but middle-aged car-owners usually employed chauffeurs. Now owners put themselves, their chauffeurs and their cars at the service of the government.* On the first day of the strike, indeed, so many cars came onto the London streets offering lifts to office workers that they almost defeated their own object, causing the worst traffic jam London had ever seen. After this it was better organized. The Ministry of Transport set up a big car park in Horse Guards Parade to which drivers reported and were sent on journeys, and there were other organizations like Mrs Baldwin's arrangement for women drivers to carry office workers in and out. It was reported later that 40 per cent of the car-drivers who reported at Horse Guards Parade were women.[20]

Certain highly-qualified professional groups played a key role in the strike-breaking apparatus. The Electrical Power Engineers Association offered its services to the government with the firm support of most of

* Not only their cars, but in some parts of the country, their horses. The Chief Constable of Newcastle reported after the Strike that 22 horses had been 'supplied gratuitously' for the use of the mounted section. The mounted police in Newcastle, including specials, were involved in a number of disturbances and baton charges.

its members. It was they in many places who kept the power stations going when the manual workers moved out, supervising and instructing the naval ratings and undergraduates who were sent in to do the job. In Bristol, scientific students who had been taking a course in electricity at the university formed the main workforce in the power station.

Journalists were another highly-qualified professional group who felt the government's cause to be their own. The National Union of Journalists was not affiliated to the TUC. At the beginning of the strike the NUJ Executive took up an attitude which would in normal times have been acceptable to the members; it instructed them not to go on strike, but also told them not to do the work of other newspaper workers who were on strike. This instruction however was met by angry protests from a number of branches, and a few days later the Executive revised it, saying that it was permissible for members to work on the makeshift newspapers which the proprietors were trying to bring out, so long as these were produced by labour which could not permanently displace men on strike. The journalists had a special reason for feeling indignant; they were outraged by what they regarded as an attempt by the TUC to 'muzzle the press' – an attempt which seemed to violate a cherished principle. So the journalists volunteered at newspaper premises for any jobs of which they were capable from packing and loading newspapers to proofreading. On the *British Gazette*, which was being produced at the premises of the *Morning Post*, they made up crews for operating the rotary presses in the machine room under the supervision of the *Morning Post*'s machine room overseer, its chief engineer and its works manager. The *British Gazette* itself told the story as follows:

> The Editorial Staff . . . clothed itself in dungarees, and marched down to the machine-room to be initiated into its job. Such a sight was never seen before. Leader-writers, art and music critics, reporters, sub-editors, financial experts – every able bodied man, of whatever rank or station, was recruited for the occasion, and all responded to the call with a 'frolic welcome'.[21]

On the *Yorkshire Post*, where all the compositors, linotype operators, proof pullers, readers, stereotypers, machine room men and dispatch men went on strike, the paper was got out by the combined efforts of the journalists, the clerical staff and the apprentices under the supervision of the overseers and assistant overseers. The paper's own account of this affair stressed the good humour and the 'camaraderie', 'as men and women got themselves into difficulties and helped each other out.'

Businessmen and people engaged in commerce came forward to help the government in numbers. The Home Secretary stated that 'the large London institutions in which men congregate for business purposes are answering the call with great vigour. From the Stock Exchange I am promised 1400 or more Special Constables and I am assured that I shall get proportionate responses from the Baltic, Corn Exchange, Lloyds, Commercial Salesrooms and other big markets.'[22]

Finally, the propertied classes, the well-to-do, automatically embraced the cause as their own. High society came into the struggle with characteristic self-confidence. *The Times*, endeavouring to get out a makeshift sheet, became, in its own words, 'the very centre of fashion'. Among its lorry-drivers were the Duchess of Sutherland, the Duchess of Westminster, Viscountess Masserene and Ferrard, and Lady Maureen Stanley, while bank and company directors offered their services in all sorts of capacities. On the *Daily Express* Lady Louis Mountbatten acted as a telephone operator; the Honourable Mrs Beaumont, with several other society women, undertook stable duty at Paddington Station (most railway vans were horse-drawn); Lord Monkswell was a signalman at Marylebone; the Honourable Lionel Guest drove a train; Lord Weymouth was a lorry-driver for the Great Western.

In conversation at the time and afterwards such people created the impression that the whole affair had been a bit of a jolly romp. Except in the West End of London, where there were hardly any strikers to be seen, the reality was often uglier. In some areas the special constables earned themselves a reputation as arrogant bullies. In Glasgow the behaviour of the students provoked a resentment in the working-class movement which endured for many years afterwards.

Support for the government was not of course universal among the middle classes during the Strike. Here and there were intellectuals, journalists, professional people and undergraduates who threw themselves into helping the strikers. They were small in number – much smaller than they would have been if a similar strike had taken place in the Thirties, or later after sizeable left-wing movements had developed in the universities. A very much larger number of middle-class people stood on the sidelines watching, perplexed but inarticulate. Many were habitual readers of the Liberal press. Their voice was not heard, nor were they permitted to know that the Archbishop of Canterbury, for one, was urging conciliation and a settlement involving the ending of the Strike in return for the withdrawal of the coalowners' lockout notices.* Instead something which most Liberals had always rejected, the concept of the class struggle, was being stridently emphasized, not only in government propaganda, but in the class composition of those active on the government's behalf. The very appearance of the volunteers, the undergraduates in their Fair Isle jerseys and their plus-fours, the society women, the men from the Stock Exchange, seemed to argue that this was a struggle of the upper and middle classes and their followers against the great mass of the working class. The government was proclaiming that it was 'saving the nation', whereas only part of the nation appeared to be on its side in the clearest class confrontation ever seen in Britain.

The View from the Top

The Cabinet was in a better position than the general public to know what its volunteers were and were not achieving. Their use for maintaining the morale of all those who sided with the government was unquestionable. Their success as strike-breakers was limited. The emergency plans to distribute food had worked reasonably well, though it had to be admitted that the TUC had only offered a confused challenge to them. On the other hand it was a different picture where the strike call had been clear. Only a small proportion of buses and trams had managed to get going with volunteer drivers, and a much smaller proportion still of passenger trains. As for railway goods

---

* Kingsley Martin was one of those who believed that the TUC made a mistake in calling out the printers, since it meant the suppression of the Liberal press which had been very critical of the government before the Strike and would probably have gone on being so, and would anyhow have given space to the TUC case which was virtually suppressed during the Strike except in the *British Worker*. See his book, *The British Public and the General Strike* (1926).

traffic, it was virtually paralysed.* Meanwhile there were whole areas of industry where strike-breakers could not be used at all; moreover after the first week, many factories where the workforce had not been called out were closing down because coal had run out, or electricity was cut off, or they could not get delivery of supplies. It was clear that if the Strike went on much longer, almost all industry would come to a standstill.

The response to the Strike had been a surprise to Baldwin and his colleagues. It had been assumed that many rank-and-file members of the trade unions would be reluctant to obey the strike call. When it became clear that the opposite was true, various explanations began to be advanced. Some Cabinet members were convinced that the trade union members feared to defy their leaders because, if they disobeyed orders, they would risk benefits for which they had paid. One school of thought believed there should be much stronger action – perhaps the wholesale arrest of TUC leaders and the call-up of army reserves. The object would be to break the power of the trade unions even if this provoked a violent struggle. In partial recognition of the need for a tougher line, the Cabinet began to prepare plans to declare the Strike illegal and freeze strike pay. They were persuaded to postpone any such action, partly by the intervention of the King, who thought that any-thing done to touch the pockets of those existing on strike pay might provoke reprisals from those who 'until now had been remarkably quiet'.[23]

Another school of thought much less influential in the Cabinet but very weighty just outside and around it, held that the government had made a mistake in precipitating the Strike; that the coalowners were like dinosaurs, buried in the past, and that the government should concentrate on achieving a compromise settlement. In the end the government was not obliged to follow either course of action, because the TUC itself acted.

The dominant leaders on the TUC General Council had been pushed into a situation which they did not want and had not expected. Never-

---

* In London the London General Omnibus Co managed to get 86 buses onto the road on 5 May and the number rose to 526 on 11 May, many doing partial runs only. The normal number was 3,293. None of London's 1,584 trams got out for the whole of the Strike. On the LMS Railway, by the end of the Strike, passenger trains had risen to 12 per cent of normal, goods trains to 3 per cent. On the GWR the comparable figures were 19 per cent and 8·4 per cent.

theless, once the Strike was forced upon them, they plunged into the practical work of carrying it out with considerable vigour, some being very gifted organizers to whom the chance to take action after days of knife-edge uncertainty came as a relief. And even those who had tried hardest to avoid the Strike could not help being elated just at first by the response to it from their members.

But elation soon gave way to misgivings. In spite of their reiterated statements emphasizing that the Strike was no more than an industrial dispute, Baldwin and the *British Gazette* were insistently proclaiming that it was an attack on constitutional government. Their greatest fear was that the Strike would lead to widespread civil disorder. Day after day they urged their members to be 'exemplary in conduct', to give no opportunity for police interference. Pickets were told to 'avoid obstruction'. Local strike organizations were told to keep strikers happily occupied with various forms of entertainment.

On the whole their members were obeying these instructions. Nevertheless there were reports within the first day or two of police baton charges in Poplar and of lorries set on fire, of crowds stopping cars at Blackwall Tunnel and insisting that their occupants get out and walk, of a tumultuous crowd at Camberwell forcing trams back into the depot. There were violent clashes in Edinburgh, with bottle-throwing and looting, and fights between strikers and specials in a number of provincial towns. It did not add up to very much – indeed, relations between strikers and police appeared to be unexpectedly good in some towns – but no one could know how quickly matters might turn really ugly.

They were uneasily aware that they were not really in control of what went on in the localities. Innumerable cyclostyled strike bulletins were being issued, and though many of them confined themselves to reproducing items from the *British Worker*, others contained matter which they thought both dangerous and irresponsible. People were being arrested in some numbers, some for assaulting strike-breakers, others for spreading rumours about the unreliability of the armed forces, others for selling Communist strike sheets. Some councils of action were coming under the influence of the Communists and the Minority Movement, who were continually saying the one thing that the TUC did *not* want said: namely that the Strike was a political struggle, that it should not be limited to beating off the employers' wage offensive, but should be directed towards nationalization of the mines and forcing the resignation of the government.

But the horizons of the dominant TUC leaders had never stretched beyond getting the mining lockout notices withdrawn while negotiations were resumed. Even this modest goal appeared to be receding. They did not now believe the government would capitulate easily, and they dreaded a long-drawn-out struggle with their funds melting away. When on Friday 7 May Sir Herbert Samuel told them that he was unofficially prepared to help towards a settlement, they grasped at the opportunity. Who better to help them than the author of the Report they thought so highly of? Secret meetings began.

The stumbling block however was the miners' leaders, headed by Herbert Smith and A.J.Cook, who were adhering to their stand that they could not agree to a longer working day or reductions in wages. The TUC leaders became increasingly impatient with this obdurate attitude. Although they had publicly stated that any further degradation of miners' wages would be 'indefensible', they knew that negotiators always adopted public postures as part of the bargaining process; the idea that you should hold fast to such postures, insisting that come what may you meant what you said, was not common sense. When the Samuel negotiations once more produced a formula which clearly contemplated a revision of wage-rates, and the miners' leaders once more rejected such a formula, the resentment that had been building up against the miners among other trade union leaders boiled over.* On 12 May a deputation went to see Baldwin and told him that the General Strike was to be called off unconditionally so that negotiations could proceed.

---

* Citrine in *Men and Work*, pp. 199, 200, describes the mood of General Council members as follows: 'Hayday ... pointed out that the miners were not aware of the general industrial situation. They were not trade unionists in the general sense ... They lived in villages, and they thought in the mass. They did not realize that we could not keep people out much longer ... Thomas followed and said ... that the miners were not big enough. They were not trade unionists in the proper sense, and did not understand or very much care about what happened to the rest of the movement! Beard said, "Those men have never readily put themselves into the hands of the General Council. That has never been the state of their minds. I am not prepared to put everything our unions have into the pawn shop and feel that it is not appreciated by those people." '

Afterwards

The announcement calling off the Strike was received by the strikers at first with the belief that a victory must have been won, then with utter incredulity. The engineers had only been called out the night before, and in many areas the Strike had seemed to be going from strength to strength. Soon disbelief turned to dismay and fury. Drivers threw bundles of the *British Worker* back into the officials' faces; local strike committee leaders broke down and wept; in East London and elsewhere angry crowds paraded the streets.

Next day it became clear what unconditional surrender involved. Strikers turning up for work found new and worsened conditions of employment imposed and refusals to re-employ them. Railway workers, busmen, dockers, print workers and others came out on strike again, and for two days the Strike appeared to be more complete than it had been before. Ultimately the unions concerned were forced to sign agreements admitting that they had been wrong to call the Strike, and promising not to do it again until negotiating procedures had been exhausted.

As the weeks passed, anger with the leaders merged into disillusionment. Up above there was also much bitterness. Some members of the General Council felt that their negotiating committee had misled them: they had understood that Baldwin had given unofficial guarantees that if the Strike was called off he would make the coalowners withdraw the lockout notices. 'There was a gentlemanly pledge of honour floating about, and the Trades Union Congress trusted it,' Ben Turner said afterwards.[24]

There was naturally much argument and counter-argument, the miners alleging that the General Council had gone behind their backs, and the General Council answering that the miners had entrusted them with the conduct of the dispute. Indeed when at last a post mortem took place on 20 January 1927, and the General Council's report was accepted by 2,840,000 to 1,095,000, much of the argument was not so much concerned with whether the General Council had been right to call the Strike off as whether they had been given power to do so by the unions concerned. But at this conference the total change in climate was apparent, as members rose to say they had never believed in the Strike.

C.T.Cramp, President of the National Union of Railwaymen, said: 'I do not believe in a general strike ... I have never believed in a general strike ... but I knew this perfectly well, that at the time of the Memorial Hall conference the great bulk of the workers of this country did believe in a general strike, and the few of us who did not were in a tiny minority.'[25]

What Cramp said of himself was not quite true of all the leaders. A few of them – including Bevin and Ben Turner – had believed in a general strike, had believed that if the movement showed its strength in such a way the government would be forced to come to terms. After 1926 they believed in it no longer and turned resolutely towards different tactics and a different strategy, seeking to increase their influence by a policy of collaboration with the employers which later became known as 'Mondism'.

The miners' lockout meanwhile continued until the end of November, a seven-month struggle endured by the miners with a stubbornness which has not been equalled in trade union history before or since. In this war of attrition the miners' families subsisted on a dwindling pittance, made up of Poor Law allowances and relief funds collected outside the mining areas, some of which came from trade unionists abroad, in particular from Soviet Russia, and provoked an indignant reaction from the government. The reports of hunger and hardship became more and more pitiful as the months passed. Yet in September 1926, after the lockout had been in operation for more than four months, not more than 5 per cent of the mining workforce had drifted back to work. By November, however, resistance at last collapsed, and the struggle was over: the men were forced back on the mineowners' terms. Earnings were beaten down and it was more than ten years before they recovered to pre-1926 levels. Meanwhile the government had already in July passed a measure which suspended the treasured seven-hour day.

The government followed the defeat of the miners with the Trade Disputes Act of 1927, which outlawed sympathetic strikes. Trade unionism's confident hopes were over at last.

13
Women

Just before Easter 1927, the Prime Minister, Stanley Baldwin, announced that women were to be given the same political voting right as men. Since the war virtually all men over 21 had had the vote. But a woman could only vote if she was over 30 and was a householder or the wife of a householder. 1·8 million women over 30 were excluded by this definition, among them all resident domestic servants, women living in furnished lettings, widows who went to live with married sons or daughters, sisters keeping house for their brothers. Now these women were all to be given the vote. And, more important, so were 3½ million young women between the ages of 21–30. The new proposal meant that the number of women on the electoral register would rise to 14½ million altogether, compared with 12¼ million men.

GIRLS' EASTERTIDE GIFT was the joyful headline in the *Daily Sketch* and inside were interviews with three 21-year-olds: a mannequin who thought it right she should have the vote, an artist's model who was against votes for women – she thought they could pull the strings without taking an outward part in politics – and a waitress who was quite indifferent to the news. 'I never read politics', she said. 'They are so dull. Give me human stuff, news of actresses, kinema stars, the darling little Duchess of York and her baby.* People like her are more interesting than anything that happens in the House of Commons.'[1]

Most newspapers did not take the announcement so lightheartedly. While the Liberal and Labour press welcomed the news, the reaction of the Conservative papers was mixed. The *Daily Mail*, which had the largest circulation of any newspaper, expressed alarm at a proposal which would place women voters in a majority over men. 'The time may come when, if women decide to use their power, they will be able

* The baby was, of course, the future Queen Elizabeth II.

to dominate the State,' the paper suggested.[2] At best, the proposed measure was a 'hazardous experiment'. 'At the worst it might lead to a national calamity,' since 'cautious and far-seeing persons well acquainted with electoral conditions' believed that it might mean the exclusion of the Conservatives from office for the next 30 years.[3] The *Mail* continued in the ensuing weeks to emphasize the 'risks from the voting of impulsive and politically ignorant girls' whose votes were likely to reflect the 'foolish Communistic sentiments' of their boyfriends.[4]

As the days passed, fear of domination by women seemed to be submerged in fear of the young and propertyless voter, whether male or female. The *Daily Mirror*, the largest circulation tabloid, ran a regular correspondence column headed FLAPPER VOTE FOLLY. It suggested that 'there is indeed a special case for *raising* the age of political privilege – for *removing* votes from thousands who prove, by not using them, that they don't want them. There is no case for showering more votes upon muddle headed amateurs.'[5]

The *Morning Post*, paper of the die-hard right wing, also urged the need to raise the minimum voting age for men to 25 while lowering that of women to the same age. Objecting to the grant of the vote to 'politically inexperienced people' of only 21, the paper observed: 'At that delightful age, and for several ensuing years, few young men or young women take the smallest interest in public affairs ... Such political views as they hold are either culled from the casual observations of one whom they admire, or are the immature fruit of the generous enthusiasms of youth.'[6] The same theme, a universal voting age of 25, was aired in the correspondence columns of *The Times*. The drawback to equal votes at 25 was that it would still put women in a majority over men. Perhaps to overcome this difficulty, it was suggested that no existing male voter under the age of 25 should be disenfranchised, only future ones. Presumably this would postpone female domination for some years to come.

Two Conservative newspapers showed wholehearted support for Baldwin's move: the *Daily Telegraph*, which observed that once any women had been given the vote, as they had been in 1918, it was inevitable that they should all get it in time, and Beaverbrook's *Daily Express*, which reassuringly carried out numbers of interviews with 21-year-old girls, the majority of whom said they would vote Conservative when the time came.

The newspapers were not just following the whims of their owners. They were, in part, reflecting the emotions of their readers. Eight years after the first woman had taken her seat in Parliament,* many of the older generation still viewed participation by women in politics with distaste and the possibility of what was called 'petticoat government' with a sense of outrage. To some, the solidarity and militancy of the pre-war suffragette movement lent a special menace to the concept of 'petticoat government'. To others it was the proposal to give the vote to *young* women that seemed especially monstrous. 'Petticoat' was the last word to be associated with them, for their very appearance – their short skirts and short hair – seemed to violate all the cherished concepts of womanliness.

In part, however, the newspapers were reflecting the doubts and fears and calculations of the politicians. Indeed, had it not been for considerations of short-term party political advantage and disadvantage, equal suffrage might have been introduced some years earlier. A Bill for the purpose had been sponsored by the Labour Party in 1919 and actually carried in the Commons against government advice, but it had been thrown out by the House of Lords. In 1922 Lord Robert Cecil, a Conservative, had tried to bring in a Bill; in 1923, Isaac Foot, a Liberal, had tried to do the same. In 1924, under the first Labour government, a Bill had been introduced and its Second Reading had been carried by 290 votes to 74, but the government had been brought down before it got any further.

During the subsequent general election in the autumn of 1924 the Labour Party in its election manifesto reminded electors that its Bill to give votes to women at 21 on the same terms as men had been killed. Perhaps in the belief that this gave the Labour Party an electoral advantage, Baldwin told the press that the Conservative Party was in favour of equal political rights for men and women and intended to refer the question to a Speaker's conference of all political parties to get agreement.[7] In fact not only were many members of the Conservative Party opposed to the measure but a number of the leading statesmen were exceedingly uneasy about it. When at last in April 1927 Baldwin

---

* Viscountess Astor, who was elected MP in a 1919 by-election and always said she had to surmount much prejudice and hostility. The first woman actually elected was the Countess Markievicz for a Dublin Constituency in 1918, but as an Irish Republican she refused to take her seat at Westminster.

announced his decision it was rumoured that many of the Cabinet were really opposed to it.* But Baldwin nevertheless secured the endorsement of the annual Conservative conference in October 1927 and by the time the new Bill was published and came up for its Second Reading on 29 March 1928, open opposition from Conservative MPs had dwindled.

In this debate speakers who used arguments which had been taken quite seriously by the previous generation provoked laughter; indeed nothing could have demonstrated more clearly the contrast between the attitudes of the pre-war and post-war worlds. Such a speaker was Colonel Applin, MP for Enfield, who said:

> I have looked up the wills for last year and I find that men left £58,000,000 whereas women left merely £6,000,000. That means that, if we are to have majority rule by women in this country, we are handing over to them the taxable wealth of the country, to which they have contributed only one-tenth (laughter). That is a very important point. It is all very well to treat it as a jest, but if we pass a law to permit women to take over the finances of this country, whence are we going?

> We are governing a great Empire . . . and that Empire comprises not only our great self-governing Dominions but the largest Mohammedan population in the world. Among the Mohammedans, women not only have no voice, but are not seen. What will be the effect on the great Mohammedan population of the world of granting the franchise in this country – the governing country – to a majority of 2,200,000 women over men? (laughter).

Colonel Applin continued:

> Hitherto men have done all the heavy work in this country (Miss Wilkinson: 'Oh really! Good gracious.').† You find no women in the stokehold of a ship in the Navy; you find no women down the coal mines today and I thank God for it; you find no women in blast furnaces. Women cannot physically perform these duties. Therefore it is a very dangerous thing for women to demand the vote on equal terms with men, without realizing what that may involve.

---

* The rumours were true. A Cabinet member, Lord Birkenhead, wrote to a colleague on 13 April 1927: 'The Cabinet went mad yesterday and decided to give votes to women at the age of twenty-one. Every speaker was against the proposal on its merits.' He went on to describe the change as 'dangerous and revolutionary' and said that Winston Churchill was one of those who protested. (Quoted in D. Butler, *The Electoral System in Britain 1918–1951*, p. 28.)

† Ellen Wilkinson, Labour MP for Middlesbrough East. She was the only woman Labour MP at the time; there were three Conservative women MPs.

Whatever happens, it must involve going into the rough and tumble of life. It must mean taking on grave responsibilities, which would perhaps be too grave a burden on women.

Sir Frederick Hall, MP for Dulwich, said:

No one has greater respect for women than I have but I have yet to learn that, considering the hundreds of years that the country has been governed by men through the House of Commons, and that a vote was not given to any woman previous to 1918, there has been any bad effect to this country because it has been governed by men (laughter).

Sir Charles Oman, MP for Oxford University, a Professor of Modern History and one of the strongest opponents of the Bill, made answer to those who said that the Bill was only a logical step:

Logic is not the thing by which the governance of England has ever taken place. Logic may rule the minds of our Latin neighbours, but it is our pride that England and its institutions are illogical to a degree, and we are proud of the fact.

'The swan-song of the die-hards' was how Viscountess Astor MP described such speeches. 'They may be singing like swans, but they are thinking like geese,' she observed, and most of the House appeared to agree with her. In defence of his Bill, Baldwin argued that it was a fallacy to suppose that women would vote by class or by sex:

There has been a unity amongst them which has been evoked by the struggle in which they have engaged to obtain these elementary rights. And with the obtaining of these rights, that particular unity which bound them together in the pursuit of a common end will be gone and they will judge of political affairs according to their temperament and according to their experience, in exactly the same way as we do.

Most of those who still had doubts about the measure found it expedient to keep quiet, and when the vote came it was 389 in favour and 12 against. When it got to the House of Lords it was 114 in favour and 35 against. Here, however, the Earl of Birkenhead, who answered the debate on behalf of the government, performed his task in a most unusual way. 'I was against the extension of the franchise to women,' he said. 'I am against the extension of the franchise to women. I always shall be against the extension of the franchise to women.' He explained the situation in which he found himself: 'I have spent nearly the whole of my political life in giving wise advice to my fellow countrymen which they have invariably disregarded, and if I had resigned every time that my wise and advantageous advice was rejected, I should seldom, indeed, during that critical period have been in office.'⁸

At the subsequent general election held on 30 May 1929, the Conservatives lost heavily and Labour emerged for the first time as the largest single party in the House and, with the support of the Liberals, once more formed an administration. It seemed that the prophecies that the flapper vote would lead to the downfall of the Conservative Party had come true, and Baldwin was much blamed.

The number of women candidates rose from 41 to 69, and the number of women MPs elected from 4 to 14. Ramsay MacDonald, the Labour Prime Minister, marked the occasion by appointing a woman to the Cabinet for the first time in British history. It was Margaret Bondfield, a trade union organizer, who had already made history in 1923 as the first woman chairman of the TUC. She recorded in her diary that when she was summoned with other newly-appointed members of the Cabinet to go to Windsor to be sworn in, she felt horribly nervous and was worried about what to wear. But after the special train had left Paddington Station she began to enjoy it because 'all the porters and travellers were so jolly and friendly – cheering, blowing whistles from the engines at the stations as our train came through.'⁹

It was one more sign of the changing status of women in society. The change had been very considerable and had been underlined by the alteration in their appearance begun during the war when, mainly for utilitarian reasons, women had thrown off their whalebone corsets and with them their hourglass figures. At the same time skirts had risen above the ankles. When the war ended no one wanted to be once more imprisoned in tight-laced stays and cumbersome skirts. Instead skirts began to rise, waists disappeared so that dresses clung round the hips but nowhere else, bosoms were flattened. Black stockings went out and 'flesh-coloured' ones came in, a delicate hint that legs might be looked at instead of hidden away. By the middle Twenties the transformation was complete; skirts had risen to the knees. The heavy swathes of high-piled hair had gone; instead there was the bob, the shingle and even the Eton crop. In place of the elaborate hats had come close-fitting, helmet-shaped little cloches under which hair was hardly visible. The heroines of popular novels now all had 'neat' heads and their figures were unfailingly 'slim and boyish'. It seemed that the surge towards equality of status with men was being emphasized by the disappearance of the more womanly characteristics.

Alongside the change in appearance went a change in behaviour. Men and women began to mix much more freely with one another than before. Women smoked in public and used the same slang as men. The more free and easy manners appeared to be adding to the enjoyment of both men and women. A new law was passed to give equal rights in divorce; under the Matrimonial Causes Act of 1923 women could, like men, sue for divorce on grounds of adultery alone, whereas previously, unlike men, they had had to prove cruelty or desertion as well as adultery to obtain a divorce.

The law also promised the right to a career, the promise being enshrined in the 1919 Sex Disqualification (Removal) Act, which said that: 'A person shall not be disqualified by sex or marriage from the exercise of any public function, or from being appointed to or holding any civil or judicial office or post, from entering or assuming or carrying on any civil profession or vocation.'

It seemed that women were no longer to be barred from equality of opportunity. At last they could put their foot on the ladder to high position. Apparently in confirmation of the great changes now in train, the census compilers in 1921 drew attention to a 'remarkable feature': the increased number of females who had entered the more learned professions which, until recently, had included hardly any women at all. Thus whereas in 1911 there had been only 477 female medical practitioners, there were now 1,253. Whereas in 1911 barristers, solicitors and engineers had been exclusively male, now there were 46 female consultant engineers, 20 barristers and 17 solicitors. Female veterinary surgeons had gone up from 2 to 24 and female architects from 7 to 49.[10]

But in fact those who had hoped and believed that women would henceforth play an equal part with men in public life, would get to the top as often as men in their chosen career or profession, were going to be disappointed. The way to the top was still very hard. In 1921 5·1 per cent of all 'higher professionals' were women. In 1931 it had only crept up to 7·5 per cent. In the higher Civil Service, though many posts were, after a good deal of haggling, nominally made available to women, a regulation under the 1919 Act laid it down that women must resign their appointments if they married, thus, it seemed, entirely nullifying the intention of that Act. And although the same Act had provided that a person should not be exempted from jury service by reason of sex or marriage, it remained very exceptional to have more than two or three women out of twelve on any jury, and all-male juries were common. As for the top political jobs, Margaret Bondfield's appointment was a landmark, but a very solitary one.

Women had originally been given the vote because of their services during the war. Formal recognition of woman's equal status followed so far as the law was concerned; manners and customs also accorded woman an equality she had not known before. But in the sphere of occupation no such equality took place.

This was in spite of the fact that during the war women had shown themselves capable of many jobs commonly reserved for men. They had gone into engineering, onto the land, into transport as bus and tram conductors, into government offices and private offices where they replaced male clerks. In engineering, where the demand for vast quantities of standardized articles permitted a great extension of repetition jobs on which semi-skilled or unskilled labour could be used, the employment of women at low rates of pay created acute problems for the trade unions; the skilled men, fully trained with long apprenticeships behind them, saw their standards undermined by the introduction of cheap female labour. Early attempts to ensure that where a woman replaced a skilled man she should get the skilled man's rate were bypassed. For women were not really replacing skilled men; the processes were altered and broken down so that they could perform repeatedly one part only of the work of a skilled man. For such work the pay of a semi-skilled man might have been appropriate, but this the unions failed to secure, and women's rates were for the most part below the lowest unskilled male rate. From the employers' point of view the motive was the obvious one of cheapening the costs of production. But they supported their actions with arguments which have been familiar ever since: that work for girls was a temporary affair until they married; that for married women it was only for 'pocket money'; that a single woman had no family to support. These arguments were not on the whole resisted by the workpeople concerned. The women were accustomed to put a low value on their services; the men fought for the principle that, once the war was over, the women should go.

And that in fact is what happened. The war ended, the men returned to claim their old jobs and women were discharged wholesale. For many it was as though the war had never been. They went back to their former occupations in textiles, clothing, shops, above all in domestic service.

But there were nevertheless certain changes of great significance. The first was that in the newer branches of engineering, particularly electrical engineering, the pattern set in the war of using women as cheap labour on repetition jobs was resumed and tended to increase year by year thereafter. The second was that typing and clerical work began to be looked on primarily as women's work. Whereas only one fifth of the clerical labour force had been female in 1911, by 1931 nearly half of it was female. Since clerical work as a whole was increasing, the number of women office workers rose from 178,000 in 1911 to 560,000 in 1921 and to 646,000 in 1931. The pay was nowhere near the male rate for the job. (See Table 26, p. 218.)

The third main change brought about by the war was the reduction in the number of women employed as domestic servants from 1,400,000 in 1911 to 1,072,000 in 1921.[11] The drift of women into war work had caused an acute shortage of domestic servants; but it had been widely assumed that when the war ended the shortage would disappear. This did not happen altogether. True, with over a million women employed as servants in private households in 1921, it remained overwhelmingly the most important industry for women, absorbing one fifth of all women employed. But even on this scale it was not as large as before, so that questions were persistently asked about it in the Commons, and two government committees were set up, one in 1919 and another in 1923, to examine the problem and report on it.

There had grown up a widespread resistance to entering domestic service. Its unpopularity had less to do with the pay than with the circumstances of the job. Though a resident servant was not expected to work all day without stopping she often had to be *available* for work all day, and had no definite hours off duty except, perhaps, a Sunday afternoon every fortnight and one evening a week. Girls working in a factory, shop or office could do what they liked with their Sundays and spare evenings; moreover they usually worked alongside others of their own age. The young girl in service often had no such companionship, and her opportunities of meeting the opposite sex were much reduced, and with them the chances of marriage.

So the young girls went on resisting the idea of domestic service, but after the onset of the slump in 1921 many were forced into it by unemployment and pressure from the employment exchanges, and during the decade the numbers rose again from 1,072,000 to 1,268,000 in 1931. It was estimated, however, that not more than 60 per cent of these were resident; to a much greater extent than formerly domestic service was carried out on an hourly or daily basis.

There were various categories of female domestic servants. At the top came highly-skilled specialist workers: cooks, ladies' maids, children's nurses, parlourmaids, housemaids. In the great houses all these categories were employed, the scale and numbers being only marginally reduced as compared with pre-war. In the houses of the comfortably-off upper middle class also it was normal to employ at least a resident cook, a housemaid, a parlourmaid and a nurse for the children. Lower down the social scale the pattern was changing. The middle-class family who had formerly employed a resident 'cook-general' might now have to pay rather more for a cook who came in by the day. The lower middle-class housewife who had formerly employed a 'general servant' – often an inexperienced little girl acting as 'mother's help' – now could not always find such a little girl; she might have to make do with a daily cleaning woman.

The multitudes engaged in domestic service were in fact absorbed by relatively few families. The 1931 census showed that only 4·8 per cent of all families employed resident domestics; less than half a million families out of a total of 10 million. It appeared that 95 per cent of the population managed without resident servants. But they did not manage without heavy domestic labour. Much more significant than the contribution of paid female domestic labour was that of unpaid domestic labour from both married and unmarried women.

Throughout the decade the vast majority of women expected to cease work when they married. Except in the textile areas, where it was traditional for married women to continue at work, it was taken for granted that a married woman didn't work unless there was some special reason such as a husband's illness or unemployment. In 1921 over 90 per cent of all married women stayed at home; less than 9 per cent were classed as 'gainfully occupied'.[12] Even in 1931, when unem-

ployment among men was forcing wives back into work, the proportion of married women working was hardly more than 10 per cent.
(See Table 25, p. 218.) In the 45–54 age-groups – i.e. post child-bearing
age – the proportion working was only 8½ per cent.

In previous decades there had been two basic reasons for married
women to stay at home. The first was preoccupation with childbirth
and child rearing. The second was the burden of household work.
Society had regarded women primarily as home-makers, and women
had so regarded themselves. It had long been recognized that the
standard of comfort in a man's home depended primarily on the
efficiency, devotion and stamina of his wife; moreover housing conditions were such that a comfortable home meant very heavy labour.
Not only was home-making looked on as a married woman's special
mission; it was seen as *woman's* special mission regardless of marriage,
so that nearly 30 per cent of single women of working age (i.e. aged
14–55) were classified as 'not gainfully occupied'.

A few (very few) single women will have been still at school or
full-time students. A few will have been young women in comfortable
homes occupied in the social round prior to marriage, or well-heeled
spinsters living on private incomes. A few will have been prostitutes.
But most of these single women were acting as unpaid home helps.
There was the elder sister who stayed at home to help an ailing mother
cope with the young ones. There was the young woman who left work
to keep house for a widowed father or bachelor brother; the middle-
aged woman who left work to care for a bed-ridden parent; the maiden
aunt who came to give a hand in some crisis of illness or death and
became a permanent and indispensable part of the family circle. Added
together their numbers were formidable; among them was the generation of 'surplus women' who never married because there were not
enough men to go round. One way and another it appears that during
the Twenties about two thirds of all women were primarily concerned
with domestic duties, whether as married women, as paid domestic
servants, or as unpaid domestic helps.

This preoccupation with home-making to the exclusion of other
things continued to dominate throughout the decade. But simultaneously the new technology was reducing the burden of home-
making for those who could afford it, and in time for nearly everyone.
The housewife in a well-equipped modern little house with a couple of

H

children only had begun to find that domestic toil was not quite the endless backbreaking process which had prematurely aged her mother. She found that she could afford a few hours of leisure, that indeed her domestic duties could often be managed in part of the day instead of the whole day. Streamlining the home and easing its burden began with the middle class but was all the time filtering down to the working class. The housewife in her thirties began to look much younger than her predecessors.

The most fundamental change concerned the number of children born to each couple. All through the decade the birthrate was falling. It had been gradually falling for about 50 years before that, but the Twenties saw a sudden sharp decline denoting a dramatic change in behaviour and attitudes to personal and family life. Thus whereas over one quarter of women married between 1900 and 1909 had five *or more* children, only one tenth of the women who married in 1930 had families of this size. Thirty-three per cent of the women who married in 1900–9 had small families consisting of one or two children only; 46 per cent of the women who married in 1920 and 51 per cent of those who married in 1930 had families of this size (see Table 27, p. 219). The smallest families were those of the salaried and professional classes, but the trend towards smaller families was noticeable in all classes.

The trend was a reflection of a new attitude to marriage and the role of women. Up till the war the vast majority of men took it for granted that their wives would have as many children as nature dictated, and women accepted the idea that this was their role. But after the war came the gradual spread of a realization that they could choose whether or not to have children and if so how many; moreover more and more couples began to believe that they should make this choice. Before the war only a small minority of couples had deliberately practised family limitation or used any form of birth control. But the majority of those who married after it did so or were going to do so one day.*

* See E. Lewis-Faning, 'Report on an Enquiry into Family Limitation and its influence on Human Fertility during the past Fifty Years'. (Papers of the Royal Commission on Population (1949), vol I.) The result of a sample survey of several thousand women in 1946 carried out by the Council of the Royal College of Obstetricians and Gynaecologists revealed that about 15 per cent of those who married before 1910 had ever used any type of birth control; of those married between 1925–9, 61 per cent had done so. Of those, 22 per cent had used artificial contraceptives and 39 per cent other methods – mainly *coitus interruptus*.

The change went hand-in-hand with a new frankness about sex – in particular, about sex from the woman's viewpoint. This did not come about without violent controversy during which certain determined reformers such as Dr Marie Stopes achieved an extraordinary notoriety. Dr Stopes was not a doctor of medicine but a scientist of some standing (which was already very unusual for a woman), and was distinguished for her studies on the origin of coal. Unhappy personal experience in her first marriage gave a new direction to her research and she was led to the realization that for innumerable wives, sex was a duty rather than a pleasure, while the husbands believed that their wives' lack of enthusiasm was the result of innate coldness.

Marie Stopes attributed this unhappy situation largely to ignorance of physiological facts. 'About the fundamental and vital problems of sex, there is a lack of knowledge so abysmal and so universal that its mists and shadowy darkness have affected even the few who lead us, and who are prosecuting research in these subjects,' she wrote.[13] Her book *Married Love: A Contribution to the solution of sex difficulties*, first published in 1918, was dedicated 'to young husbands and all those who are betrothed in love', and was intended to dispel some of this ignorance. And it attacked many of the attitudes to sex which had prevailed for so long. It challenged the assumption that a 'nice' woman did not have any sexual impulses and that sex was a low and degrading necessity to a pure woman. It also opposed those who held that the control of conception was immoral, and argued that it was important for the health of the mother and for the happiness of the couple concerned that the births of children should be spaced.

Marie Stopes had difficulty in finding a publisher and had to help finance her book herself. But within five years it had sold 220,000 copies. Marie Stopes was a Quaker, and believed that her mission was divinely inspired. This belief was reflected in her book, and no doubt helped its entry into thousands of respectable and, by later standards, rather unsophisticated homes. Indeed Marie Stopes' supporters held that her theme could not have been treated in more beautiful and delicate language. Others however characterized the book as a 'romantic, emotional, rhetorical rhapsody'.[14]

The sequel to *Married Love* was entitled *Wise Parenthood*, and gave practical guidance on artificial contraceptives. In 1921 Marie Stopes founded the first birth control clinic for working women, where free advice could be obtained and contraceptives could be fitted by a qualified nursing staff. Believing that a chain of such clinics should be set up as a public service by the state she also founded a Society for Constructive Birth Control, which was launched with the benevolent support of some well-known names in the medical and political worlds at a packed meeting in the Queen's Hall London in May 1921.

Inevitably this campaign aroused the active hostility of the Roman Catholic Church. In 1922 a Dr Sutherland, himself a Roman Catholic and a doctor of medicine at Edinburgh University, published a book entitled *Birth Control* in which he accused Marie Stopes of taking advantage of the ignorance of the poor to subject them to experiments of a most harmful and dangerous nature. He commented: 'It is truly amazing that this monstrous campaign on Birth Control should be tolerated by the Home Secretary. Charles Bradlaugh was condemned to jail for a less serious crime.' Marie Stopes sued Dr Sutherland and his publishers for libel.

The case came up in front of the Lord Chief Justice, Lord Hewart, during the last week of February 1923, and the defence hardly touched on the religious or theological objections to birth control of the Roman Catholic Church, but dwelt rather on the kind of arguments which might be expected to carry weight with the all-male jury. Distinguished medical men were asked whether they would leave *Married Love* lying about for their young maid-servants to read; whether it was desirable that young girls (particularly young girls of 16) should learn about such matters before marriage. Would they let their own daughters read it? Was it wise to scatter such knowledge among the uneducated classes? Would not an increased knowledge of artificial contraceptives lead to an increase in fornication? And if it was really necessary for people to know more about such matters before marriage should it not be done in private, the father in a talk to the son, the mother in a talk to the daughter?

The judge did not conceal that his sympathies lay with the defendants. But the jury, evidently unmoved by all the suggestions about their daughters, brought in a confused verdict which held that the statements made by Dr Sutherland were true, but that they were defamatory and were not fair comment and that Dr Stopes was entitled to damages. On this the judge held that Dr Stopes had lost the case. This finding was reversed in her favour by the Court of Appeal, but was reversed again in the Lords in 1924.

The voluntary campaign for birth control clinics continued on its course. Organizations of working-class housewives such as the Co-operative Guilds and Women's Sections of the Labour Party took up the campaign with fervour. And how greatly times had changed was underlined by a debate in the House of Lords which took place, oddly enough, on the very eve of the General Strike. At the time maternity and child welfare committees were not allowed by the government to give information on birth control to women attending the welfare centres. Lord Buckmaster moved on 28 April 1926 that this prohibition should be removed. On the issue of family limitation he observed:

> Some fifty years ago it was new. Its advocacy was attempted to be punished by the Criminal Law, it startled and shocked people, but today the only thing that is left is this: Will you take steps to withhold from the poor the knowledge that is possessed and practised by the rich?

On behalf of the government the Lord Privy Seal, the Marquess of Salisbury, resisted Lord Buckmaster's motion, expressing as he did so an attitude which was on its way out:

> Everybody knows that the movement for birth control is largely supported by women who could have children but who prefer not to have them – married women, women who do not do their duty, women who prefer their own ease to the obligations that they have undertaken, women whose duty not only to their husbands, but to their country, is to bear children and who will not do so . . . What is the impression which will be given to the public throughout the country? It will be said: 'The House of Lords or His Majesty's Government have agreed that henceforward, so far as their official sanction is concerned, a woman may choose for herself. It does not matter even what her husband thinks.'

But Lord Salisbury was fighting a losing battle, and this was demonstrated by the vote; Lord Buckmaster's motion was carried against the government by 57 votes to 44.

By the end of the decade discussion of such matters had ceased to be questionable and had become fairly respectable. Family planning, as it began to be called, was accepted. It made a more significant change in the lives and status of women than any other single factor. Equality with men in the economic sphere had proved to be an illusion; the introduction of women to men's jobs had turned out to be temporary; equal pay never materialized; equality of opportunity granted in theory had been denied in practice. But release from incessant involuntary child-bearing – this was a reality.

Table 25   Women aged 25–54: Proportion Working

	Single	Married
1921	70·7	8·9
1931	74·8	10·7
1966	85·5	44·4

(Source: extracted from tables in A.H.Halsey (ed.), 1972. *Trends in British Society since 1900*. This table excludes widowed and divorced.)

Table 26   Female Employment

	1911		1921		1931	
	No.	Per cent	No.	Per cent	No.	Per cent
	000		000		000	
Total females gainfully occupied	5,425	100	5,697	100	6,264	100
– of which:						
Private indoor domestic servants	1,403	26	1,072	19	1,262	20
Textile workers (skilled)	654	12	526		533	8
Other domestic, catering or personal service	375		467		551	9
Clerical workers	179	3	570	9	646	10
Leather & textile goods (skilled)	483		328		293	
Shop assistants etc	342		425		503	

(Source: Guy Routh, *Occupation and Pay in Great Britain 1906–60*.)

Table 27 Family Size: Number of children by date of marriage

	1900–9 %	1920 %	1930 %
No children	11·3	13·8	16·5
1 or 2 children	33·5	45·6	51·1
3 or 4 children	27·7	25·8	22·0
5 or more children	27·5	14·8	10·4

(Source: Halsey, op. cit., p. 55.)

14
New Enjoyments

The Car

The motor was having an impact as great as the coming of the railways in the previous century. It was altering people's habits of life in innumerable ways, influencing their choice of home, their environment, their style of living. It was creating new dangers but also new kinds of enjoyment. Motor manufacture was a growth industry which affected many other industries, demanding new skills, offering work in fresh areas. In the ten years from 1919 to 1929 it had made every town and village look different, sound different, smell different.

Motor-cars had existed before 1914, but in an undeveloped form, although hansom cabs had begun to give way to taxis and petrol-driven buses were supplanting horse-drawn ones. But electric trams were still the standard means of moving about towns. Pedal cyclists were numerous. Long-distance travel depended on the railways. Most commercial vehicles were horse-drawn. Merchandise was carried by the railways, and the roads were, to a large extent, designed to act as feeders to them. Loads which were too heavy to be taken from the railways by horse and cart were hauled away by steam locomotives which chugged along the road at the legal maximum of 4 mph. During the war development of the motor for civilian needs was held up while the manufacturers concentrated on army trucks.

In the early Twenties all the old forms of transport were still in operation, but they were being rapidly overtaken by the motor-bus, the motor-lorry, the motor-van, the long-distance motor-coach, the motor-cycle and, above all, the private motor-car. 'Be a motorist and have your own railway' was the slogan of a Scottish Motor Show in 1924.[1]

The contrast between 1919 and 1929 can be illustrated from the

London traffic counts of those years. On 14 May 1919, a fine day, a record was taken of the traffic crossing Blackfriars Bridge between 8 am and 8 pm. The bridge linked Fleet Street, the City, and Smithfield meat market with South London, and was a busy commercial thoroughfare. On that day it was crossed by 14,150 vehicles classified as follows:

Electric trams	2,012
Motor omnibuses	604
Horse-drawn trade vehicles	6,286
Motor trade vehicles	2,078
Cabs: *horse-drawn*	48
motor	885
Carriages: *horse-drawn*	24
motor	501
Cycles: *motor*	55
pedal	1,434
Barrows *etc*	223
	14,150

Ten years later the census-takers had changed their terminology and their record of the traffic crossing Blackfriars Bridge on a fine day in July 1929 looked like this:

Electric trams	2,568
Omnibuses	1,548
Light cars (a)	7,399
Heavy cars (b)	2,397
Horse-drawn carts, vans, drays	2,898
Cycles: *motor*	270
pedal	2,294
Barrows *etc*	244
	19,618

a)   i.e. private cars and taxis and motor-cycles with side cars.
b)   i.e. commercial vehicles.

On this bridge the volume of traffic had risen by 38 per cent, and its composition had changed in the following way:

	1919 per cent	1929 per cent
Horse-drawn	45	15
Petrol-driven	29	59
Electric	14	13
Pedal cycles *etc*	12	13

In 1919 a private car was an expensive luxury which only the rich could afford. They employed chauffeurs, for the older generation had never learnt to drive; moreover the cars were unreliable and repair shops scarce. Manufacturers and dealers did not, on the whole, expect to service the cars they sold, and the chauffeur had to be a mechanic as well. The sons and daughters of the wealthy took up driving themselves with enthusiasm, but they too relied on the chauffeur to look after the car.

When cars began to be mass-produced they became cheaper, and the number of owner-drivers increased rapidly. By the end of 1923 the Citroen was being advertised at £230 as the most inexpensive coupé obtainable. This was more than a skilled engineer earned in a year, but it was a figure within reach of upper middle-class and higher-paid professional people. There was also a market for second-hand cars, particularly among ex-army officers and others who had had driving experience during the war. The most reliable car for rough roads was the American Ford, known as a 'tin Lizzie'. But soon two British firms, Morris and Austin, began to dominate the market for small cheap cars. All the time they were getting safer and more reliable. Four-wheel brakes were introduced, and corded tyres. There were still many technical problems to be overcome. It was noted that when the RAC conducted its trial of small cars in May 1924 a common defect was loss of water caused by boiling on the steeper hills.

Most of the new owner-drivers took up motoring for its own sake. Driving a car, tinkering with it at weekends, was a new hobby. The cheaper mass-produced cars tended to be tourers with folding canvas hoods, so that driving was more like an open-air sport than a convenience. Many were only used in the summer for trips into the country or to the seaside. The roads were very inadequate, but they were also relatively deserted. A car meant you could 'get away from it all' a desire well understood by the advertisers. An advertisement in the *Daily Mail* for a Standard put it like this:

Every week-end a holiday. Where shall it be this week? Through highways to old world towns and villages or byways to the woods and fields; a quick straight run to the silvery sea or a dawdle amid hills and dales? Each weekend a new scene – a new delight. That is what this 'Standard' Light Car means to the family. £235 and £375.[2]

The adventurous were intoxicated by speed. The law imposed a universal speed limit of 20 mph; it was almost entirely disregarded – indeed cars were continually advertised as guaranteed to do 50, 55, 65 and even 85 mph. To the drivers speed brought a new kind of exhilaration and a sense of power. They raced one another on the main roads and tore along country lanes followed by clouds of dust. The Bright Young Things used their cars for clue-chasing games; in July 1924 the Hon. Lois Sturt was prosecuted for driving round Regent's Park at 51 mph on the wrong side of the road; it was stated in Court that a line of clues had been put down by the servants, who were stationed at various points in and around London, and the drivers had been racing one another from point to point.

The less affluent who could not afford cars shared in the gaieties and excitements of the motor age by buying motor-cycles. They scorched along the roads with as much speed and dust and rather more noise than the motorists. Young men took their girlfriends riding pillion. Sometimes there would be two people clinging on behind one rider. More utilitarian were the motor-cycles with sidecars attached. They had a number of advantages over the car. They were cheaper to buy and run, the tax was lower and the running repairs were often simple enough to be tackled by the owners themselves. In the years 1922–4 the number of motor-cyclists on the roads exceeded the number of motorists.

Even the poorest participated in the glories of the motor age. There was a new form of treat, the charabanc outing, for which you saved up for half a year in order to spend a day at the sea or at the races. Country-dwellers were sour about the charabanc crowds who invaded country pubs and were driven along quiet country lanes shouting and singing.

Initially, motorists were hampered by the absence of self-starters. This was a particular drawback for women drivers. Cranking the engine with a starting-handle was a heavy and sometimes dangerous job; a slight miscalculation and you could do yourself an injury. By the early Twenties most new cars were being equipped with electric self-starters, though there were many complaints that these were feeble and sluggish; and every car carried a starting-handle in case of emergency. Other aids to driving, such as electric windscreen-wipers, began to be installed. However, the Minister of Transport refused in 1924 to make driving mirrors compulsory, saying: 'I am not satisfied that the universal adoption of mirrors or reflectors to enable drivers to see overtaking traffic would generally assist in the prevention of accidents though their use in cases where the driver is unable to hear or see signals from behind is no doubt a convenience for overtaking traffic.'[3] Hand signals were introduced to show oncoming traffic whether the driver was turning right, left or stopping. A careful driver was expected to blow his horn at every intersection, round every bend and at any pedestrian in the road or looking as though he might step into the road. When there was an accident the magistrate usually asked the driver whether he had blown his horn; it appeared that if he had done this, he had done all that could be expected of him.

Anyone who had reached the age of 16 could buy a driving licence; one for a motor-cycle was permitted at 14; there were no learners' tests. Fast drivers were called 'road hogs' and were blamed for the rising number of accidents. A London judge remarked that road accidents would never decrease until a few motorists had been hanged.[4] Motorists blamed pedestrians for the accidents; they habitually crossed the roads without looking, it was said; they threaded their way diagonally across the streets; they stood in the road talking just near a bend; they walked along the edge of the pavement with their backs to the traffic, idly stepping off into the path of oncoming vehicles. Also blamed were pedal cyclists who, it was alleged, rode with their heads down over the handlebars not looking where they were going.

Pedestrians complained that the police did not stop motorists who were exceeding the 20 mph speed limit. But it seemed that the police had difficulty in proving that drivers were speeding. On some deserted country roads they did prove it; they set up police traps and made a rich haul in fines. The motorists complained bitterly about petty police persecution for minor breaches of regulations when no danger was involved. Elderly people found it difficult to get used to the new hazard. They continually misjudged the speed of oncoming cars, perhaps instinctively expecting them to move at a horse's pace.

In May 1924 the House of Lords debated London street accidents. It was said that walking in the streets of London was now a more dangerous occupation than coalmining. 'My experience is that the narrow escapes which most of us have from time to time do not occur in the crowded parts,' said Lord Lamington, who initiated the debate: 'You are walking along and see nothing in the shape of a motor vehicle, and then all at once you hear the swish of one of these juggernauts rushing along at a speed far in excess of twenty miles an hour. You are almost overwhelmed by it before you realize that there is any vehicle anywhere in your neighbourhood. It is not fair that these frightful risks should be incurred by the general public.'[5]

By this time the number of motor-vehicles going past Hyde Park Corner had reached over 50,000 a day. Immense traffic blocks were building up in the centre of London. Some said that the congestion was due to slow-moving horse-drawn traffic holding up the cars, others that the streets were too narrow. It was known that the Ministry of Transport was planning some major circular roads which would divert traffic round London rather than through it. In other parts of the country bypasses round built-up areas were bringing some relief.

More and more women were learning to drive and created much controversy in the correspondence columns of the newspapers. Some male motorists were affronted by the growing female participation in what should be a man's affair. An article in *The Motor* headed 'Women – and Safety Last' observed that 'Vanity, of course, is the chief reason why a woman ever seeks to learn to drive,'[6] and dwelt at length on woman's incompetence and total absence of road sense, her indecisiveness and lack of consideration for others.* But women drivers were coming on the road in ever-increasing numbers.

Women were encouraged to take up driving by the appearance in

---

* The accusation that women drivers were a danger on the road did not appear to be substantiated by the figures given to the Royal Commission on Transport in 1929. The National Safety First Organization collected figures of the cause of fatal accidents on the road from coroners' returns. 97·8 per cent of the drivers involved in these accidents were men, 2·2 per cent were women. (See *First Report of the Royal Commission*, Cmd 3365, p. 52.) This was at a time when women formed a much higher proportion of all drivers than 2·2 per cent. It was estimated that 40 per cent of volunteer drivers in the General Strike were women.

the middle Twenties of cheap mass-produced saloon cars. Bit by bit motoring was becoming less an outdoor sport than a convenient way of getting about. In 1925 for the first time the number of private cars exceeded that of motor-cycles. In the next few years the demand for small saloons rose quickly. By 1929 the Morris Cowley saloon cost £195. It was fitted with Triplex glass in every window and had chromium plating. 'So excellent is the protection from the elements provided by the modern saloon car that this type of vehicle is kept in use throughout the winter by many motorists who at one time made a practice of forgoing the driving of a car from October to March,' reported *The Motor.*[7]

Even so there were no car-heaters, so that motoring in winter was a chilly business, while the problem of freezing radiators troubled everyone. 'Fur Rugs, Foot-muffs and Fur-back gloves make ideal presents at Yule-tide,' said one advertisement to motorists. 'Foil Jack Frost in his evil designs. No necessity to empty the radiator every cold night. Just use an "Ever-Warm",' said another. The Ever-Warm was a radiator lamp. A new invention, the zip fastener, was adapted for many uses. 'Motoring Comfort is increased by equipment fitted with the Lightening Zipp Fastener,' ran one advertisement: 'Radiator muffs, overshoes, tyre covers and hundreds of other articles. ZIPP! Its Open! ZIPP! It's Closed!'

More and more police had to be put on traffic duty at busy intersections, to the neglect of their ordinary work. The Wolverhampton Town Council sent a delegation to study automatic traffic signal systems in Berlin and other continental towns and decided to instal some themselves as an experiment. Some other towns, including Manchester, followed suit. The Royal Commission on Transport in 1929 described this novel method of using red, green and amber lights at crossroads: 'We watched the system in operation at various busy crossings both at Manchester and Wolverhampton and were greatly impressed with its success. We only saw one driver cross the white line when the red light was showing and he explained that he was a stranger and did not understand the signal.'[8] Soon after, the first experimental traffic lights appeared in London.

All this time the law on motoring was derived from an Act passed in 1903. For years people had been saying that it was ridiculously out of date. At last in 1930 a Bill supported by all parties was piloted through the House by Herbert Morrison, Minister of Transport in the 1929 Labour government. It abolished the general speed limit altogether for motor-cars and motor-cycles on the recommendation of the Royal Commission, which found that the 20-mph speed limit had for long been disregarded nearly everywhere and that 'such flagrant and universal breaches of the law tend to bring the whole law of the country into contempt.' Proposals that the speed limit should be raised to 30, 35, or 40 mph were turned down on the grounds that the psychological effect of a speed limit on motorists was bad, since it encouraged them to think that if they did not exceed it they were driving safely, whereas 40 mph could be safe under certain conditions and 5 mph dangerous in others. The suggestion that a speed limit should be imposed in built-up areas only was rejected on the grounds that it was difficult to define built-up areas. A minority in the House of Commons was very worried about the decision to abolish the speed limit,* but the majority was prepared to accept the considered judgment of the Royal Commission. By this time many MPs were motorists themselves.

A proposal that licences should be granted only after a driving test was also rejected. Though Hall Caine MP named a large number of countries in which driving tests were compulsory, and insisted that the accident-rates in these countries were lower than those of Britain, the House again preferred to abide by the recommendations of the Royal Commission, which had asserted that accidents were seldom caused by beginners, but by drivers who were deficient in 'road sense' and also by a certain type of motorist quite properly called a 'road hog' who took unnecessary risks such as 'cutting in'.

Under the new Bill, however, those taking out a licence would have to make a declaration that they were not suffering from any disability which would make driving a danger. The minimum age for driving a car was raised to 17; that for riding a motor-cycle to 16. Speed trials or organized races on the road were made an offence, and penalties for dangerous driving much increased. Uniform road signs were to be enforced throughout the country. It was laid down that a motor-cycle

---

* One was Dr Salter, MP for Bermondsey, who said that 10,000 trees had been planted in his borough and every year 600 were knocked down by motor-cars. 'We found that it was due to vehicles mounting the pavement. In practically every case this was owing to the excessive speed. Being obliged to apply the brakes suddenly in order to prevent a catastrophe they mounted the pavement and knocked down the trees' (18 February 1930).

must not carry more than one pillion rider at a time, that the pillion must be properly constructed and that the person on it must ride astride. 'I think that for Miss 1930 that will present no great problem,' said Morrison.[9] The debate revealed, as such debates have so often done since, that nobody was really happy about what was being done. One MP wanted much tighter regulations over drunken driving; another regretted the hazards created by the tramways; another complained that vibration from enormous commercial vehicles was shaking down historic buildings in Oxford and Cambridge; another asked in vain that all commercial vehicles should be compelled to have pneumatic tyres.* Another spoke with emotion of the 1,782,000 horses in the country and said: 'Our success in connection with horse-breeding is one of the reasons why this country has been looked upon with so much pride.' Herbert Morrison wound up his speech by saying: 'I hope that the House will consider the Bill as a big Bill, one of the great legislative milestones that we see from time to time like the Municipal Corporations Act, the Public Health Act, the Local Government Act and so on.'[10] It was an unfortunate peroration, for only four years later much of it had to be put into reverse; a speed limit of 30 mph in built-up areas was imposed, and driving tests were introduced.

The Bill became an Act towards the end of 1930. That year road accidents reached 156,000, of which 7000 were fatal. The number of vehicles on the road reached 2 million, and of these private cars topped 1 million. In spite of accidents, motoring had ceased to be an exercise for the adventurous. It had become a quite ordinary thing.

Cinema

From the beginning to the end of the decade the cinema dominated the world of mass entertainment. Like the motor-car, it had been in its infancy before 1914. By the time the war was over, technical progress had overcome the jerkiness which had made the early films suitable for little but knockabout farce and crude melodrama, and had eliminated

---

* Pneumatic tyres were in almost universal use on cars and buses but many commercial vehicles still had solid tyres.

the long pauses between reels. Now smooth-running, full-length story pictures revealed a fast-growing mastery of the new medium. The films were shown initially in buildings designed for something else, such as music hall, but by the middle Twenties new and luxurious cinema palaces were springing up.

The virtual cessation of film production in Europe during the war gave the Americans the chance to establish supremacy. Hopes for the revival and development of the British film industry were not fulfilled. The American film companies bought up English cinema houses, and imposed block bookings on the others as a condition for allowing them to hire the most popular films.

The films were black and white and all silent; captions enabled the audience to follow the story. The sophisticated laughed at the choice of language revealed in these captions; one critic complained of their 'sickening illiteracy . . . their horrible clichés of phrase, their emphasis of the obvious, their flatulence of style'.[11] In London's West End, where cinema seats were as costly as those in a theatre, the films were accompanied by live orchestras. In the humble local 'flea-pit', where you could get in for a few pence, background music was supplied by a piano. The newest cinemas built in the late Twenties were equipped with giant organs.

Everyone went to the cinema: the well-to-do and the unemployed, the highly-educated and the hardly literate, the sophisticated and the naive. For the most part they all saw the same films. As a leisure activity the cinema superseded the music hall and competed not unsuccessfully with pub, church and political meeting. It involved much less audience participation than these other activities. At the music hall you had cheered or booed or bandied words with the comedian and joined in singing popular songs. But at the cinema you sat silent in the dark holding your girlfriend's hand. For though the earliest film audiences booed the villain in time-honoured fashion, the custom quickly died; only the habit of whistling when the lovers kissed lingered on. There was rather a lot of kissing, close up and long-drawn-out. But love scenes were subject to stringent rules. No couple was ever seen in bed together, and a minimum of clothing was required. To a later generation they were the reverse of daring. Violence on the screen, of which there was plenty, was less deliberately savage and sadistic than in later decades.

For working women the cinema eclipsed all other forms of entertainment; for men it took precedence over the football match. It
enabled innumerable people leading cramped and deprived lives to
escape into a world of glorious make-believe. The camera could
mirror and respond to the private fantasies of millions in ways never
possible before. It could move more swiftly than reality, calling up an
illusion of speed and the sensations of freedom and excitement that go
with it. Such was the appeal of the Westerns, which showed men
galloping much faster and more dangerously than on a race course,
while the prairie rolled out behind them, or of the thrillers, in which
cars tore round bends, gangsters jumped onto fast-moving trains,
escaping prisoners leapt from one rooftop to another. The camera
could create scenes of massive and unprecedented splendour, convey
sensations of space and distance. It could show turbulent crowds in
action, armies of warriors going into battle. All this, so commonplace
to later generations, was novel in the 1920s.

Robin Hood, which appeared in 1922, was a film which combined
many of these elements. Against the monumental grandeur of
Nottingham Castle (specially constructed for the purpose in Hollywood, complete with moat and drawbridge), crusaders marched with
pennants flying, and tournaments were staged. Douglas Fairbanks, the
hero, who was genuinely athletic in real life, displayed superhuman
agility, vaulting into the saddle, scaling walls, leaping chasms. Single-
handed he outwitted the army sent against him, thumbing his nose at
them like a schoolboy. It was a film for everyone, parents and children,
educated and uneducated.

The 'spectacle' films were indeed among the most expensive and
impressive. For *The Hunchback of Notre Dame*, first shown in 1923, the
cathedral was recreated in Hollywood in painstaking detail and at
enormous cost. It formed a noble background to the pygmy human
beings who, it was thought, re-enacted Victor Hugo's tale with much
talent. The story was carefully doctored to produce a happy ending.
In the same year *The Covered Wagon* was being advertised as 'The Film
Sensation of the Century'. It was an 'epic' of American pioneer history,
depicting the long trek of men and women west across the plains. For
its opening weeks in London, some real Red Indians were shipped over
and grouped in a tableau on the stage at the end of each performance.
Ben Hur, first shown in 1926, presented another 'gorgeous spectacle'

with, among other things, chariot-racing in a giant Roman circus and a battle between Roman galleys and a fleet of pirate ships. It also included scenes from the life of Christ, whose face was never seen, however. More than a million people went to *Ben Hur* at the London Tivoli before it was generally released.

The camera could create new comic situations. Harold Lloyd, amiably puzzled behind his horn-rimmed spectacles, would be seen balanced terrifyingly on a ledge at the top of a skyscraper, peering down a drop of heart-stopping dimensions at the ant-like movements of traffic below. Supreme among the comic films of the period were those of Charlie Chaplin. *The Kid*, in which Chaplin, the tramp, inadvertently becomes the foster-parent of a small boy (Jackie Coogan), came out as early as 1920. In 1925 came *The Gold Rush*; it included one episode only possible on a film; the log hut of Chaplin and his mate is blown to the edge of a cliff and a little beyond; they are inside and unconscious of what is happening. This scene lasted nearly a quarter of an hour, during which audiences became exhausted with laughter.

Another technical innovation was the animated cartoon. The adventures of Felix the Cat who kept on walking were very popular until superseded by Mickey Mouse, a character who first appeared in 1928 in a cartoon created by Walt Disney, a young man of 27.

The 'star' system was deliberately fostered by the film companies so that people should queue up to see their favourite no matter in what film. The great 'stars' of the period included Rudolph Valentino, who first appeared in the *Four Horsemen of the Apocalypse* in 1920; Ramon Novarro, who starred in *Ben Hur* among many other films; Adolphe Menjou, who acted in polished drawing-room comedies; Tom Mix, the hero of innumerable Westerns; Gloria Swanson, who appeared in love dramas; the slinky Pola Negri; the bouncing Clara Bow, known as the 'It' girl ('It' meant sex appeal). By the late Twenties Greta Garbo had taken her place as a star who promised to outshine all others.

In 1927 Cecil B. de Mille produced his spectacle *The King of Kings*. It was Hollywood's version of the life of Jesus Christ. Despite the careful reverence with which the subject was treated the film deeply offended many people whose feelings on the matter did not quite coincide with those of Hollywood.

But something else was bringing spectacle films to a temporary halt. In 1928 appeared the announcement: 'See and hear Al Jolson in

The Jazz Singer with Vitaphone; A Singing and Talking Film.' The advent of sound plunged Hollywood into confusion. As cinema houses began to be wired for it many stars were subject to premature fade-out; their voices and manner of speech did not, unfortunately, match up to their appearance. For a time visual considerations took second place to the technical problems of synchronizing sound with sight. Everything that had made the camera unique as a medium was over-looked, and film directors, convinced that all they needed to do was to transfer existing stage plays to Hollywood and photograph them, produced what some said were the worst films of the decade. Initially the new soundtracks were excruciating, and grossly distorted speech and song. But the technical problems were quickly overcome. Before the decade was over Metro-Goldwyn-Meyer had set a new fashion with *The Broadway Melody*, the first film musical comedy, with singing and dancing and chorus work. It had vitality and pace and heralded a new generation of song and dance films to be born in the Thirties.

Radio

While the cinema was revolutionizing mass entertainment, the radio was transforming life at home. By 1931 one family in three had a wireless set. Ten years earlier people had hardly heard of wireless except as a means of sending messages to ships at sea. But as with so much else, the war had proved a forcing house for its technical develop-ment, and by 1920 the manufacturers had begun to be aware of its commercial potentialities. There were already several thousand amateur enthusiasts dabbling in the new science in their own homes, both sending and receiving messages. Among them were ex-soldiers, sailors and airmen who had come out of the war equipped with techni-cal knowledge.

The possibilities of wireless were being demonstrated in America, where hundreds of radio stations had been set up by private firms. They were broadcasting gramophone records and concerts; the result had been a boom in demand for receiving sets. Soon the station owners were financing programmes by selling advertising time. The multiplicity of broadcasting stations was leading to competition for wavelengths and much interference and confusion in the air.

In Britain, the Post Office had been in control of wireless telegraphy since 1904, and had power to issue licences to transmitters and receivers of wireless signals. The Postmaster General, who was a member of the government, now faced some difficult choices. The kind of chaos which competing enterprise on the American pattern could cause in a small country like Britain was unthinkable. Moreover in the armed services departments there was already concern lest the proper use of the ether waves by the army, navy and airforce should be jeopardized by concerts and other frivolities. On the other hand, it would be politically unacceptable to allow broadcasting to be concentrated in the hands of one company only – for example the Marconi Company – thus giving to a private concern a monopoly of this new means of communication. In the end, after a period of indecision, the manufacturers came together to form the British Broadcasting Company, which was to be licensed by the Post Office to build broadcasting stations and to transmit programmes. The project was to be financed by the sale of receiving licences at 10s a year. Any British wireless manufacturer could have shares in the Company, which was however limited to the payment of a nominal dividend only. The reward to the manufacturers was expected to come from the sale of receiving sets and components.

The BBC began regular broadcasting in November 1922. By March 1923, 125,000 people had receiving licences, and it was thought that probably about 200,000 'home constructors' were listening without a licence. The status of the 'home constructors' was regularized a little later and by the end of 1924 the number of licences had topped 1 million. In 1927 the Company was transformed into the British Broadcasting Corporation, an independent, publicly-appointed, body, with which the manufacturers no longer had any connection. It continued to be called the BBC.

The home constructors who assembled their own sets did so partly because it was cheaper. The amateur sets looked to the uninitiated like a jumble of wires and components clustered together on a bench. But the ready-made sets were scarcely more compact. Most people listened through earphones; a loudspeaker was a separate attachment, a large free-standing horn, perhaps 2 ft high. Loudspeakers distorted the sound unless it came from a very high-powered and expensive set. A two-valve set with one pair of earphones cost about £25 in 1923; a four-valve set £35. If a loudspeaker was added it would cost an extra £6. One firm recommended, in addition, a 'power amplifier' costing £27. This was at a time when the average earnings of a skilled industrial worker were £3 6s. So a high proportion of listeners depended on a simple crystal set with earphones, and the quality of the sound that came to them was often superior to that through the loudspeaker on a much more powerful set.

During 1923 the BBC was broadcasting from 6 stations; London, Birmingham, Manchester, Cardiff, Newcastle and Glasgow. It was reckoned that the simple crystal set had a range of 20 miles through the earphones, a one-valve set 30 miles, a two-valve set 50–80 miles, and a four-valve set 120–250 miles. To get good results through a loudspeaker, one or two extra valves were needed in each case.

In its first issue, published on 28 September 1923, the *Radio Times* gave hints on aerials:

Before deciding what sort of wireless set the intending listener should buy, he must consider the following. Firstly, what is the best aerial he can erect? The deciding factor in this case is height, and we will take as standard a single wire aerial 40 ft high and 60 ft long with the lead in the ground floor. Of equal importance is the earth connection which should be to a main water pipe or to an earth plate sunk in the ground.

Two or three years later, ways of achieving the same result with an indoor aerial were being advertised. For example.

Don't spoil your garden with a clumsy pole, with its mass of wires and ugly china insulators . . . A simple, indoor (Electron or Superial) Aerial may be looped in the loft out of sight, one end tied to the rafters and looped back again, the other end brought under the eaves direct to the set through the nearest window.[12]

Expense was not the only reason why so many people built their own sets. Wireless had its own special fascination, particularly for a rising generation of schoolboys. Teachers were surprised to find that boys classed as dull at their lessons had often absorbed a knowledge of radio much in advance of their elders, and had acquired a scientific vocabulary in connection with it which they had certainly not been taught at school. Boys were saving their pennies to buy components and persuading their parents to let them build sets. For them, building the set and fiddling with the reception was much more important than listening to the programmes put out by the BBC. A *Radio Times* correspondent described such activities in his own village.

There are forty-one houses and cottages in it and in those dwellings are sixteen sets . . . None of the sets, I believe, has been installed by strangers. Two at least were the unaided work of the owners. Most if not all of the others I fancy the wheelwright's son was responsible for. The repository of wireless theory in the village from the beginning has been the parson's son.[13]

The rural communities were among the keenest. Villagers were never again going to feel as isolated from the rest of the world as they had done before. They were helped by the improvement in reception which followed the construction of the biggest transmitting station in the world at Daventry in Northamptonshire in the summer of 1925. It meant that 85 per cent of the population could listen in even with a crystal set. There were some villages with a wireless in every house. Village pubs began to install radios with powerful loudspeakers. There were grumbles about oscillation – a high-pitched howling and whistling. But sets were getting cheaper. Soon a two-valve set could be bought for under £10.

The programmes were limited by commercial and sectional pressures. Chief of these was the powerful newspaper lobby, from the beginning hostile to the BBC, regarding it as an unfair competitor. The newspapers secured the prohibition of news broadcasts earlier than 7 pm and were able to impose a condition that any news given out must be obtained and paid for from the news agencies. These restrictions were dropped during the General Strike when, in the absence of newspapers, the BBC was permitted to give out news five times a day and found itself not particularly well equipped for the task. Directly the Strike was over, the 7 o'clock news rule was reapplied, though in 1930 it was modified to allow news bulletins to be read at 6 o'clock.

In addition to this, and much more limiting for the development of the new medium, the newspapers were able to prevent running commentaries on sporting events, and even to restrict eye-witness descriptions of public ceremonies and the relaying of important speeches. Meanwhile the Postmaster General intimated that the BBC was expected to avoid matters of political and industrial controversy.

Most of the entertainment industry also looked on the BBC as a threat to their prosperity. The theatre managers believed that listening at home could mean a drop in box office returns, so they barred live broadcasts from theatres. So did the managers of the music halls, which had been in decline since the advent of the cinema. They also put pressure on performers to refuse broadcasting engagements. The manager of the Queen's Hall, London's leading concert hall, banned its use to the BBC and stopped artists under his control from broadcasting. The ban was not just used to prevent the relay of concerts. In 1923 the BBC tried to arrange a live broadcast of the speeches of the Prince of Wales and Earl Haig to the annual meeting of the British Legion, but the Queen's Hall authorities refused to allow the microphones to be installed. Gramophone companies were among the few to take a different attitude. They were acute enough to recognize that broadcasting could stimulate their sales.

The programmes were also influenced by the personal outlook of the BBC's Managing Director, John Reith, a deeply religious man who saw broadcasting in terms of high moral responsibility and was determined to give the public what he thought they ought to have. This influence was particularly marked on Sundays, when daytime broadcasting might be expected to command its largest audience. Though music was broadcast on most mornings during the week, on Sunday mornings there was silence, while frivolous items were carefully excluded on Sunday afternoons and evenings.

The following was the programme for Whit Sunday, 23 May 1926:

3.30–4.40 A popular orchestral concert from the wireless orchestra conducted by Herman Finck, including Masque 'The Merchant of Venice' (Sullivan); selections from a Midsummer Night's Dream (Mendelssohn); Suite, 'Choppiano' (arranged by Finck); Roy Henderson, baritone, singing 'Largo al Factotum' (Rossini) and other songs by Frank Bridge and Arthur Sandford.

4.40–5.30 Orchestral works by Herman Finck, including 'March of the Giants'; Entract, 'Idle Dreams'; Pot Pourri, 'Finckiana'; Dance Suite, 'Vive La Danse' etc.

5.30–6.00 Shakespeare's heroines, No. 4. Three scenes from the Merchant of Venice with Cathleen Nesbit as Portia.

6.00–6.30 Close Down.

6.30–7.45 Service from Carlisle Cathedral with address by the Bishop of Carlisle.

8.00–8.10 Bow Bells rung by the Ancient Society of College Youths relayed from St Mary-le-Bow.

8.10–8.55 Wesley Memorial Service.

8.55–9.00 The Week's Good Cause: The John Groom Crippleage and Flower Girl's Mission.

9.00–9.15 Weather forecast and news.

9.15–10.30 Albert Sandler, violinist, and the Grand Hotel, Eastbourne orchestra with Kate Winter, soprano in a concert of popular classics by Liszt, Haydn, Mendelssohn, Verdi, Gounod, Kreisler.

10.30 Close Down.

The programme for Whit Monday, a Bank Holiday, was a bit jollier:

10.30 Changing of the Guard relayed from Buckingham Palace Courtyard.

3.00–5.00 Popular Orchestral Programme with Fred Lake (tenor) Grace Ivell and Vivian Worth (songs at the piano) Louis Hertel (Entertainer).

5.00–5.15 'Le Lac' and its author by Mdme de Walmont.

5.15–6.00 For the children.

6.00–6.40 Talk by the Wireless League.

7.00–7.25 Weather forecast and 1st News Bulletin. Desmond MacCarthy: Literary Criticism.

7.25–7.40 Mozart piano sonata.

7.40–8.00 A.W.Carr (England's Cricket Captain) talking on the Test Matches.

8.00–9.00 The Royal Park's Band with soloist singers relayed from Hyde Park Bandstand.

9.30–10.00 Weather and second General News Bulletin. Mr L. de G. Sieveking reading from Kathleen Mansfield's works.

10.00–11.00 Special Empire Day programme.

11.00 Close Down.

There was much music to remind the older generation of good times in the pre-war days, for example 'Palm Court Hotel' music, and military bands. More to the liking of the younger generation was the post-war jazz music from America. On most weekday evenings the last item was dance music by Jack Payne and his orchestra or the Savoy Orpheans. Dancing meant the foxtrot, the Charleston, the 'blues', with the odd tango and slow waltz thrown in. It meant the saxophone, and syncopated rhythms surging out with a gaiety and vitality that was new. Jack Payne argued that syncopated music was popular simply because it was so cheerful and 'we all want to be happy'.[14] The words were very often happy too. Like the song hit of 1927–8:

> Sing Halleluja! Halleluja!
> And you shoo the
> Blues away!

Children's Hour between 5 and 6 pm had a wide audience. Variety and revue programmes were popular. But radio drama was in its infancy. 'Quiz games' and other radio features of the kind had hardly begun. Among those who got most out of radio were the serious music-lovers, those for whom a live concert had been a rare treat, but who could now familiarize themselves with the works of great classical composers, and hear world-famous performers previously only read about. The BBC enriched the lives of existing music-lovers and enlarged their number.

After 1927 the BBC was at last able to break the ban on running commentaries of sporting events, and rapidly developed a new technique in eye-witness descriptions of football matches, cricket matches, Wimbledon tennis, the Boat Race. The Derby became a high-speed *tour de force* spoken in an accelerating crescendo of excitement. The quality of the loudspeakers was improving all the time, and listeners began to rely less on earphones. By 1929 radio sets had become more compact. There were portable sets which did not need elaborate aerials, and sets that could be run off the mains with no batteries to be replaced or accumulators to be recharged.

As loudspeakers developed, people began to value the radio as background music rather than as an occasion for which you sat down and listened with conscious deliberation. By 1930 the radio was, like the car, an ordinary thing. It had a comfortably familiar sound when you got back from work, a sound which was as much part of home as the fire in the grate or the cup of tea on the table.

Table 28 Number of Road Vehicle Licences

Quarter ending 31 August	Cars 000	Motor Cycles 000	Commercial 000	Buses 000	Total Motor 000	Horse-drawn 000
1922	315	378	151	78	976	233
1923	383	430	173	86	1,132	207
1924	473	495	203	94	1,326	179
1925	579	571	224	99	1,537	151
1926	676	629	248	99	1,718	126
1927	778	672	276	96	1,889	103
1928	877	691	294	93	2,028	83
1929	970	705	318	96	2,163	66
1930	1,042	699	334	99	2,251	52

(Source: *Statistical Abstract for the United Kingdom*, No. 78.)

Table 29 Wireless Licences Current at 31 March

1922–3	125,000
1923–4	748,000
1924–5	1,350,000
1925–6	1,960,000
1926–7	2,270,000
1927–8	2,488,000
1928–9	2,730,000
1929–30	3,091,000
1930–1	3,647,000

(Source: *Statistical Abstract for the United Kingdom*, no. 78.)

15
Second Thoughts about the War

By the late Twenties a marked change in attitudes to the 1914–18 war had come about. Bit by bit the orthodox view of the war which had prevailed only 10 years earlier had been discarded.

In 1919 most people still took it for granted that the war had been fought for a noble purpose. Britain had been bound in honour to enter the struggle for the preservation of freedom and the rights of small nations, it was said. Now it was over, we must make Germany pay.

While the war was on, few civilians had had a very clear idea of its physical realities, or of the feelings of those who were doing the fighting. Soldiers home on leave found it difficult to share their thoughts with those at home, who in turn derived their picture of life in the front line from newspapers which habitually hid quite as much as they revealed, and from streams of war fiction which laid stress on the splendid and heroic aspects of the war and the wonderful spirit of both officers and men. Famous among such war books was Ian Hay's *The First Hundred Thousand*, which came out in 1915 and told the story of a unit of Kitchener's army, one among 'those battered decimated indomitable legions which saved us from utter extinction at the beginning'.

After the Armistice books of another kind began slowly to appear, revealing a less conventional and more disturbing attitude to the war. One of the earliest was a novel by A. P. Herbert called *The Secret Battle*, about a young man who had joined up imbued with idealistic eagerness for self-sacrifice, but who, after displaying great bravery and endurance, was eventually shot for cowardice. The book came out in 1919. It made little impact. Neither did the poems of Siegfried Sassoon, which appeared in 1918 and amounted to a savage repudiation of the war. Wilfred Owen had been killed in the last week of the war; his poems were published posthumously in 1920. 'My subject is War and the pity of War . . . All a poet can do today is warn,' he had written in a preface. Some of the war poems of Isaac Rosenberg, who was killed in 1918, came out in 1922.

The quality of writers like Owen, Sassoon and Rosenberg came to be recognized by a later generation. In the years just after the war they were hardly noticed outside a small circle of intellectuals and dedicated pacifists. Rupert Brooke, who had died on his way to Gallipoli in 1915, was the most highly regarded poet; he had been fired with enthusiasm for the war. 'Now God be thanked Who has matched us with His hour, And caught our youth, and wakened us from sleeping,' he had written on the outbreak. His *1914 and Other Poems* had been a best-seller after his death.

Less than 10 years later a very different mood prevailed. Part of the change was of course attributable to the spread of socialist ideas, and to the growing influence of the Labour movement. The Labour Party's declared aim, for example, in 1928 was to establish peace 'by renouncing war as an instrument of national policy, by disarmament, by political and economic cooperation through the League of Nations'.[1] But the changed attitude was not confined to Labour and its supporters; it went much wider.

Many things had helped to undermine the old ideas about the war, not least disenchantment with the peace that had followed it. It was hard to go on believing that it had been a war to end wars and to make the world safe for democracy. The promises of a land fit for heroes had not materialized. Some people had done well out of the war, but it was not the returned soldiers, nor the bereaved parents and widows. A new generation was growing up anxious to test the validity of its parents' assumptions. 'Debunking' myths about the war became popular.

The new attitude showed itself from about 1928 onwards in a flood of war memoirs and war novels of a new kind. Simultaneously some earlier war books which had not done well at the time were quickly reprinted. Suddenly the publishers who had avoided war books could not get enough of them. Many were written by authors who had served as junior officers. Once no one had wanted to share their thoughts. Now the opposite was true. Some of the books were of lasting value, and were still being reprinted and read 40 years after. Most were of less consequence and soon forgotten. They had one thing in common: they challenged the orthodox view of the war.

Inevitably most of them faced up to the physical realities of war; the prolonged shellfire which stupefied and drove men mad, the wounded who died in no-man's-land calling for help which never came, the endless mud, the corpses that swelled and stank, the bloated flies in the Gallipoli campaign, the well-fed rats on the Western front. They were attacked in *The Times* for so doing. In an outburst of irritation a leading article declared that some contemporary authors were 'determined, like the old fresco painters when they pictured Hell, so to scare, horrify and revolt the reader that he shall never think of war again without trembling and nausea'.[2]

Yet the suggestion that the war books dwelt on horror for horror's sake was misleading. Indeed, among the more chilling were those in which physical horrors were referred to only casually, as though part of a landscape so familiar as to be taken for granted. One of the most celebrated, Edmund Blunden's *Undertones of War*, which came out in 1928, scarcely mentioned horrors at all.

The chief characteristic common to the new books was that their authors had ceased to assume that the war had been fought for a noble purpose. They expressed a growing uncertainty about motives on both sides. People were not now sure that Germany had been solely to blame. And many of those who thought the war had been unavoidable also believed that it had been unnecessarily and brutally prolonged by the Allied governments for ignoble purposes. Some of the books merely threw doubt on these central questions. Others made clear the conviction of their authors that the war had been, in the words of Siegfried Sassoon, 'a crime against humanity'.

Around these central issues crowded a host of subsidiary themes: the imbecile bureaucracy, the helplessness of the individual in the clutches of the military machine, the blunders of the higher command who nonchalantly sent courageous and idealistic young men to their deaths, the futility of life in the army where so much time was spent drearily undoing work which others had previously carried out, and where men were so often marched long distances for no apparent purpose than to be marched back again exhausted. Another subsidiary theme was the mendacity of the newspapers, which had invented tales of German atrocities and given civilians an entirely false picture of the state of affairs at the front. Another was the complacency of the Church, always so certain that God was on the side of the Allies.

Preaching in St Paul's Cathedral in 1928, on the 10th anniversary of the Armistice, Dr Lang, Archbishop of Canterbury, showed himself acutely aware of the new unease. He did his best to reassure those among the bereaved who, surrounded by a loss of faith in the justice of the war, found it difficult to bear:

> The bravery and self-sacrifice which met the onslaught of war, which . . . kept the honour of the nation's pledged word and defended and preserved its freedom – were they worth while? Surely the answer must ever be a strong and thankful 'yes'. To answer otherwise would be to wrong not only the memory of the dead but the heart of the living.

And he quoted the words of a man who had said to him: 'To think otherwise would be enough to drive me out of my mind. It would mean that my fine son was thrown away.'[3]

It was with the subsidiary themes, rather than the central issue, that R. C. Sherriff's enormously popular war play *Journey's End* was primarily concerned. It opened at the Savoy Theatre in January 1929, after having been rejected by most of the London theatre managements. The action of this play was set in a dugout on the Western front. The hero, Stanhope, a courageous and much respected officer, had been three years in the trenches and now only kept himself going with the help of the whisky bottle. The nearest thing to doubt about the objects of the war in general came in a casual reference to the Germans as being 'really quite decent . . . outside the newspapers', and the suggestion that blowing one another's trenches to blazes seemed rather silly. But the picture of life at the front, and the grim inevitability of death which overshadowed the play from first to last, came as a shock to a younger generation who had been brought up to think of the war as a splendid if terrible affair. Some got from it an anti-war message to which others remained deaf. All were utterly gripped by it. The play's commercial success may have been partly due to the fact that it clung to a convention familiar to West End audiences: the leading characters were ex-public school boys, and their attitudes, emotions, interests and conversation were those commonly associated with the public school. So acceptable was it that a special performance was staged for men who had won the vc. while the bbc, a body very sensitive to what was and was not fitting, broadcast a studio performance on the evening of Armistice Day, 1929. At the end of the year the Editor of the *Radio Times* invited readers to name the broadcast item they had enjoyed most in 1929. *Journey's End* came top of the list.

Unlike *Journey's End*, there was no mistaking the message of many of the war books which came out in 1929 and 1930. They included Robert Graves's autobiography *Goodbye to All That*, in which the author, who had served as an officer in the Royal Welch Fusiliers, described his growing conviction that the war was merely a sacrifice of the idealistic younger generation to the stupidity and self-protective alarm of the elder. *Goodbye to All That* touched on nearly all the sub-sidiary themes: the offensive behaviour of the regular officers to those among them who had not the correct public school/Sandhurst back-ground; the 'Quetta manners'; the bayonet instructors who ordered men to HATE the Germans ('Hurt him now! In at the belly! Tear his guts out!'); the blunders of the higher command who, for example, launched a gas attack in a dead calm so that their own side were gassed despite frantic messages from those on the spot; the flights of journalis-tic imagination in the newspapers. ('The battalion enjoyed the bit about how they had gone over the top shouting "Remember Kitchener" and "Avenge the Lusitania". "What a damn silly thing to shout," said someone.')

Among the war novels of 1929 was Richard Aldington's *Death of a Hero*, with a prologue which read like an angry manifesto. But the novel that made the greatest impact was the translation of one which came from Germany, Erich Maria Remarque's *All Quiet on the Western Front*. This was the war seen through the eyes of a very young soldier serving in the ranks. It described the physical terror and de-gradation of war with shattering effect. It also conveyed the decency and loyalty shown by men to one another when near to death, the comradeship which in retrospect was for some the only redeeming feature of the war. This story of a German soldier seemed to mirror the experiences of his British counterpart. Here was the same behaviour under fire, the same sensation of not belonging when on leave, the same press bromides for civilians, the same petty tyrannies in training camp. Robert Graves's joke about a system in which the old men would fight while the young ones stayed at home was matched in *All Quiet* by a proposal that the politicians and generals from both sides should be armed with cudgels and made to fight it out among themselves, while every one else paid for their seats as at a bullfight, and looked on with the band playing. The message of *All Quiet*, though never spelt out, was very clear. Ordinary people of different countries had no quarrel with one another, had indeed a greater affinity with one another than they had with their own rulers. Those who had done the fighting and the dying had been, on both sides, the victims of a monstrous deception.

The English edition of *All Quiet* first came out in April 1929. By September it had already been reprinted 19 times and sold 260,000 copies. That year other war books from abroad included Ernest Hemingway's *A Farewell to Arms*, a love story set against the Italian retreat after Caporetto, and Arnold Zweig's *The Case of Sergeant Grischa*. The output and sale of war books, some very mediocre, continued to boom. The reading public, it seemed, was at last determined to find out 'the truth about the war'.

As though anxious to restore the war's former image, on 11 November 1929 the British Legion staged in the Albert Hall a 'Festival of Empire and Remembrance' at which old wartime songs like 'Tipperary' were sung. A curtain drawn aside above the organ disclosed a Field of Remembrance with a white cross standing amid poppies; with bands playing and flags unfurled, holders of the v c marched in, followed by representatives of all the services, including the Boy Scouts and Girl Guides. Carrie Tubb sang 'How Sleep the Brave?' There was a tableau of Britannia and her Empire. When the Prince of Wales appeared the audience of thousands burst spontaneously into 'For he's a Jolly Good Fellow'. At the end, the Hall was darkened, the notes of the Last Post were sounded, and the lines of Laurence Binyon, 'They shall not grow old as we that are left grow old,' were quietly read.

In spite of such endeavours, those who thought that the new books distorted the truth about the war were finding it difficult to make their voices heard. One writer, Douglas Jerrold, was full of indignation at the slur cast on the motives and behaviour of those who had fought, and was bitter at the suggestions that the war had been useless, futile and wicked. In a booklet published early in 1930 entitled *The Lie About the War* he conducted a polemic against some 16 books currently on sale at his favourite bookshop,* alleging that they presented a picture

---

* The books attacked by Jerrold were: *Under Fire* by Henri Barbusse (1918); *The Secret Battle* by A.P.Herbert (1919, but reprinted in 1929 with a special introduction by

of the war which was fundamentally false even when superficially true. To suggest that they told the truth about the war, he argued, was as ridiculous as to suggest that Dostoevsky was the man who told the truth about Western civilization. The war, he affirmed, could have been avoided only by the sacrifice of honourable principles honourably held. Evidently inspired by the voice of Jerrold, *The Times* leader already referred to appeared on 10 April 1930, asking how it was possible that only 12 years after the war ended 'the new legend of the War, almost as naked of truth as the Emperor of his clothes' could have succeeded 'with so many qualified to accuse its nakedness'. The flood of war books 'is only now receding and showing us what deposit it has left upon fair pastures . . . It is testimony to the sticking power of mud that, twelve years after demobilization, the Army should be appearing before an unofficial Court-martial.'[4]

This leader was accompanied by a correspondence in which even *Journey's End* (specifically exonerated by *The Times*) did not escape stricture. Generals and colonels wrote in to deny that officers had been heavy drinkers, and one letter suggested that if officers had really behaved as in *Journey's End* 'we should certainly have lost the war'.[5]

In assuming that the flood of war books was by this time receding, *The Times* was premature. That year (1930) saw the publication of many more, including Siegfried Sassoon's fictional autobiography *Memoirs of an Infantry Officer*, which described how the author renounced war and threw away his Military Cross, and Richard Aldington's *Roads to Glory*, which contained among other things a short story about an English captain meditating over a German grave

---

Winston Churchill); *The Enormous Room* by E.E. Cummings (1922); *The Spanish Farm* by R.H. Mottram (1924); *Rough Justice* by C.E. Montagu (1926); *These Men Thy Friends* by Edward Thompson (1927); *War Birds*, Anon. (1927); *Goodbye to All That* by Robert Graves (1929); *Death of a Hero* by Richard Aldington (1929); *Red Cavalry* by Babel (1929); *The Storm of Steel* by Ernst Junger (1929); *A Farewell to Arms* by Ernest Hemingway (1929); *Squad* by James B. Wharton (1929); *The Path of Glory* by George Blake (1929); *The Case of Sergeant Grischa* by Arnold Zweig (1929); *All Quiet on the Western Front* by Erich Maria Remarque (1929).

Of these books, Jerrold appeared most to dislike the Hemingway: 'As to Mr Hemingway's hero, it is impossible to write of him with reasonable restraint. A man who breaks his enagagements, deserts at the height of a battle, and aids and abets the desertion with him of a nurse whom he has seduced, would on any reading not be a man I should care to meet except in circumstances which allowed me to say what I thought about him . . . This unspeakable cad . . .' etc.

and saying: 'Brother, what have we done to each other?' There was also Frederick Manning's *Her Privates We*, one of the few books written through the eyes of a man in the ranks. From abroad came Jaroslav Hasek's satire *The Good Soldier Schweik*.

Few of the writers of the British books subscribed to what was already the accepted view in the Labour movement, that the war had been caused by imperialist rivalries, and that the capitalist system had within it forces which drove countries to war. Indeed the authors attributed the war to a variety of causes, including militarism, stupidity, greed, fear and even overpopulation. They had an immense influence on the reading public, and formed the background to the peace movements of the Thirties, including the celebrated Oxford resolution of 1933 ('That this House will in no circumstances fight for its King and Country'), the formation of the Peace Pledge Union and the Peace Ballot of 1935. They made it certain that people would never again go into a war with the illusions of 1914.

16
The End of the Decade

The atmosphere at the end of the decade was very different from that which had prevailed at its beginning. 'Make Germany Pay' had given place to a tentative hope that the League of Nations might save mankind from future wars. In the same period many rigid social conventions had been discarded. Theories about the working of the human mind and about human behaviour which had seemed revolutionary in 1920 were taken for granted, by 1930. Greater frankness about sex offered the chance of happier personal relationships.

Women had achieved a new independence, dramatically illustrated by Amy Johnson's hazardous solo flight to Australia in 1930. She was a trained mechanic as well as a pilot. By that year most young married women were consciously deciding for themselves whether to have babies and if so how many, whereas 10 years earlier it was more likely to have been nature which decided. As a result the birth-rate fell from 25·5 per thousand population in England and Wales to 16·3. But many more babies were surviving. Infant mortality per 1000 births had dropped from 80 in 1920 to 60 in 1930.

New industries had transformed everyday life. Cars and radios were now commonplace. Electrical appliances had brought more comfort and convenience into the home. Less and less money was going on alcohol, more and more on the cinema and football.

But side by side with the signs of prosperity for some had come privation for others. Since 1921 there had not been a single month when the number of workless had fallen below a million. It was in the main the older basic industries – coalmining, iron and steel, shipbuilding, cotton – which seemed unable to escape from depression. Since most of them were concentrated in the North and Wales, unemployment had begun bit by bit to take on a new geographical pattern. By the end of the decade this pattern was clearly defined, and funds were organized for the relief of what had come to be called the Distressed Areas. The Prince of Wales visited them and met skilled colliers who had not worked for 5 years, housewives who sent the whole family to bed on washday because they had no change of linen, children who never tasted milk.

In spite of the strains and stresses through which society had passed, its foundations had remained relatively undisturbed. The criticism made so forcefully by the Webbs in 1920 when they observed that nine tenths of all accumulated wealth belonged to one tenth of the population was still as valid as ever. Just as marked was what they had described as the 'central wrong of the capitalist system': 'the power which the mere ownership of the instruments of production gives to a relatively small section of the community'.[1] The pressure of the Labour movement had not resulted in any change in these fundamentals. The confident hopes of the miners in 1919 that the coal-mines would be nationalized had been dissipated. Indeed, nearly everything the miners had gained in the immediate post-war years had been taken from them, even their seven-hour day.

There had been no advance towards the 'common ownership of the means of production' which had been embodied as an aim in the Labour Party's new constitution in 1918. Instead there had been a very considerable growth of state activity, much of it designed to improve the living standards of working people. There had been new social legislation of enormous consequence to future generations, including the birth and growth of council housing, the first contributory pension scheme for the elderly, and major developments in unemployment insurance. The existence of unemployment benefit, pushed up to something approaching the levels needed for maintenance and extended over many months for the long-term unemployed after 1924, greatly hindered the drive to bring down wages, a drive which hardly let up throughout the whole of the decade, though falling prices meant that there was little reduction in real wages in the long run for most industrial workers.

The defensive strength of the trade unions, though still very considerable, had however been weakened in the aftermath of the General Strike. Membership affiliated to the TUC had declined to 3·7 million, as compared with 6·5 million in 1920. Part of the loss arose from the Trades Disputes Act, passed by the Baldwin government in 1927, which had severed members employed in government service from the TUC. At annual congresses nobody discussed the merits of 'direct action' as they had done in the heady days of 1920. Indeed the TUC had outlawed its chief advocates, the Minority Movement and the National Unemployed Workers' Movement, prohibiting local trades councils from further association with either. On the TUC General Council the desire to avoid repetition of large-scale conflicts such as the General Strike was now overwhelming. The members had turned instead to the possibilities of improved industrial relations through a policy that became known as 'Mondism'. They thought in terms of cooperation with employers in the reorganization of industry, in return for trade union recognition and consultation. Labour's paper, the *Daily Herald*, had long lost the revolutionary fervour of its early post-war days and appeared anxious to demonstrate its respectability to its readers, who by this time numbered a million.

At local level the mood of hope and confidence which had shown itself during the General Strike had evaporated. There was little left of it but an instinct of class solidarity more marked than in earlier decades. 'We're all Labour here,' it would be said over and over again to door-to-door canvassers at election time. The members of the households concerned were quite impervious to arguments from either right or left; it was simply that Labour was 'us' and all other parties 'them'.

Rather like the TUC, by 1929 the leaders of the Labour Party seemed anxious to parade their attitudes of moderation. Ramsay MacDonald had long since and with some difficulty persuaded his followers that the ballot box was the sole key to social change. But he and his closest colleagues appeared now to have lost much of their appetite for change itself. The Party's 1929 general election manifesto showed little anxiety to storm the citadels of financial and industrial power. True, there was a promise to nationalize the mines (without which the support of the mining areas might have been in jeopardy), but it was a pledge that stood in splendid isolation. Otherwise there was a promise to deal with unemployment by schemes of national development, and a list of measures to improve existing social legislation. It was markedly less radical than the manifesto which had heralded the return of the 1924 Labour government, which had called for state ownership of mines, railways and power stations, and a capital levy.

Returned as the largest single party, but still with no over-all majority, the second Labour government came into being in June 1929, once more a minority government, dependent on the support or forbearance of the Conservatives or Liberals in the House for whatever it wanted to do. The supreme issue was unemployment, and on this it did little but fumble for its first year of office, to the growing discontent of its supporters.[2] There was even much hesitation concerning the abolition of the 'not genuinely seeking work' disqualification for unemployment benefit, which had caused mounting indignation in the distressed areas. But it was not finally abolished until there had been a behind-the-scenes revolt by the trade union group of Labour MPs.

The vast work schemes of road-building and other industrial developments which everyone had thought would be put in hand seemed slow to materialize, even though these had not only been prominent in the Party's pre-election programme but had also formed a major plank in that of the Liberal Party, which had put forward detailed plans with the help and approval of J. M. Keynes. But this was before the era of 'managed capitalism', and the Treasury experts and industrialists and financiers called in for consultation by the government were all pulling in different directions, so the upshot was that little was done to provide work.

In any case government moves were being rapidly overtaken by events in the outside world. The Wall Street crash in the autumn of 1929 was followed by an economic crisis in the United States of a magnitude never seen before. It spread rapidly to country after country, each of which was engulfed in turn. It was immeasurably the worst depression ever known, and except for the Soviet Union no nation escaped, both advanced industrial countries and backward colonial countries suffering its devastating impact. In Britain unemployment, which had totalled 1·1 million when the Labour government first took office, rose steadily, reaching 2·8 million by August 1931. Twenty-two per cent of all insured workers were unemployed.

It was at this point that an acute financial emergency was superimposed on the trade depression. There was a crisis of confidence in the pound and a drain on gold. At Cabinet level it was argued that drastic economies in government spending, including pay cuts for the armed forces, civil servants and teachers, were urgently needed to restore confidence, otherwise the pound would collapse. But when a proposal for major cuts in unemployment benefit came before it, the

Labour Cabinet was divided. This was the supreme issue around which conflict and controversy had raged ever since 1921, on which one committee of inquiry after another had been followed by a Royal Commission. It was the issue over which society itself was most sharply divided, one side resenting the heavy cost and convinced that the system was inhibiting the proper adjustment of wage levels, the other side passionately convinced that if a man could not be offered work he must be protected from both hunger and humiliation.

In the end the Labour Cabinet resigned and Ramsay MacDonald, the Prime Minister, and some of his Labour colleagues crossed over to join forces with Conservative and Liberal leaders to form a 'national' government.

For the Labour voters it was the culminating point of months of disillusionment. To the active Labour Party workers it was total betrayal. In the general election that followed shortly afterwards Labour was demoralized and lost 1¾ million votes, the Liberals were split and their vote fell by 3 million, while the Conservatives, standing as 'National' candidates, achieved an overwhelming majority. A new 'National' government was installed with MacDonald at its head, surrounded by men who represented big business. It was a government of unusually old men who were still looking back with longing to the values and standards of pre-war days. The turbulent decade was finally over.

Notes and References

Chapter 1   The Political Setting

1   Sidney and Beatrice Webb, *A Constitution for the Socialist Commonwealth of Great Britain* (1920), Introduction p. xll.
2   See W.L.Guttsman, *The British Political Elite* (1965).
3   *Herald*, 16 November 1918.
4   Speech 13 December 1918, quoted in *Liberal Magazine*, January 1919.
5   Speech 11 December 1918, quoted in *Liberal Magazine*, January 1919.

Chapter 2   The Post-War Industrial Confrontation

1   Coal Industry Commission, *First Interim Report*, 1919, Cmd 84
2   ibid., vol I, Minutes of Evidence First Stage, Cmd 359, p. 363.
3   ibid., p. 362.
4   ibid., vol. II, Minutes of Evidence Second Stage, Cmd 360, Q. 18,572.
5   ibid., p. 724.
6   ibid., Q. 24,395.
7   ibid., Q. 24,473.
8   ibid., p. 1016.
9   ibid., Q. 23,838–58.
10   ibid., vol. I, First Stage, Q. 3,688–718.
11   ibid., vol. II, Q. 24,473.
12   ibid., p. 648.
13   ibid., Q. 15,678, 15,683.
14   ibid., Q. 14,199.
15   ibid., Q. 15,112–212.
16   ibid., Q. 15,251–67.
17   ibid., vol. I, Q. 5,208.
18   ibid., vol. II, Q. 23,805.
19   *The Times*, 6 December 1918.
20   *The Times*, 11 December 1918.
21   *The Times*, 12 December 1918.
22   House of Lords Hansard, 16 July 1919.

23   This account is based on that given in Philip S. Bagwell, *The Railwaymen* (1963).
24   *The Times*, 1 October 1919.
25   *The Times*, 2 October 1919.
26   Transport Workers Court of Inquiry, vol. I, *Report and Minutes of Evidence*, Cmd 936, p. 43.
27   ibid., p. 153.
28   ibid., p. 31–2.
29   ibid., p. 132.
30   ibid., p. 266.
31   ibid., p. 144.
32   ibid., p. 137, 135.
33   ibid., p. xiv.
34   ibid., p. 20.
35   ibid., p. 186.
36   ibid., p. 194.
37   ibid., p. 184.
38   ibid., p. 195.
39   ibid., p. 127.
40   ibid., p. 90.
41   ibid., p. 135.
42   ibid., p. 393, 395.
43   ibid., p. 409.
44   ibid., p. 275, 384.
45   ibid., p. 246, 263.
46   ibid., p. 36.
47   ibid., p. 497.
48   National Transport Workers Federation, *Report of Tenth Annual Meeting*, 1920, p. 46.

Chapter 3   The Attitude to the Outside World

1   *Daily News*, 8 May 1919.
2   *Manchester Guardian*, 12 May 1919.
3   *Daily Herald*, 17 May 1919.
4   League Covenant.
5   House of Commons Hansard, 20 May 1920.
6   *Trades Union Congress Annual Report*, 1919, p. 298.
7   ibid., p. 217, 219.
8   ibid., p. 338.
9   *Daily Herald*, 19 May 1920.

10   *Daily Herald*, 14 August 1920.
11   House of Commons Hansard, 28 April 1920.
12   *Manchester Guardian*, 3 May 1920.
13   National Transport Workers Federation, *Report of Tenth Annual Meeting*, 1920, p. 149.
14   *Daily News*, 29 October 1920.
15   House of Lords Hansard, 24 November 1920.
16   ibid., 23 November 1920.
17   ibid., 15 December 1921.
18   ibid., 14 December 1921.
19   ibid., 15 December 1921.
20   ibid., 19–20 July 1920.
21   *The Times*, 23 April 1924.
22   ibid.
23   *Daily Herald*, 24 April 1924.
24   *The Times*, 24 May 1924.

Chapter 4   Slump: The Dole and the Poor Law

1   *Report of the Unemployment Insurance Committee*, 1927 (commonly known as the Blanesburgh Report).
2   T. Macnamara, Minister of Labour, House of Commons Hansard, 24 October 1921.
3   Sir Alfred Mond, House of Commons Hansard, 15 June 1921.
4   *Ministry of Health Report 1921–2*, Cmd 1713.
5   *Trades Union Congress Report*, 1922, p. 337.
6   *Third Winter of Unemployment*, 1923, p. 105.
7   Article by George Lansbury in *Labour Monthly*, June 1922.
8   House of Commons Hansard, 13 February 1924.
9   Quoted in Michael Rose, *English Poor Law 1780–1930* (1971), p. 300.
10   House of Commons Hansard, 20 May 1924.
11   *Report of the Unemployment Insurance Committee*, 1927.
12   Minutes of Evidence, Unemployment Insurance Committee, 1927.

Chapter 5   Upper and Lower Middle

1   See F. M. L. Thompson, *English Landed Society in the Nineteenth Century* (1963), the final chapter of which has some detailed information on landownership and sales after the war.
2   According to *Who's Who* (1929), which, as pointed out in Chapter I, furnishes an incomplete record and particularly so from the 1920s

onwards, when it became the practice to transfer estates to private companies in which the family were the major shareholders.

3   See D. Butler and J. Freeman, *British Political Facts 1900–1960* (1963), p. 118.
4   House of Lords Hansard, 17 July 1922.
5   House of Lords Hansard, 29 June 1922.
6   See Chapter I, Table 2.
7   D. H. Lawrence, *Pornography and Obscenity* (1929).
8   John Collier and Iain Lang, *Just the Other Day* (1931).
9   H. G. Wells in his introduction to the 1930 edition of *The Outline of History*.
10 *Daily Mail*, 25 May 1925.
11 *Sunday Express*, 19 April 1925.

Chapter 6   Housing: The State Moves In

1   *Mrs Beeton's Family Cookery*, 1923 edition.
2   *Report of the Royal Commission on the Housing of the Industrial Population of Scotland*, 1917, Cd 8731, para. 481.
3   ibid., para. 404.
4   ibid., para. 2232.
5   *Report of the Local Government Board on questions of Building Construction in connection with the Provision of Dwellings for the Working Class in England, Wales and Scotland*, 1918, Cd 9191.
6   ibid., para. 86.
7   ibid., para. 98.
8   House of Commons Hansard, 18 April 1919.
9   Departmental Committee on Increase of Rent and Mortgage Interest (Restrictions) Act. Interim Report 1922. Final Report 1923.
10 Minutes of Evidence to Departmental Committee, 17 October 1922.
11 ibid.
12 ibid. p. 207.
13 ibid., p. 233.
14 ibid.
15 House of Commons Hansard, 23 June 1924.
16 House of Commons Hansard, 22 February 1924.

Chapter 7   Education: 'Elementary' or 'Advanced'?

1   Cmd 2443, pp. 23, 37–40.
2   *Secondary Education for All* (1922), p. 33.
3   ibid., p. 54.
4   Speech at Plymouth, 7 May 1921.

5   House of Commons Hansard, 13 March 1922.
6   House of Commons Hansard, 22 July 1924.
7   *Secondary Education for All*, p. 95.
8   *Report of Board of Education, 1924–5*, Cmd 2695, p. 87.
9   Quoted in an article by R.H.Tawney in the *Daily News*, 14 February 1918. The article is reprinted in the volume of essays *The Radical Tradition*, 1964.
10   House of Commons Hansard, 22 July 1924.
11   *Report of the Consultative Committee on the Education of the Adolescent*, 1926.
12   ibid., Appendix III, Table III.
13   *Secondary Education for All*, p. 26.
14   *Report on the Education of the Adolescent*, p. xxiii.
15   ibid., p. 84.
16   ibid., p. 131.
17   ibid., p. xxii.

Chapter 8   Old Age Pensions: Means Test or Insurance?

1   Quoted by Neville Chamberlain, House of Commons Hansard, 18 May 1925.
2   Appendix to *Report of Departmental Committee on Old Age Pensions*, 1919, Cmd 411, Q. 4977.
3   ibid., Q. 2405.
4   ibid., Q. 3060.
5   ibid., Q. 4473.
6   ibid., Q. 4535.
7   *Report of Departmental Committee on Old Age Pensions*, Cmd 410, p. 9.
8   Cmd 411, Q. 2150.
9   ibid., Q. 2604.
10   ibid., Q. 2383.
11   ibid., Q. 6761.
12   ibid., Q. 7537.
13   *Report of 56th Annual Trades Union Congress*, 1924, p. 112.
14   House of Commons Hansard, 25 June 1924.
15   ibid.
16   House of Commons Hansard, 18 May 1925.

Chapter 9   Industrial Change

1   The percentage figures of reductions in the workforce are all taken from the estimates in Agatha Chapman, *Wages and Salaries in the United Kingdom 1920–1938* (1955). These figures are used because the

official figures are not available on a comparable basis for the years concerned.

2   Cmd 3156.
3   *Factors in Industrial and Commercial Efficiency*, Part I, 1927.
4   See Sidney Pollard, *The Development of the British Economy 1914–1950* (1962) for a detailed analysis.
5   Article by J.M.Keynes in the *Evening Standard*, 22 July 1925.

Chapter 10   Hours, Wages and Organization

1   *Annual Report of the Chief Inspector of Factories*, 1920, Cmd 1403, p. 150.
2   ibid., 1921, Cmd 1705, p. 83.
3   Richard Stone and D. A. Rowe, *Consumer Expenditure and Behaviour in the United Kingdom 1920–38*, vol. 2 (1966).
4   *Report of 57th Annual Trades Union Congress*, 1925, p. 149.
5   ibid., p. 150.
6   ibid.
7   *The Worker*, 3 January 1925.

Chapter 11   The Mining Crisis

1   The miners' allegation appeared in the *Daily Herald*, 31 July 1925. According to R.Page Arnot in *The Miners: Years of Struggle* (1953), a denial that the statement had been made was issued from Downing Street several months afterwards.
2   *The Times*, 3 August 1925.
3   *Report of the Royal Commission on the Coal Industry*, 1925, vol. II, Minutes of Evidence, p. 997.
4   ibid., p. 931.
5   ibid. p. 933.
6   *Report of the Royal Commission on the Coal Industry*, vol. I, p. 223.
7   ibid., p. 229.
8   Ministry of Health Circular 636 to local authorities, dated 20 November 1925.
9   *Report of 57th Annual Trades Union Congress*, 1925, p. 437.
10 ibid., p. 382.
11 See Fred Bramley, then TUC General Secretary, in *Labour Magazine*, October 1925.
12 TUC Report, *The Mining Crisis and the National Strike*, p. 62A.
13 ibid., p. 61A.
14 ibid., p. 8.
15 ibid., p. 10.
16 ibid., p. 17A.

17   ibid., p. 32A.
18   TUC Memorandum, para. 6b.
19   *Mining Crisis and the National Strike*, p. 34A.
20   Recalled in Lord Citrine, *Men and Work* (1964), p. 160.
21   ibid., p. 172.

Chapter 12   The General Strike

1   From the *Industrial Syndicalist*, March 1911, quoted in Sidney and Beatrice Webb, *History of Trade Unionism*, revised edition, p. 658.
2   See Philip S.Bagwell, *The Railwaymen* (1963).
3   TUC Strike and Progress Report No. 3, TUC Library.
4   Amalgamated Union of Building Trade Workers, *Monthly Issue*, June 1926.
5   S.Higenbottam, *Our Society's History* (1939), p. 264.
6   Amalgamated Society of Woodworkers, *Monthly Journal*, July 1926.
7   This report and the subsequent ones from AEU district delegates are taken from the Amalgamated Engineering Union *Monthly Journal*, June 1926.
8   See H.J.Fyrth and Henry Collins, *The Foundry Workers* (1959), p. 174.
9   United Society of Boilermakers, *Monthly Report*, June 1926.
10   National Amalgamated Furnishing Trades Association, *Monthly Report*, June 1926.
11   *New Dawn* (journal of the National Union of Distributive and Allied Workers), 15 May 1926.
12   TUC Progress of Strike Report No. 2, TUC Library.
13   Ben Turner, *About Myself* (1930), p. 300.
14   TUC Progress of Strike Report No 1, TUC Library.
15   Emile Burns, *General Strike: Trades Councils in Action* (1926), p. 187.
16   *The Mining Crisis and the National Strike*, p. 186A.
17   TUC Progress of Strike Report No 4, TUC Library.
18   *British Gazette*, 6 May 1926.
19   *The Motor*, 18 May 1926.
20   ibid.
21   *British Gazette*, 13 May 1926.
22   ibid., 6 May 1926.
23   Harold Nicolson, *King George the Fifth* (1952).
24   Ben Turner, *About Myself*.
25   *The Mining Crisis and the National Strike*, p. 184A.

Chapter 13   Women

1   *Daily Sketch*, 14 April 1927.
2   *Daily Mail*, 14 April 1927.
3   ibid., 16 April 1927.
4   ibid., 20 April 1927.
5   *Daily Mirror*, 14 April 1927.
6   *Morning Post*, 14 April 1927.
7   *The Times*, 8 October 1924.
8   House of Lords Hansard, 21 May 1928.
9   Margaret Bondfield, *A Life's Work* (1949), p. 277.
10   *1921 Census of England and Wales*, General Report, p. 125.
11   These figures did not include charwomen and comprise only servants in private households. Service in hotels and restaurants, not included in these figures, was increasing.
12   The 'gainfully occupied' included people who normally worked but were temporarily unemployed. See Table 26, p. 218, for figures.
13   Marie Stopes, *Married Love* (1918).
14   See Muriel Box (ed.), *The Trial of Marie Stopes* (1967), p. 363.

Chapter 14   New Enjoyments

1   *The Motor*, 29 January 1924.
2   *Daily Mail*, 4 July 1924.
3   H.Gosling, House of Commons Hansard, 5 August 1924.
4   *The Motor*, 12 February 1924.
5   House of Lords Hansard, 14 May 1924.
6   *The Motor*, 24 June 1924.
7   *The Motor*, 3 December 1929.
8   Cmd 3365, para. 36.
9   House of Commons Hansard, 18 February 1930.
10   ibid.
11   *The Times*, 3 October 1923.
12   *Radio Times*, 9 July 1926.
13   ibid., 24 September 1926.
14   ibid., 18 June 1926.

Chapter 15   Second Thoughts about the War

1   *Labour and the Nation*.
2   *The Times*, 10 April 1930.
3   *The Times*, 12 November 1928.
4   *The Times*, 10 April 1930.
5   *The Times*, 9 April 1930.

Chapter 16   The End of the Decade

1   Sidney and Beatrice Webb, *A Constitution for the Socialist Commonwealth of Great Britain* (1920), p. xii.

2   See Robert Skidelsky, *Politicians and the Slump* (1967).

Short Guide to Further Reading

General

C. L. Mowat, *Britain Between the Wars* (1955).
R. Graves and A. Hodge, *The Long Weekend: A Social History of Great Britain 1918–39* (1940).
J. Collier and I. Lang, *Just the Other Day* (1931).
R. Bennett, *A Picture of the Twenties* (1961).
M. I. Cole (ed.), *Beatrice Webb's Diaries, 1912–24* (1952). *1924–32* (1956).
Thomas Jones, *Whitehall Diary*, vol. 1, 1916/25, vol. 2, 1926/30 (1969). vol. 3, Ireland 1918/25 (1971).

Economic

Derek Allcroft, *The Inter-war Economy: Britain 1919–1939* (1970).
E. J. Hobsbawm, *Industry and Empire* (1968).
Sidney Pollard, *The Development of the British Economy 1914–1950* (1962).

Occupation and Pay

A. L. Bowley, *Wages and Income in the United Kingdom since 1860* (1937).
A. M. Carr Saunders and D. Caradog Jones, *A Survey of the Social Structure of England and Wales* (1937).
Guy Routh, *Occupation and Pay in Great Britain* (1965).

Statistical Reference Works

Agatha Chapman, *Wages and Salaries in the United Kingdom, 1920–1938* (1955).
E. H. Halsey (ed.), *Trends in British Society since 1900* (1972).

R. A. Stone and D. A. Rowe, *Consumer Expenditure and Behaviour in the United Kingdom, 1920–1938* (1966).

White-Collar Workers

G. S. Bain, *The Growth of White Collar Unionism* (1970).
F. D. Klingender, *The Condition of Clerical Labour in Britain* (1935).

Industrial and Trade Union

R. Page Arnot, *The Miners: Years of Struggle* (1953).
P. S. Bagwell, *The Railwaymen* (1963).
A. Bullock, *The Life and Times of Ernest Bevin*, vol. I (1960).
Lord Citrine, *Men and Work* (1964).
H. Clegg, *General Union* (1954).
G. D. H. Cole, *British Trade Unionism Today* (1939).
H. J. Fyrth and H. Collins, *The Foundry Workers* (1959).
A. Hutt, *The Post War History of the British Working Class* (1937).
J. Jeffreys, *The Story of the Engineers* (1946).
H. Pelling, *A History of British Trade Unionism* (1963).
M. L. Yates, *Wages and Labour Conditions in British Engineering* (1937).

1926 General Strike

Contemporary
R. Page Arnot, *The General Strike* (1926).
Emile Burns, *The General Strike: Trades Councils in Action* (1926).
W. H. Crook, *The General Strike* (1931).
K. Martin, *The British Public and The General Strike* (1926).

Recent
C. Farman, *The General Strike, May 1926* (1972).
J. Klugmann, *The General Strike, 1925–6* (History of the Communist Party vol. 2) (1969).
A. E. Mason, *The General Strike in the North East* (1970).
Margaret Morris, *The British General Strike* (Historical Association Pamphlet) (1973).

Education

J. Graves, *Policy and Progress in Secondary Education, 1902–42* (1943).
K. Lindsay, *Social Progress and Educational Waste* (1926).
G. A. N. Lowndes, *The Silent Social Revolution* (1969).
B. Simon, *The Politics of Educational Reform, 1920–1940* (1974).
R. H. Tawney (ed.), *Secondary Education For All: a Policy for Labour* (1922).

Leisure

Asa Briggs, *The Birth of Broadcasting* (1961).
        The Golden Age of Wireless (1965).
Paul Rotha, *The Film Till Now* (revised edition, 1967).

Social Policy

Marian Bowley, *Housing and the State* (1945).
Muriel Box (ed.), *The Trial of Marie Stopes* (1967).
Bentley B. Gilbert, *British Social Policy 1914–1939* (1970).
Paul B. Johnson, *Land Fit for Heroes* (1968).
R. Postgate, *The Life of George Lansbury* (1951).
Dan Rider, *Ten Years' Adventures among Landlords and Tenants* (1927).
E. D. Simon, *The Anti-Slum Campaign* (1933).
Robert Skidelsky, *Politicians and the Slump* (1967).
The Third Winter of Unemployment (1923). Report of an Enquiry by a
group of investigators published by P. S. King and Son.

Appendix

Table 20 Wage Standards Compared with 1920

	Cost of Living Index	Stone's Price Index	Wage-rates	Manufacturing earnings
1920	100	100	100	100
1921	91	92	80	95
1922	73	78	62	76
1923	70	74	62	69
1924	70	74	63	69
1925	71	74	63	70
1926	69	73	64	70
1927	67	71	64	70
1928	67	71	62	70
1929	66	70	62	70
1930	63	69	62	69

	Earnings Manufacturing	Earnings Building	Earnings Iron and steel	Earnings Coal
1920	100	100	100	100
1921	95	92	95	a
1922	76	72	60	57
1923	69	66	55	61
1924	69	68	57	63
1925	70	69	56	59
1926	70	70	55	a
1927	70	70	55	56
1928	70	69	54	51
1929	70	69	54	53
1930	69	69	54	51

(a) strike years.

Index